Homeplaces

Duke University Press *Durham and London* *2026*

Home-places

Dwelling and Habitability in Critical Times

EDITED BY JOÃO BIEHL AND FEDERICO NEIBURG

Printed in the United States of America on acid-free paper ∞
Project Editor: Livia Tenzer
Designed by Courtney Leigh Richardson
Typeset in Freight Text Pro Book by Westchester Publishing Services

Library of Congress Cataloging-in-Publication Data
Names: Biehl, João Guilherme editor | Neiburg, Federico G. editor
Title: Homeplaces : dwelling and habitability in critical times /
edited by João Biehl and Federico Neiburg.
Other titles: On habitability and livingness in critical times
Description: Durham : Duke University Press, 2026. | Includes
bibliographical references and index.
Identifiers: LCCN 2026011320 (print)
LCCN 2026011321 (ebook)
ISBN 9781478039129 paperback
ISBN 9781478034162 hardcover
ISBN 9781478062738 ebook
Subjects: LCSH: Dwellings—Social aspects | Housing | Homelessness |
Equality | Home—Psychological aspects | Belonging (Social psychology)
Classification: LCC GN414 .H654 2026 (print) | LCC GN414 (ebook) |
DDC 307.3/36—DC23/eng/20260608
LC record available at https://lccn.loc.gov/2026011320
LC ebook record available at https://lccn.loc.gov/2026011321

Cover art: Anastasia Taylor-Lind / *5K from the Frontline*, Collecting firewood from abandoned apartments in Krasnohorivka, Ukraine, 2021. Courtesy of A. Taylor-Lind.

Contents

Part II. Homeostasis

Part III. Afterlife of Slavery and War

Part IV. Disasters and Displacements

Part V. Domestic Experimentality

Part VI. Toxic Environs

A Note on the Cover Art

The cover art shows a resident of Krasnohorivka, in the Donbas region of Ukraine, collecting firewood from abandoned apartments in 2021—the city's seventh winter without heating. In their project *5K from the Frontline* (https://www.5kfromthefrontline.com/), photographer Anastasia Taylor-Lind and anthropologist Alisa Sopova describe the scene:

> Since the outbreak of hostilities, the gas distribution station had been stranded in no man's land. Authorities were reluctant to invest in front-line towns that might be attacked again or change hands. People were, for the most part, left to their own devices. To survive, many residents installed makeshift wood-burning stoves; those who couldn't afford firewood salvaged furniture, doors, windows, and beams from abandoned apartments. The dull, suffocating cold of unheated rooms was

almost worse than the frost outside. The knowledge that there wasn't a single warm place in the entire town was the hardest part. In 2024, whatever remained of the town was demolished in battle and then occupied.

Here domicide and house-ing converge in a single frame: a home dismantled to make another home habitable. *Homeplaces* begins in this tension—the unrelenting work of crafting habitability from the very wreckage of dwelling.

Acknowledgments

Homeplaces is the culmination of a long-standing collaborative project exploring the idea of home and homemaking in our beleaguered times, bringing together scholars of different generations, countries, institutional affiliations, and ethnographic commitments. The project began a decade ago as a collaboration between the Department of Anthropology at Princeton University and the Graduate Program in Social Anthropology at the National Museum of the Federal University of Rio de Janeiro in Brazil. Over the years, we have been fortunate to include more people and hold multiple meetings that have reinforced the project's intellectual cross-pollination, international scope, and experimental character.

We thank all the colleagues who accompanied and inspired us on this journey, as well as the institutions that supported us, especially the Brazil LAB at the Princeton Institute for International and Regional Studies (PIIRS), the

Princeton University Center for Human Values (UCHV), the Brazilian Center for Research on Culture and Economy (NuCEC), and the Brazilian Council for Scientific and Technological Development (CNPq).

In March 2022, we had the privilege of hosting an advanced seminar at the School for Advanced Research (SAR) in Santa Fe, New Mexico. This fantastic weeklong gathering of intense and creative reflection helped us focus our collective concept making on "house-ing," or home as a verb. It also gave us the joyous sense of having a book in the making. We are very grateful to our SAR hosts, Paul Ryer and Leslie Shipman.

As this collective endeavor unfolded and *Homeplaces* took shape as a book, we were fortunate to have the wonderful support of a brilliant group of young anthropologists who contributed greatly to the research and exchanges of ideas: Naomi Zucker, Onur Günay, Nikhil Pandhi, Aaron Su, Ayluonne Txai Tereszkiewicz, and Vinicius Cardoso Reis. Kendra Juskus's keen editorial eye, sharp pen, and generous spirit gave the manuscript wonderful literary cohesiveness, enhancing diverse storytelling and the book's inner connectivity.

Special thanks to Ken Wissoker, editor extraordinaire, for his enthusiasm for this project as well as for his vision and guidance throughout. We are grateful for the inspiring support that the reviewers and the stellar editorial team at Duke University Press provided in bringing *Homeplaces* to life.

The book benefited from the production support of the Brazil LAB at the Princeton Institute for International and Regional Studies and a generous publication subvention from Princeton University's Committee on Research in the Humanities and Social Sciences. Our deep gratitude goes to photographer Anastasia Taylor-Lind and anthropologist Alisa Sopova for permitting us to place an image from their project *5K from the Frontline* on the cover of *Homeplaces*—a gesture as generous as the image itself is arresting.

JOÃO BIEHL AND FEDERICO NEIBURG

Introduction

Oikography

It is no accident that this homeplace, as fragile and as transitional as it may be, a makeshift shed, a small bit of earth where one rests, is always subject to violation and destruction. . . . For when a people no longer have the space to construct homeplace, we cannot build a meaningful community of resistance. —BELL HOOKS, "Homeplace: A Site of Resistance"

House-ing: On People Making Houses and Houses Making People

Destruction and erasure do not tell the whole story. The quest for dwelling creates homeplaces. Against end-times thinking and through cuts and bleedings, this book focuses on home as *house-ing*: the reciprocal process of people making houses and houses making people. We are engaged in a collective effort to think with and through the contingency, ingenuity, and indeterminacy involved in carving out places we call home amid ongoing calamity—from environmental disasters, racialized segregation, police violence, and Indigenous and gendered servitude, to infectious and toxic landscapes, mass-engineering projects, and human displacement, to body mutilation and experimentation, familial escapes and fleeting sanctuaries, and the reckoning with ancestral wars.

In *Homeplaces*, anthropologists move across a range of landscapes and histories, taking the house to be a built shelter, a collection of relations, affects, memories, and moralities, and a lively nexus within neighborhoods, communities, and larger political, economic, and ecological systems. We explore how lifeworlds and imaginations are shaped by homemaking. The places we live in are simultaneously open and closed, composed of hard-won certainties and overwhelming uncertainties. They are places of shelter and entrapment, of autonomy and interdependence, where hierarchy and care coexist, and desire lingers.

What do ethnographies of housed and dehoused subjects thus bring into view? And what comes into play when the house itself becomes the subject of ethnography?

In the aftermath of the devastating 2010 earthquake in Port-au-Prince, Haiti, we find houses realized at diverse scales, with the homeless living in temporary camps and in movement. They belong to unstable, yet persistent, configurations of houses articulated against the backdrop of the plantation and Black geographies. Victims of the Fukushima nuclear disaster in Japan move between their contaminated homes and new settlements, reclaiming irradiated ancestral objects to restore a sense of belonging. Displaced by Brazil's largest hydroelectric dam complex, riverbank dwellers re-Amazonize their new concrete houses. Here, their intricate use of debris and plants subverts the sameness of a massive housing development.

In a feverish Rio de Janeiro engulfed by racist police violence, favela residents mourn the deaths of young Black men, which led to the demise of entire families and the dying of homes. In the rapidly urbanizing outskirts of La Paz, Bolivia, Indigenous women navigate servitude and leverage kinship ties to plot a house of their own for themselves and their loved ones. Farther north, in the hills of Soacha, a town south of Bogotá, Colombia, the war-displaced rural poor are now targets of social cleansing by militias. While some houses are marked as harboring deviants to be killed, an atmosphere of fear pervades the neighborhood and the unprotected intimacy of all dwellings.

In the persistently segregated American Southeast, the restoration of a nineteenth-century prayer house by a Black Gullah Geechee community is an act of returning to and reclaiming home ecologies and transcendence. It is also a political claim to alternative livability in a contaminated landscape. Some eight hundred miles away, in Chicago, people refuse to leave collapsing buildings that are filled with unresolved repair needs. Instead, they eke out an existence amid mold, refuse, weeds, rodents, and dogs that roam vacant units and the same common grounds that also nourish enjoyable gardens.

Consider how domestic and laboratory spaces bleed into each other, and how technologies both rehouse and reshape science. After losing limbs in work-related accidents, Swedish subjects in an experimental study redesign the terms and uses of their neuroprosthetics through an embodied domestic science. Meanwhile, local malaria scientists in Tanzania are paying attention to bodily movements in peridomestic spaces. This is prompting experimenters to reorient technocratic prevention away from the indoor-insecticidal approach and toward the design of protective communal atmospheres. Mosquitoes expose the fantasy in public health of controlling the home, which is inextricably linked to social relations, material underpinnings, and interspecies actants.

And see how young people in the American Southwest, scarred by historical violence and dispossession and dismissed as seedy, create fables of home and intimacy with strangers in temporary communal spaces where they are together and alone with the unknown. Finally, for the impoverished and unlettered elderly heirs of a bygone settler war in southern Brazil, the ancestral home is more than just a memory. It is a residual, shared sentience that invokes the spirit of nature and the healing power of storytelling.

The housed and the dehoused, as well as homes as ethnographic subjects, shift our perception toward relationality. With their incompleteness and openness to worlds and ways of life beyond the domestic sphere, they challenge our restrictive notions of habitability and livingness. Contrary to the idea that we "build and have built because we dwell,"[1] in *Homeplaces* we explore how people actively create provisional forms of dwelling amid ongoing calamity in historically shaped territories.[2] These are not returns to an authentic past. Rather, they are dynamic quests and adaptations to critical times.

While dislodging the dominance of crude universals, the immanence of house-ing also detonates restrictive concepts, such as the domicile. Bourgeois ideology enshrines the home as private, stable, and bounded—the natural refuge of the nuclear family, sealed away from others and from history. Hardened into the sociological category of the household, this fiction underwrites public policies on housing, reproduction, and public health that are at once disciplinary and exclusionary.[3]

Our ethnographic approach reveals that houses are never static entities, but rather "live forms" that are constantly remade through human and other-than-human interactions.[4] Displacement, violence, and environmental degradation force individuals to devise fluid house-ing strategies and creatively appropriate technologies. Thus, through participation in multiple intellectual lineages and cross-pollinations, *Homeplaces* grounds abstract notions of dwelling in the tangible, sensory realities of people struggling to endure in precarious environs, maintain livability, and find some form of transcendence.

The book's title references bell hooks's idea of "homeplace," which she developed in the book *Yearning: Race, Gender, and Cultural Politics*.[5] For hooks, "homeplace" refers to the ways Black women have historically created and maintained domestic spaces that serve as sites of resistance and healing against white supremacist oppression.[6] These spaces were not merely physical homes, but rather, they represented safe havens where Black individuals could affirm their dignity and humanity, where "all that truly mattered in life took place."[7] They were sites for nurturing counterhegemonic worldviews, spaces for "renewal and self-recovery, and communities where cultural practices and knowledge could be preserved and transmitted."[8] hooks emphasized that these homeplaces were political constructions deliberately created as spaces of mutual affirmation and healing from racist domination.

Yet implicit in hooks's account is the fragility of such spaces. Homeplaces had to be made and remade precisely because they could be—and often were—unmade. We extend her concept to foreground this transience: homeplace in our framing is not an achieved ideal but an ongoing, often unsettled endeavor. It is at once a site of solidarity and of tension, a refuge shadowed by displacement, a place of healing that still bears the imprint of the violence it resists.[9] The embodied dwellings examined in *Homeplaces* are not bounded units. Instead, they are entangled in various affective, institutional, and para-infrastructural configurations.[10] These house-ings exhibit multiscalar and metamorphic characteristics that transcend biopolitical capture and escape the binary of subjection and resistance. At their heterotopian best, these real places—unfolding across generations and through fragile webs of relationships—offer us an alternative perspective and encourage us to recognize ongoing efforts to repair the increasing precariousness that affects much of the world.[11] They embody life's insistence against decay and destruction. Lively yet dying, they serve as counterpolitical harbingers, defying ever-encroaching tyranny.

Oikography

We put forth *oikography* as an ethnographic approach that deconstructs ideological premises and statistical assumptions about homes and homemaking. The term oikography combines two ancient Greek roots: *oikos* (house or household) and *graphia* (drawn or written). We created this term to describe the methodological approach and theoretical orientation of this book to field research centering on how people create homes and how homes create people, as well as on the associated storytelling and representational practices. While countering universalizing assumptions about home and homemaking, oikography helps us approximate the plasticity and relationality of households across space and time. It also illuminates domestic spaces as critical nodes where microlevel practices connect to macrolevel processes.

Oikos, with its multiple senses and significations—including house, family, estate, patrimony, private space, and economic and moral spheres and related social hierarchies—opens up our imagination to many possible forms of dwelling, entrapment, exclusion, and becoming in the worlds people are thrown into. The *oikos* is similarly constituted by a set of dynamic relationships between bodies, buildings, rules, infrastructures, and other nonhuman elements (be they geophysical and biochemical matters, construction materials, or spiritual entities) as well as between intimacy, publicness, and the *polis* (Greek city-state or political community). Seen from this perspective, the house is a vital nexus between material, political-economic, affective, and aesthetic forces at work, and it is a place where public life and private life blur and these very terms are recast. When the word is combined with the Greek suffix *graphia*, as is the case in oikography, matters of the house are also inextricably linked to recordkeeping, archiving, and regimes of visualization, including the ethnographic account.

The concept of house-ing is central to each essay in this collection. It refers to the sensory processes by which people and houses mutually constitute one another. As a gerund—a verbal noun—house-ing elicits the home as a dynamic human-nonhuman entity shaped by intricate interplay between stability and instability, boundaries and flux, and stillness and movement. Engaging with house-ing in critical times prompts the question: What prospects remain for the "modes/genres of being human" under such persistent duress?[12] This approach also opens new vistas onto the shifting ground of the social, material, political, and moral.

Our collective oikography intentionally engages with house-ing in contexts of chronic precariousness (exacerbated by emergencies and new uncertainties) in the global South and among vulnerable communities in the global North, seeking to advance creative comparative work on the anthropology of the house. As we worked on this book together, the figure of the house became increasingly important for understanding today's most pressing planetary issues—from the governance of epidemic and pandemic life to the limitations of technocratic responses to climate-related disasters, to the dynamics of ongoing brutal wars.

The COVID-19 pandemic has thrown the house and its significance to public health and the economy into sharp relief. The tensions between mobility and immobility and between protection and risk that run through where we live have become central to debates about which labor is essential to life, whose life is worth saving, and who is destined to die, in hospitals or at home. As evidenced by the ongoing conflicts in Ukraine, Palestine, and Sudan, to name a few, the house is also increasingly being utilized as a strategic target—not only to enact collective annihilation and expand colonial occupation, but also to extinguish the enduring forms of liveliness that homes sustain.[13] A recent report by the United Nations special rapporteur on the right to adequate housing calls for "domicide"—the massive, arbitrary destruction of civilian housing in violent conflict—to be prosecuted as a crime against humanity.[14]

For most of our subjects, who have experienced a history of dehousing and rehoming, the notion of stability as a counterpoint to crisis is, at the outset, untenable: They have not inhabited or experienced bounded or intact dwellings in contradistinction to breakdowns or critical events. People's house-ing efforts, rather, speak to the *longue durée* of critical times and to creative repertoires of material and affective "mediants."[15] Oikography is thus attuned to such multirelational efforts to instantiate provisional homeplaces: grounds from which to gauge the past, make the present habitable, and forge future horizons. Designating an emplaced yet embattled and energetic milieu, *oikos* subverts and overflows. House-ing dynamics are more confounding and generative than hegemonic theoretical schemes account for.[16]

The contributors to *Homeplaces* work in a wide range of languages, each of which has different words for *house*, animated by local senses and meanings—*casa, maison, kay, nyumba,* 家, *Haus, hus*, and *home*. Yet, in our comparative and juxtapositional work, we take the Greek *oikos* as a common starting point, particularly because the term and its troubled history conjure up the house as a site where domination is legitimized and inscribed in the bodies of enslaved people—men, women, and children—challenging us to focus on patriarchy, racialization, exploitation, and hierarchy as integral to processes of house-ing. As we foreground the *oikos*, we remain alert to the shifting and uneven relations between the domestic and the political—between *oikos* and *polis*. Moreover, *oikos* serves as the etymological root for many innovative arrangements: *oikos* + *nemein* = *oikonomia* ("economy"), referring to the management of the house and of material resources in general; and *oikos* + *logos* = *oikologia* ("ecology"), referring to the interactions of organisms and their physical environments.[17]

The essays that compose this book evince an ethos of incompleteness and an invitational quality. Excerpted from ongoing studies and longer writings, the chapters resemble the porous houses and actions they describe. They are filled with unsettled figures who come and go, haunted by their pasts and uncertain about their lives in the future. Simultaneously illuminating the emergent and the elsewise and reckoning with structural and historical recognition, they might well be called oikographic short stories.

Taken together, our essays articulate an ethnographic approach to contemporary house-ing efforts at the generative intersection of five strands of research, always rooted by local concepts and practices: (1) the anthropology of kinship, patriarchy, care, and violence; (2) the economic dynamics of households related to the provision of shelter, the circulation of money, and the use of technology; (3) the anthropology of public policies and infrastructures concerning housing and services, risk and health, security, and rights and citizenship; (4) human and other-than-human alignments and the house as a material entity acting on residents and the environment, eliciting varying degrees of agency; and (5) the anthropology of aesthetics and poetics, showing how figures of home and forms of homemaking constitute the house as a kind of sensory archiving machine that shapes affective pasts and the stories and trajectories of tomorrow.

Each oikography in this collection reflects a collaborative mode of knowing—copresence and coknowledge—through the figure of the house as a verb over time. Attention to the multifaceted nature of house-ing requires ethnographic agility and humility on the part of the fieldworker. It also requires an openness to traversing people's labor and imagination—a homeplace for thought and interference, if you will.

Politics of Homemaking

The multiplicities of the house complicate our understanding of the intimate and the political as well as of the blurring of the two. In her seminal work *The Human Condition*, philosopher Hannah Arendt traces the shifting roles of public and private life from ancient Greece to the postwar modern period in which she was writing. She argues that ancient political thought took the division between public and private spheres—the *polis* and the *oikos*—and the distinction between activities related to the common world and those related to the mere maintenance of life as self-evident and axiomatic. However, with the emergence of the social sphere in the modern age, the line between the public and the private became "entirely blurred."[18] The economic question of individual life and species survival has ceased to be an apolitical household affair and has been integrated into a "gigantic, nation-wide administration of housekeeping."[19] In this early articulation of biopolitics, formerly domestic matters become collective concerns, and the two spheres are reconfigured. No longer separate or opposed, they "constantly flow into each other like waves in the never-resting stream of the life process itself."[20]

With the blurring of boundaries, both spheres are destabilized. Society's overwhelming intrusion into the private sphere hijacks the household for the sake of the good life of the *polis*. "Mass society," Arendt writes, "not only destroys the public realm but the private as well," thereby depriving people not only of their place in the world but also of "their private home, where they once felt sheltered against the world."[21] Without the protection of the private realm, people experience "a rebellion of the heart."[22]

Arendt was deeply troubled by the modern experience of worldlessness—the erosion of a shared world—and the diminished capacity for critical thinking and action that resulted from the destruction of public and private spaces. This left people vulnerable to totalitarian manipulation and unable to take collective responsibility for their shared human condition.

Oikography allows us to consider Arendt's philosophical account from a more nuanced perspective, tracing her insights into the real consequences of shifting configurations of the *oikos-polis* for human experience and political life into the here and now. This approach eschews totalizing claims in favor of close attention to the politics of domesticity and domestication.[23] Through the lens of house-ing, we can critically think and write about power, insurgency, the nature of social change, and agency in the present moment. This approach also provides a means of creatively challenging the blanket application of dominant theoretical frameworks associated with settler colonialism, neoliberalism, biopolitics, and control societies.[24]

By taking the house as an ethnographic subject, we can focus on form and structure without losing sight of how social fields emerge and transform over time. This brings us closer to the places where the boundaries between public and private life, and between the human and nonhuman, become blurred, now that fantasies of the good life in the *polis* have collapsed.[25]

Contemporary theorizations of materiality as a means of rethinking the political and our place within it are helpful here, to a point. In *Vibrant Matter*, for example, political theorist Jane Bennett writes against "the idea of matter as passive stuff, as raw, brute, or inert," and against the supposed "division of meaning" that separates "dull matter (it, things)" from "vibrant life (us, beings)."[26] She argues that matter itself is vital, lively, and, in its own way, agentive. She is less interested in the specifics of human action than in the broader forms of "distributive agency" that characterize different actants (as Bruno Latour puts it) and the ways in which they make a difference in the world.[27]

The call for attention to the vibrancy of matter and its "thingly power" offers another entry point or perspective for oikography.[28] In this conceptual framework, the house is regarded as a material entity, and it is understood in relation to its capacity to act on and through its human and other-than-human inhabitants, as well as its impact on the surrounding milieu. However, while the house does indeed "make things happen," focusing solely on the material place fails to acknowledge the intricate webs of systems, decisions, and human agencies that determine who can live in the house and how. To bring these machineries into view—and with them the questions of "ethics, accountability, normativity, and political critique"—the house must be peopled, so to speak.[29]

Environmental Attunements

These matters are not new territory for anthropology. In fact, there is a rich archive of anthropological work that directly or indirectly sheds light on homemaking as generative social domain. Time and again, even when anthropologists have not explicitly focused their studies on houses, the homemaking they have encountered in the field has challenged them to slow down analytically. Throughout the anthropological record, there are hints of the agency of the house in expanding conceptual work on the nature of social life and in breaking open modes of representation.[30]

In his early twentieth-century armchair monograph, *Seasonal Variations of the Eskimo*, Marcel Mauss, for example, offers detailed descriptions of Inuit territory and housing and living arrangements. He is attentive to the ways in which "the material form of human groups . . . affects different modes of collective activity."[31] Mauss meticulously outlines how the settlement "takes on quite different forms according to the seasons."[32] Describing the contrasting dwellings and organizational forms that characterize the summer and winter seasons—from concentrated single-family tents to dispersed multifamily longhouses—the anthropologist elucidates a close relationship between morphology and the social group itself.

There is a plasticity to Mauss's human-environment analysis (to which *Homeplaces* subscribes) that refuses facile determinisms. He does indeed frame his project against the geographical determinism of the then-popular anthropogeography, arguing for a more nuanced attention to the entanglements of inhabited, built, and lived worlds: "The land factor," he writes, "must be considered in relation to a social context in all its complex totality."[33]

In his account of seasonal variations in residence and human-animal livingness patterns, Mauss refuses to view houses and social groups as fixed, bounded entities. Instead, he recognizes how these entities are reconfigured over time in response to different forms of sociality and activity that are related to the territory itself and changing environmental factors.[34]

Such land-based dynamics are evident in the diasporic Haitian mobile landscapes studied by Federico Neiburg as well as in the stories of peoples facing nuclear disaster in Japan and dam-related resettlement in Amazonia, as demonstrated by Ryo Morimoto and Thiago da Costa Oliveira and Carlos Fausto, respectively, in their essays. Here, dwellings are permeable, adaptable, and influenced by contested histories, land use, and management. They flow through "vicinage," as João Pina-Cabral would say, echoing South African anthropology of the 1960s.[35] They are made and remade through ecobiosocial connections and are inflected by expert knowledge and power relations. Thus, in contrast to Mauss's stable environment/seasonality, house-ing under ongoing calamity is suffused with world-historical violence and the "runaway nature" of the Anthropocene, technocratic intervention, and scientific experimentation.[36]

Homeplaces challenges the fantasy of a stable and analytically graspable social morphology and advocates against a mere cataloging of losses. Instead, it emphasizes the negative plasticity at play in house-ing, namely the dissolution of forms, bodies, and buildings that has been long and intensely underway and is always situated. This dissolution is the very material with which people create a sense of habitability and keep house-ing alive. Our collective ethos is powerfully exemplified in Catherine Fennell's essay on "the house underfoot" in Chicago's late-industrial racialized urban ecologies, in which she describes houses constructed from ruins. People exert agency over ravaged, worked landscapes, and living is a continuous process of domesticating corroding spaces while securing the right to housing.

More than resilience is at play here. In Thiago da Costa Oliveira and Carlos Fausto's photographic essay, we witness the "bricolage" of Amazonian riverine communities displaced by a gigantic clean energy and urban development project.[37] Countering the company's cataloging of land appropriation and ruination, the anthropologists and their cameras accompany the displaced as they recover experiences from their former lifeworld and rebuild their new cinderblock/homogeneous residences with the debris of a space that no longer exists. All sorts of technocratic equivocations are fleshed out, and resettlement has a method of its own. Here, the homeplace is a testament to the stubborn human will to domesticate the time of displacement.

Houses bleed. In their essay, set in Tanzania, on the domestic as a global health research infrastructure, Ann H. Kelly and Javier Lezaun present houses as inherently leaky sites of multispecies coexistence. As a kind of immune and atmospheric system, houses are conduits for the transmission of disease since the homely is communal and unfolds beyond the walls. In line with some of Mauss's key insights, the ethnographies of house-ing reveal expansive diasporic subjects scarred and shaped by the shifting landscapes and geographies they or their codwellers have traversed. In Mauss's striking human-animal rendering, one could "compare these individuals with the long antennae extended forward by a creature that is itself extraordinarily distended."[38]

In Alexandra Middleton's essay, we see that the house and its experiments allow for human distension. By following neuroprosthetic test subjects into their households, she shows how the experimental object is integrated into domestic routines and social interactions. This integration restores the users' abilities, reconstructs a familiar sense of home, and skillfully subverts the experiment and its expectations. Traversing such domestic experimentation and contestation within, against, and beyond technoscience, we land on the leakage and uncontainment of house-ing and its subjects.

Cry for Home

When anthropologist Franz Boas commissioned his student Zora Neale Hurston to enter the "homely life" of southern Black communities and capture elements of their "true inner life" in the mid-1920s, Hurston rushed back to her hometown of Eatonville, Florida.[39] Little did Boas know that the budding ethnographer/writer and her interlocutors would collaborate polyphonically to create a multigenerational record of African American life and insurgent subjectivities. Through exchanges in residences, gardens, porches, and other communal spaces, they crafted a bold methodological and theoretical detour from the emerging science of culture/cultural relativism (championed by figures such as Ruth Benedict and Margaret Mead), pivoting to a sensory and literary anthropology that in turn yielded insights into the power of refusal as well as the dynamics of affective states and domestic politics.[40]

This is the theory behind "our tactics," Hurston writes in *Mules and Men*, drawing from both her pioneering ethno-poetic fieldwork in one of the country's only all-Black towns and her own novelistic sensibility: "The white man is always trying to know into somebody else's business. All right, I'll set something outside the door of my mind for him to play with and handle. He can read my writing but he sho' can't read my mind. I'll put this toy in his hand, and he will seize it and go away. Then I'll say my say and sing my song."[41]

The anthropologists of *Homeplaces* embrace Hurston's critique, which is rooted in radical ideas of Black agency and justice that have too long been relegated to the periphery of the discipline. We also leverage the potential of the detour she opened up with her dehoused and rehoused interlocutors and their trajectories as they experimented with form, genre, technique, and textuality, thereby affirming the capacious power of storytelling and the multiple senses of home that "the soul lives by."[42]

In the opening essays, João Biehl and Angela Garcia return to where they were raised, in southern Brazil and the American Southwest, respectively, to reckon with their ancestral sense of home and the ruptures and heterotopias wrought by world-historical violence and the reconfiguration of family complexes. In both auto-oikographies, the image of the house does not provide an illusion of stability and belonging amid daily uncertainties; rather, it serves as a platform for departures. People live discontinuously, "from one map to the next," and the desire for domesticity is a multitemporal, recuperative journey through displacements that can open onto new universes of reference.[43]

In Biehl's return to a dwelling that no longer exists, we see an incarnated home sentience that unlettered farmers forged against the specter of death and are left to ponder the mysteries of the intergenerational transmission of surges of survival. These flickering, homespun traces and poetic trails relentlessly delineate expansive cartographies of belonging and promise, transcending the racialization and necropolitics conjured by the ruling classes, and continually animated by storytelling.[44]

The main subject of Garcia's essay is the Mother Road, a house-turned-brothel-turned-hostel set against the backdrop of America's infrastructural booms and busts, migratory cycles, and marginalizations west of Albuquerque's historic downtown. In this transient communal space, we encounter the fantasies, sensory experiences, and relational endeavors of a once-dehoused young woman—the anthropologist herself—who worked as a maid as she attempted to queer a domesticity of her own making. Garcia's literature has rescued this experience of living alone together in the narrowest of spaces.

It enables us to reconsider the wound of unhomeliness and the power of alternative house-ing as well as the unknown and unspoken that accompany social life.[45]

The "cry for home" is a constant theme in Zora Neale Hurston's most iconic ethnographic interlocutor, Cudjo Lewis, the last known survivor of the brutal transatlantic slave trade.[46] Equally constant is his sense of being a displaced "cartographic subject," unmoored from ancestral coordinates yet ceaselessly yearning for connection.[47] Hurston's *Barracoon: The Story of the Last "Black Cargo"* is set at the home of Cudjo (as she mostly refers to him) in Plateau, Alabama—originally named Africatown following the US Civil War.[48] This personal reckoning with "the most dramatic chapter in the story of human existence" begins with an open house: "It was summer when I went to talk with Cudjo so his door was standing wide open," Hurston writes.[49] A hybrid of ethnographic study and oral history, *Barracoon* (the term for the structure used to temporarily shelter Africans who were to be sold and exported) is the result of a series of visits that Hurston made to Kossula (Cudjo's African name) in the late 1920s. At that point, Kossula lived alone and gardened; his wife and children were gone. In Hurston's words: "This is the life story of Cudjo Lewis, as told by himself. It makes no attempt to be a scientific document, but on the whole he is rather accurate."[50] She writes,

> But I knew he was somewhere about the house before I entered the yard, because I had found the gate unlocked. When Cudjo goes down into his back-field or away from home he locks his gate with an ingenious wooden peg of African invention.
>
> I hailed him by his African name as I walked up the steps to his porch, and he looked up into my face as I stood in the door in surprise. He was eating his breakfast from a round enameled pan with his hands, in the fashion of his fatherland.
>
> The surprise of seeing me halted his hand between pan and face. Then tears of joy welled up.
>
> "Oh Lor', I know it you call my name. Nobody don't callee me my name from cross de water but you. You always callee me Kossula, jus' lak I in de Affica soil!"[51]

Over the course of several months, Hurston and Cudjo had frequent conversations (some of which she captured on film), shared meals, and forged a strong bond over his reminiscences. In *Barracoon*, the anthropologist recounts Cudjo's journey as "contraband flesh" and relays his yearnings in their original vernacular.[52] Although Hurston wrote the story a few years after their interactions, the oral nature of the book's language as well as its racially charged editorial concerns prevented its publication at the time. It would not appear in print until nearly a century later.[53]

Cudjo himself punctuates the story around the figure of the house and the violence of being dehoused. His narrative moves back and forth between his ancestral home in Africa ("De old folks dat live two hund'ed year befo' I born don't tell me de father [remote ancestor] rule nobody"); his capture and time spent in the barracoon ("We all lonesome for our home"); the dehumanization of the Middle Passage on the *Clotilda* ("We lookee and lookee and lookee and lookee and we doan see nothin' but water. Where we come from we doan know. Where we goin, we doan know"); and his life as a slave in the United States ("We say we born and raised to be free people and now we slave").[54] Cudjo also reflects on his experience as a free man in a foreign land in the "afterlife of slavery" ("Why doan you give us piece dis land so we kin buildee ourself a home?").[55]

In Ayluonne Txai Tereszkiewicz's essay, we learn how Black communities created and maintained communal religious spaces during and in the wake of the plantation to express their cry for home and a sense of transcendence while addressing disenfranchisement. The anthropologist returns to North Carolina, where her once-enslaved ancestors worked the land before fleeing northward. There, she traces the role of a historic prayer house blending African and Christian traditions as an evolving place of refuge—a "being-at-home . . . far beyond the bounds of an explicitly domestic space" and a "central atlas of survivals and possibilities"—for Gullah Geechee captives and their descendants. The long-standing Gullah community continues to face inequities tied to their land: dispossession through development, lingering chemical toxicity from industrial activity on the repurposed plantation, and uncertainty regarding environmental remediation. For residents, the restoration of the chapel embodies the desire voiced by Cudjo: to have a "piece dis land so we kin buildee ourself a home."[56] The ancestral, spiritual place of origin embodies the power of creation in those marshes and the ability to transform what could be into what is, namely Black freedom and repair beyond injury.

Toward the end of *Barracoon*, Cudjo agrees to let Hurston take his portrait. "I'm glad you takee my picture. I want see how I look," he says. "Once long time ago somebody come take my picture but they never give me one. You give me one." Cudjo is dressed in his best suit, but he takes off his shoes. He explains: "I want to look lak I in Affica, 'cause dat where I want to be."[57] He also asks to be photographed in the cemetery among his family's graves.

In present-day Haiti, Cudjo's words "where we goin, we doan know" resonate deeply.[58] The interconnected histories of African capture, the Middle Passage, plantation enslavement, *marronage*, anti-imperial rebellion, and all forms of systemic violence have given rise to a shared sense of displacement and an unknown journey's end. The tension between captivity and the impulse to escape and rebuild lives is vividly captured by the concept of "configuration of houses," as articulated by the Haitian anthropologist Louis Herns Marcelin.[59] According to Marcelin, the sense of home is always plural and tied to "a set of houses linked by an ideal of family and ancestry" that modulates "sense systems in territories that have been historically and socially constituted."[60]

House-ing is on the move, as we learn from Federico Neiburg's essay. In beleaguered Haiti, the house is an emplacement of movement and tension as well as an ancestral and contemporary relational process. People have learned to keep their deceased loved ones close through the configuration of their houses, known as *lakou*. Even when physically destroyed by natural disasters and violent political economies, the *lakou* figure continues to nourish a sense of land ownership, collective belonging, and mutual obligation that drives the centrifugal and diasporic dynamics of house-ing. As Cudjo yearned: "I want to look lak I in Affica."[61]

Domicide

What is the grip of the world-historical on house-ing? How do we address the disfiguring and refiguring effects of this siege on our thinking and writing about the reciprocal relationship between homes and people?

In their seminal work on "uprooting" in the context of the French efforts to suppress the Algerian anticolonial struggle in the 1950s, Pierre Bourdieu and Abdelmalek Sayad chronicle the displacement of over a quarter of the largely rural population.[62] Hundreds of thousands of families were resettled and confined into heavily policed, concentration-like "regroupment camps" or fled to the alien urban environment of the capital city, Algiers.

The young Bourdieu and Sayad met in a colonial milieu and forged a bond that became a form of creative intellectual resistance. While Bourdieu, a philosophy student at the time, was serving in a French army research unit in Algiers, Sayad, a sociology student, was engaged in anti-occupation movements. Their wartime friendship led to an unexpected collaboration that transformed them both into ethnographers of people who had been uprooted, left houseless, and trapped. In turn, these subjects held a mirror to the young scholars' own sense of out-of-placeness and desire for belonging and transformational social knowledge.[63]

In *Homeplaces*, we strive for a decolonial and anticolonial scholarly and political engagement as well. Colonial oppression deprives people of the protection of a home, and this dispossession leaves its mark on disjointed bodies. As Bourdieu and Sayad poignantly observe, "It is the body language, the way one stands, looks, or walks, that expresses bewilderment better than words." While landless peasants sat idle, without the rhythms and toil of the land, desperate women and tired children wandered in search of "a piece of bread or a can of water," exposed to the gaze of the armed forces and foreigners.[64]

Here and elsewhere, colonial power implodes domestic autonomy and restructures inhabited space. The housed subject of the embattled present becomes a thing of the past—"a new framework of existence that marks colonial possession on the ground."[65] Those who have breathed a "life of proximity" among neighbors are now valueless and abruptly thrust into a "world of anonymity." However, these displaced and highly surveilled bodies and souls also find ways to collaborate in "opening up new horizons," as Frantz Fanon writes in *The Wretched of the Earth*.[66]

Meanwhile, in the name of maintaining peace, the policeman and the soldier put oppression and domination into practice, bringing "violence into the home and into the mind of the native."[67] This is what every Algerian—dehoused or threatened at home—felt in their hearts: "Colonialism is not a thinking machine, nor a body endowed with reasoning faculties. It is violence in its natural state and it will only yield when confronted with greater violence."[68] Officials tortured Algerians in the cellars and vacated houses to extract information about the anonymous resistance and the homemade weapons that had been fashioned to overthrow colonial rule and end the brutality of civilization.[69] The victims' cries of pain rose into the domestic spaces of orderly citizens, solidifying a sensorium of terror and generalized complicity with dehumanization.

The use of violence against houses as a way of controlling territory and mind remains a present-day technology of power throughout our volatile world.[70] In Sebastián Ramírez's essay we learn how paramilitary groups that terrorized rural Colombian populations during the country's brutal civil war have mutated into criminal organizations controlling vast peripheral areas inhabited by refugees on the outskirts of the capital, Bogotá. Even during "peace accord" times, the war machine continues in order to maximize illicit economies and a shadowy para-sovereignty. Militias target those who cannot pay their drug-related debts or protection fees, as well as LGBTQIA+ people and community leaders deemed socially dangerous and eradicable, with threatening pamphlets and graffiti. This cleansing horrorscape renders the everyday inhospitable, turns the neighborhood into a siege zone, and transforms the threatened house into a prison. The only refuge left for people is to be seen in order to be dismissed, to be named in order to be erased, and to be fixed in order to disappear.

Set amid the unrelenting gang violence, police violence, and racism in Rio de Janeiro, Eugênia Motta's tragic oikography reveals how a house intended to shelter urban poor families becomes a place of calamitous harm. Beginning with the brutal murder of a young Black man involved in petty crime—a "bad death"—we witness the house spiral into one affective, moral, and medical crisis after another. At the center of this "dying home" is Maria, a grieving mother grappling with her inability to safeguard her loved ones and the very idea of motherhood as a generative force. Maria's own death and the resulting dispersal of kin ultimately reveal the house as an organism that lives and dies and harbors relatedness and expansive social projects, whose incompleteness and abrupt interruption continue to interpellate the anthropological imagination.

Habitability

Houses are gendered and engendering. In the early 1970s, while Pierre Bourdieu famously reified the "traditional" Kabyle house (by then already dismantled by the colonial/anticolonial war) as the embodiment of a cosmological system in which space organizes structural relationships (complementary, tense, and hierarchical) between the sexes, feminist scholars were peopling houses again with the practices of real women characters, who were both objects of domination and house makers on their own terms.[71]

In her ethnography *Women of Value, Men of Renown*, set in the Trobriand Islands, Annette Weiner powerfully challenged Bronisław Malinowski's early theory of value, developed concerning the circulation of kula objects by male argonauts.[72] Weiner entered people's houses and chronicled how women were custodians of food and the kula objects. Through their care and public display, women added value and communicated a distinct cosmic order.[73] In this context, the gendered configuration of houses and labor actively defied the idea of a male-centered politics as well as the production of value and knowledge consecrated by male ancestral researchers (excluding women and the agency of the house).

Following Weiner's pioneering work, scholars creatively adopted the gendered house as a generative locus to rethink and queer classic anthropological subjects, such as the household, kinship, and the political.[74] As Janet Carsten notes in *After Kinship*, the intimacy of houses "jumbles up" what anthropologists tended to separate: "In the sometimes haphazard 'side by sideness' of what happens in the house, we can begin to understand how ideas about bodies and about gender come to structure social relations."[75]

Houses and ideas of home not only structure social relations but also unleash relational plasticity, which is key to the work of sublimation and the creation of alternative life projects. In Susan Helen Ellison's essay we meet Brisa, a Bolivian domestic worker (*criada*) who embodies centuries of Indigenous domination and servitude and yet creatively redeploys asymmetrical relations and ambivalent kinship ties in pursuit of her own place and a dynamic future. In this "oikobiography," we see how the master's house is composed of differentiated spaces that allow for abuse and secrecy, as well as for commensality and the forging of tactical calculations and reciprocity. We also witness the calvary of the laboring house, embodied by the *criada*, as a forward-looking perseverance and an aspirational drive to build, brick by brick, a place that will finally feel like home.

Surprisingly, Claude Lévi-Strauss also embraced the house as a flexible analytic capable of transcending entrenched theoretical principles—including his own—and offering new perspectives on affiliation and collective life.

Unlike the traditional anthropological focus on descent, the house—and the ensuing "house societies"—is a hybrid social form that can change over time.[76] For Lévi-Strauss, the house is a "moral person," composed of material and immaterial goods that bind groups of people together.[77] In this framework, the traditionally rigid binaries of bloodlines, descent laws, and marital structures are no longer oppositional, but rather "tactics to be used simultaneously or alternately" (as Brisa and numerous characters of *Homeplaces* do).[78] The house borrows the language of kinship while simultaneously subverting it and forming new combinations. Such house-ing "allows us . . . to better understand how categories deemed incompatible can blend together," thus providing a window into the workings of time and the entanglements of human and more-than-human becomings.[79]

In Ryo Morimoto's essay, set in the aftermath of the Fukushima nuclear disaster, the elderly Naoko navigates the traditional layout of her house, which includes room for ancestral spirits, amid the excesses wrought by irradiation. Despite biopolitical warnings, she moves between her evacuated and temporary residences. This movement resurfaces and strengthens a domestic sensorium fundamental to Naoko's moral ideal of a satisfying death and a place of rest in the afterlife—things that cannot be technocratically redomesticated. Isotopes can coexist with humans, and houses never die completely. Like us oikographers, house-ing continually enters and reenters people's lives, even where and when habitability is threatened.

Livingness: Grounding Incompleteness

As we dehouse the planet, what practices of habitability and humanness emerge from the house?

By attending to the quest for homeplaces and the grounds of dehousing and house-making, we gain partial and meaningful insight into the shifting geographies and crossroads that shape livability.[80] Thus, the *oikos* is not only lively ontologically but also as a material manifestation—both closed and open—of the larger historical, social, political, and economic forces into which it is folded, and by which its own agentive properties are animated and sustained over time.

The ethnography of house-ings foregrounds incompleteness and unfinishedness. It offers us a means of charting the dynamics of habitability through time. This approach allows us to pay attention to material forms and the changes they mediate, to what is fluid and to what is fixed or bleeds, and to what people desire and do with mobility or stasis. Adopting this perspective allows us to consider multiple temporal registers simultaneously, addressing ancestry, the *longue durée* of history with its inheritances and ruptures, and the politics of domestication in the present moment.

Throughout *Homeplaces*, we focus on house-economic-ecological interconnections, think with and through the praxis of house-ing, and pursue six broad arcs of inquiry into this dynamic verb and related syntax: who, what, where, when, why, how?

- *Who constitutes the housed, the dehoused, and the in-between subject?* How does a focus on the housed/dehoused subject detonate ideas of the self, the governed, and the liberal subject? Who participates in domestication once we destabilize the anthropocentric?
- *What materialities and decays unfurl within the house, and what sensoria do they produce?* What surfaces when we attend to the physicality and bleeding of the house, and to house-ing as an archiving operation, that memory alone cannot capture?
- *Where are homes possible and where are they impossible?* Which places and forms of habitability and livingness emerge from attempts to dwell in uncertain and inhospitable environs? What third spaces or liminal zones are created?
- *When are homeplaces made?* In what ways do houses and their rhythms serve as an escape from the past and a platform from which to venture into the future? When do places we call home become moral arbiters, and how do their existence and demise affect the world?
- *Why do houses and the senses of home take the forms they do?* This question is as much about sense making and "the right to opacity" as it is about changing political and technological landscapes.[81] What drives a good life, the transcendence of harm, and the achievement of repair through domestic relationships, labor, and calculations?
- *How do housed and dehoused subjects perform the work of scaling and narrate their relational efforts at habitability?* How can this multitude of conceptual, political, and poetic imaginings refigure anthropological

knowledge making and enable new forms of inscription, storytelling, and visual representation?

Homeplaces emerges from our collective and ongoing engagement with the hard-to-pin-down multiplicity of house-ings that sets peoples, worlds, thoughts, and imaginations in motion. We treat houses in both their singular and plural forms. People operate with the concept of "the house" or "my home," so notions of singularity and belonging matter. Social life happens along and among houses, with houses also territorializing political collectives. Furthermore, we pay close attention to the immanent, sensory ways in which this manifold *oikos* inhabits people. We view the domestic realm as an organism, a lively dynamic of openness and closeness that transforms spaces into generative states of incompleteness. In house-ing, incompleteness is not a lack but rather a drive to relate to other houses or ideas of home. The agency of houses and peoples is intertwined as they continuously shape each other and their environs.

The essays of *Homeplaces* offer creative ways of reconceptualizing the relationship between the self, the house, the world-historical, and sensoria in the praxis of habitability, belonging, experimentation, and durability. Against the backdrop of horror and renewal, myriad temporal rhythms and gestures of intensification, resurfacing, leakage, and bleeding coalesce into collective noticing of a livingness that nourishes a different kind of insurgency and political possibility for the world.

NOTES

We want to thank the editorial guidance of Brad Weiss, Christopher Nelson, and Heather Paxson, who helped us publish a colloquium on our first collective set of reflections on the ethnography of house-ing (Biehl and Neiburg, "Oikography").

1. Heidegger, "Building Dwelling Thinking," 146. Martin Heidegger's essentializing concept of dwelling—"Only if we are capable of dwelling . . . can we build" (158)—has been criticized for its Eurocentrism and ahistoricism. Anthropologists such as Tim Ingold and James F. Weiner have shown that the philosopher's German romantic dwelling does not take into account the various place-making practices that have been documented in different societies. See Ingold, *Perception of the Environment*; J. Weiner, "Anthropology Contra Heidegger."

2. As Malcolm Ferdinand pointedly notes in *Decolonial Ecology*, "Heideggerian dwelling assumes a totalized Earth and a solitary man, immobile in his dwelling" (6).

Researchers working in urban settings and with migrant and refugee populations have further challenged Heidegger's place-bound conception and politically dangerous universalism by documenting how meaningful dwelling can emerge in transient conditions (Chavez, *Latino Threat*; Hage, *Diasporic Condition*; Joseph, "Maisons diasporas et maisons locales"; Olwig, *Caribbean Journeys*). On provisional forms of dwelling, see Guedes, "Interstícios, distâncias"; and Mello e Souza, "Formas provisórias de existência."

3. On the bourgeois ideal of domicile, see Elias, *Court Society*, chap. 1; on the disciplinary dimension of house and housing, see Foucault, *Discipline and Punish*; on the colonial roots of the disciplinary concept of domicile, see Mitchell, *Colonising Egypt*, chap. 3; and on the friction among local concepts of home and statistical concepts of domicile, see Motta, "Resisting Numbers."

4. Stewart, "Precarity's Form," 8. See also Ingold, "Building, Dwelling, Living."

5. Hooks, "Homeplace."

6. The concept of homeplace aligns with the experiences of *marronage* and *quilombos*—independent communities formed by escaped slaves to resist slavery across the Americas. See Price, *Maroon Societies*; Santos, *Colonização, quilombos*; and Dealdina, *Mulheres quilombolas*.

7. Hooks, "Homeplace," 41.

8. Hooks, "Homeplace," 49. See also Morrison, "The Site of Memory."

9. Our approach engages with a growing body of ethnographic work on the plight of the dehoused and the struggle to make home, including Jason De León's *The Land of Open Graves*, Matthew Desmond's *Evicted*, Didier Fassin and Anne-Claire Defossez's *Exile*, Brian Goldstone's *There Is No Place for Us*, and Nicholas Shapiro's *Homesick*.

10. See Das and Das, "How the Body Speaks"; Steedman, *Landscape for a Good Woman*; and Kopper, *Architectures of Hope*.

11. On "heterotopia," see Foucault, "Of Other Spaces."

12. On "modes/genres of being human," see Wynter, "Un-Settling the Coloniality," 331.

13. See Munira Khayyat's *A Landscape of War* and "Introduction: Another Season of War in South Lebanon."

14. See Rajagopalm, "Domicide"; and Porteous and Smith, *Domicide*.

15. Appadurai, "Mediants, Materiality, Normativity."

16. See Bachelard, *Poetics of Space*; and Douglas, "Idea of a Home."

17. See l'Estoile and Neiburg, "Governing the House"; and l'Estoile, "Can Economic Anthropology Escape?"

18. Arendt, *Human Condition*, 28.

19. Arendt, *Human Condition*, 28. See also Zelizer, *Social Meaning of Money*, chap. 2; Morduch and Schneider, *Financial Diaries*; and Zaloom and James, "Financialization and the Household."

20. Arendt, *Human Condition*, 33.

21. Arendt, *Human Condition*, 59.

22. Arendt, *Human Condition*, 39.

23. See Colomina, "Domesticity at War."

24. See Deleuze, "Postscript on Control Societies."

25. See Berlant, *Cruel Optimism.*

26. Bennett, *Vibrant Matter*, vii.

27. See Latour, *Reassembling the Social*, 50; Bennett, *Vibrant Matter*, ix. Things, Bennett argues, possess vital powers, serving "not only to impede or block the will and designs of humans but also to act as quasi agents or forces with trajectories, propensities, or tendencies of their own" (viii). Citing Gilles Deleuze and Félix Guattari's "material vitalism" as inspiration, Bennett is interested in the way such agencies reverberate, trying to "bear witness to the vital materialities that flow through and around us" (x). From this attention to "thing-power" as a "productive, positive power," matter becomes an active force that intervenes in the world and the public sphere. See also Connolly, *World of Becoming.*

28. Bennett, *Vibrant Matter*, xiii. See also Miller, *Home Possessions.*

29. Appadurai, "Mediants, Materiality, Normativity," 221. See also Fischer, "Peopling of Technologies."

30. See, for example, Carsten and Hugh-Jones, *About the House*; Beeckmans et al., *Making Home(s) in Displacement*; Frost and Selwyn, *Travelling Towards Home*; and Stolz and Alderman, *Houses Transformed.*

31. Mauss, *Seasonal Variations*, 20. See also P. Dawson, "Seeing Like an Inuit Family."

32. Mauss, *Seasonal Variations*, 36.

33. Mauss, *Seasonal Variations*, 21. For another instance of seasonal transhumance patterns, see Claude Lévi-Strauss's accounts of Kwakiutl mythologies as commentaries on the human-land-sea relations in "The Story of Asdiwal," and Marshall Sahlins's account on sea-land patterns of polities in both the Pacific and the Aegean in "The Stranger-King."

34. Ingold, *Perception of the Environment.* See also Liboiron et al., "Toxic Politics"; and Walley, *Exit Zero.*

35. Pina-Cabral, "Partible Houses." See also Cortado, "La force du regard."

36. See Petryna, *Horizon Work.*

37. Lévi-Strauss, *Savage Mind*, chap. 1.

38. Mauss, *Seasonal Variations*, 52.

39. Boas, foreword to *Mules and Men.*

40. See Benedict, *Anthropologist at Work*; Mead, *Coming of Age*; and Hurston, "You Don't Know Us Negroes."

41. Hurston, *Mules and Men*, 10.

42. Hurston, *Mules and Men*, 10.

43. Deleuze, "What Children Say," 63. See also Barthes, *How to Live Together.*

44. See Biehl, *Jammerthal, o Vale da Lamentação*; and Munn, "The 'Becoming-Past' of Places."

45. See Garcia, *The Way That Leads Among the Lost.*

46. Hurston, *Barracoon*, 98.

47. Biehl and Locke, "The Anthropology of Becoming," 55–57.

48. See Brown, *Descendant.*

49. Hurston, *Barracoon*, 40, 52.

50. Hurston, *Barracoon*, 38.

51. Hurston, *Barracoon*, 52.

52. Hurston, *Barracoon*, 40.

53. Womack, "Contraband Flesh."

54. Hurston, *Barracoon*, 55, 95, 96, 101.

55. Hartman, *Lose Your Mother*, 6; Hurston, *Barracoon*, 109. See also Hartman, *Scenes of Subjection*.

56. Hurston, *Barracoon*, 109.

57. Hurston, *Barracoon*, 131.

58. Hurston, *Barracoon*, 96.

59. Marcelin, "A linguagem da casa." See also Comerford and Neiburg, "A casa e a invenção da família."

60. Marcelin, "A linguagem da casa," 37.

61. Hurston, *Barracoon*, 131.

62. Bourdieu and Sayad, *Uprooting*.

63. See Pérez, *Bourdieu and Sayad Against Empire*.

64. Bourdieu and Sayad, *Uprooting*, 156.

65. Fanon, *Wretched of the Earth*, 23.

66. Fanon, *Wretched of the Earth*, 23.

67. Fanon, *Wretched of the Earth*, 37.

68. Fanon, *Wretched of the Earth*, 61.

69. Fanon, *Wretched of the Earth*, 275.

70. See Said, *After the Last Sky*; and Weizman, *Forensic Architecture*.

71. Bourdieu, "Berber House."

72. A. Weiner, *Women of Value*. See also Munn, *Fame of Gawa*.

73. A. Weiner, in *Women of Value*, asks: "When the role of women is being publicly dramatized, what statement is a woman making about the structure of the social and cosmic order?" (18).

74. See Yanagisako, "Family and Household"; Guyer, "Household and Community"; Humphrey, "No Place Like Home"; and Weston, *Families We Choose*.

75. Carsten, *After Kinship*, 26.

76. Lévi-Strauss, "Maison," 435. See also Carsten and Hugh-Jones, *About the House*; and Joyce and Gillespie, *Beyond Kinship*.

77. Lévi-Strauss, *Paroles données*, 190. See also Motta, "O que faz o dinheiro da casa," 6.

78. Lévi-Strauss, "Maison," 436.

79. Lévi-Strauss, "Maison," 436. See also Biehl and Locke, *Unfinished*.

80. See McKittrick, "I Lost an Arm."

81. Glissant, *Poetics of Relation*, 185.

PART I

Dehoused

JOÃO BIEHL

1

Home Sentience

Dehoused

"I know the house is no longer there," Vó (Granny) Armanda says. "But I want to see the araucaria [candelabra tree]."[1] She had not been to her birthplace in Riegels' Trail, a remote corner of Picada Café, for over sixty years—"since Oscar took me to be married." As a subject dehoused, Vó Armanda still harbored the desire for home that memory had yet to destroy. "Ich kann das noch immer spüren" (I can still sense it), she tells me in Hunsrückisch, the oral koine-like language that my unschooled immigrant ancestors devised and in which I also grew up.[2]

It is July 1993. I am back in the place of my beginnings in southern Brazil after two years in California, where I have been pursuing graduate studies in religion and circuitously finding my way into anthropology. As I reconnect with family, I also make further inroads into my dissertation on the nineteenth-century Mucker civil war that shattered German-Brazilian communities, of which I am an accidental descendant.[3]

I am a fifth-generation offspring of poor emigrants who fled hardships and wars in the Old World and came to the settlement of São Leopoldo in search of a new home, much like the millions of Germans who fled to the United States throughout the nineteenth century. Founded in 1824, this new smallholding colonization experiment was part of an imperial military-agricultural plan aimed at securing the frontier zone still in dispute between Brazil, Uruguay, and Argentina. In a region where about a third of the population was enslaved, these colonists were also meant to diversify the economy and whiten the labor force. The land serving as the frontier to some was also the traditional territory of the Kaingang people, an Indigenous nation that was either killed or forcibly displaced in the early 1800s during a plantation venture, which ultimately foundered, based on enslaved Black labor.

Around the kitchen table and in extended family gatherings, I grew up hearing about the hardships our ancestors faced. Yet, strangely, no one knew where exactly those ancestors had come from or, for that matter, the original history of this settler frontier. It was as if we lived in a present without political memory, a present shaped by the straits of survival and punctuated by the household's vital events. Work on the family farm from dawn to dusk, long trips on an ox wagon over perilous roads to bring agricultural products to the city, lack of access to formal health care, and a century without public education—these were fates that my *colono* parents would try to spare their children.[4]

Poignantly, tombstone inscriptions from those early days convey the *colônias* as a ravaged place and home as a wearying pilgrimage:

> Home pilgrim, now rest from life's toil and sorrow in the cemetery's silent house until the resurrection morning.
>
> Here we have no permanent place. We are looking for the future one.

This sense of unhomeliness would be my heritage, too.

Like all settler frontiers, this was a place of violence, subjugation, and systemic neglect. Ordinary *colonos* would have to find ways to fix precarious infrastructures by themselves and create their own therapeutic practices to

FIGURE 1.1. Nineteenth-century house. Photo by Torben Eskerod.

ward off untimely death—as did those who were deemed "false saints," or Mucker.

Around 1868, a pious healing movement emerged in the remote colony of Leonerhof (today Sapiranga). It centered on the trances and scriptural interpretations of a young woman called Jacobina Mentz Maurer and the herbal remedies concocted by her husband, João Jorge Maurer—both born to immigrant parents. The story goes that the unconscious Jacobina would communicate enlightenments from the "spirit of nature" and, based on these visions, João Jorge, the "Wonder Doctor," would prepare infusions for the growing number of afflicted who flocked to their house.

"After three years in perfect order," as an early participant would later put it, the group became known, first among estranged neighbors and then by the church, the press, and the government, as *Mucker*—literally, those who dig muck, who are false saints, sanctimonious and hypocritical.[5] Enveloped in rumors of apostasy, immorality, and communism, those searching for belonging and mending through the Maurers were instead framed as a threat to the very foundations of the colonial enterprise. Authorities portrayed these homegrown enemies as "bloody primitive Indians" and mutinous "white negroes"—and treated them as such.[6] In 1874, during a year of intense intra-ethnic conflict, approximately one hundred Mucker families were hunted down and killed like wild beasts by settler militias and national army troops, called in by the local elites who knew all too well how to massacre dissent.[7]

Bystanders to the conflict, like my ancestors, would thereafter dread the heavy hand of the state, conceal any traces of a nature-bound spirituality, and trust no one. Living in fear that Mucker-like creatures would steal their animals or goods at night or tear down their houses, they would sleep next to their rifles. The lesson was invariably "Man muss sich aufpassen" (You have to watch yourself), as my grandpa, Vô Oscar, would hark back to while drinking his nightly bottle of rum.

I Can Still Sense It

As I continue to wrestle with my own escapes and returns, I am enthralled by Vó Armanda's understanding of the house as something unbound by time and space and as an openness that sparks her own sense of exile. Through

FIGURE 1.2. Home pilgrimage. Photo by Torben Eskerod.

and beyond the materiality of a "house that is no longer there" (with both its gendered history and ravaged diasporic landscape), Granny conveys a lasting sensorium that shelters desire: "I want to see" the critically endangered pine tree.

What surfaces for me in this encounter is not a human submission to an ur-family complex or to the tyrannical "idea of a [primary] home" but, rather, what I call *home sentience*—a human-nonhuman archiving impulse that indexes homemaking efforts and survivals and that drives sociality and the journeying of subjects across multiple milieus.[8] "Ich kann das noch immer spüren" (I can still sense it).

Something more than merely the chronological and territorial is at play here. The evanescent edges of a poetic modulation crystallize around Vó Armanda's enduring sense of home. There is a word for this, I believe—*spüren*. In the Hunsrückisch German-Brazilian language, the verb *spüren* means to perceive something physically. The emotional term *fühlen* (to feel) cannot capture such an incarnate *Spur* (trace). In its polysemy, *spüren* also means to foresee and to lay a track, to map and reterritorialize, if you will. Yes: "The smallest cell remembers . . . a secret order among syllables . . . how do you . . . how can you . . . lose a language," the poet M. NourbeSe Philip presciently writes.[9] *Spuren*, then, are the footprints of a hunted animal.

Seen from this perspective, the sense of home or home sentience is an unwritten constellation of intensities and traces that, shaped by life circumstances and fantasy spaces, absorb and amplify everything that passes through them, like veritable prisms of light, forging a kind of sensorial, image-making pluriverse—as in Philip's poetic rendering:

Stone mourns
                    haunted
into shape and form
by its loss
              upon

                    loss
honed keen . . .
to unleash the promise
                                    in ugly
the absent in image.[10]

Home sentience reorients anthropological praxis to encompass surges of survival that relentlessly forge capacious cartographies of belonging and promise. Here, I hone the auto-ethnographic to shore up the surges of my ancestors' house-ing efforts and the interferences of their poetic trails, which upend the limits of the speakable and the known—a "loss upon loss." I am challenged to excavate the in-betweenness of lives lived elsewise and deaths deferred to elsewheres, from the sediments that have come to me through the figural.

The Absent in Image

Now widowed for over two decades, Vó Armanda lives alone in a small house that my father built. A few days after our initial conversation, I go back to plan the trip to the site of her childhood in the *Kolonien—colônias*—as we call the rural settlements we all hail from. Out of the blue, Granny says, "Letzte Nacht habe ich mit dem Haus geträumt. Du warst auch da" (Last night, I dreamed with the house. You were there, too).

The house appears here not as "a body of images that give mankind proofs or illusions of stability," as Gaston Bachelard suggests in *The Poetics of Space*, but rather as an operator of imagination, kinning, and lamentation.[11] Vó Armanda says that she dreamt *with* the material vestiges of the house: "I was in the old house in the colony; all the windows were open."

An opening of the house to the world and its unforeseens, the window image works as a portal of sorts. And in the scene that follows, I hear the haunting depeopling of her sense of home: from the windows of the house that is no more, Vó Armanda does not see the desired araucaria tree but instead sees the burial ground of her familial social body. She intuits ancestral thresholds, a vision that I now live in: "Then, all of a sudden, I was in the cemetery, next to the grave where Oscar [her husband] and Iva [her daughter] are buried."

A third grave marker, a cross, has fallen on the ground, Granny adds, enunciating a possible future through her home sentience: "Joãochen [little João, as she used to call me], you stood next to that cross, holding a newborn in your arms."

To my ears, then, Vó Armanda's dream channeled the real dread of having to witness the passing of her son—my ill father, who was being amputated,

FIGURES 1.3 AND 1.4. Vó Armanda and João at the window.
Photos by Torben Eskerod.

FIGURE 1.5. A plant grows from a grave in the Lutheran cemetery of Picada Café. Photo by Torben Eskerod.

limb by limb, by a merciless diabetes—all while trying, in her clairvoyance, to keep open the question of intergenerational transmission. It was as if the shadow of death had rekindled Granny's homespun sentience. Absence is not lack: "The absent [is] in image."[12]

Two years later, when death broke into our house, Granny's dream immediately came back to mind. Especially the image of the window, because the last words my father uttered to my mother before he passed away in July 1995 were, amazingly: "Why did you close the house? Open the window!"

As the concreteness and multivalence of the open window further splintered what remained of my historical objectivity and flat realism, it also sharpened my attentiveness to what is out of place, to the porousness between life and nonlife, and to the coexistence of the actual and unhistorical in one's sense of home and of what is to come. With every return to former familial grounds, I became ever more attuned to the ways home sentience was imprinted on the bodies of my journeying ancestors.

I reflect on the *traces-of-what-one-does-not-know* that have come my way over the years (and that have unraveled taxonomies of my own doing) in light of Walter Benjamin's early fascination with "flashes," in which "history appears to be concentrated on a single focal point," and through his idea of dialectical images that surface when "what has been comes together in a flash with the now to form a constellation," such that the image in that moment expresses "dialectics at a standstill."[13] This is because memory is mediated, and such mediations are "not temporal in nature but figural [*bildlich*]," shattering the fantasy of a philosophy of history without interruption.[14] Moreover, in these figural moments of arrest, which "can only take place in a flash," history charges to the fore and "the has-been can be grasped."[15]

With time, then, these sediments and personal flashes seeped into the historical traces I found in my work on the Mucker. While one struggles to recover "what has been lost and found and lost again and again," a conscientious empiricism wedded to a radical analytical openness to wonder is in order.[16]

As I drove back into the colonies, I talked to strangers I encountered along the roads and often stopped to visit distant relatives. I attended religious services and walked through cemeteries, enraptured by any erstwhile remnant that came my way. I encountered improvised things and wondrous surfaces, like the earthbound imagery of ancient graves: a sun, a branch of leaves, and at times a desiring heart.

Was this a nature-bound spirituality?

Insurgent Archivings

Then there were the kernels of counterhistories.

"The Mucker were not bad people," the elder Edgar told me, overlooking the serpentine road leading to Picada Café. "They were colonists like us. But they wanted power. My grandpa said that Jacobina was like Christ. More than this I don't know."

It was always an elder in the family who anchored Mucker ties and activated surviving images. As Rudolfo, the owner of a trade house in the nearby colony of Santa Maria do Herval, also conveyed: "My grandfather used to say that the Mucker did not cause trouble around here. . . . People went to Jacobina, celebrated, and then returned to their homes." Within the meanderings of the downtrodden, I sensed a different longevity of the domestic, therapeutic beginnings of the Mucker, shining light on outlying worldings and insurgent archivings.

I, too, wanted to enter into a living relationship with *what-one-does-not-know*. Folded into exteriorities and resonances that demanded further elaboration, these homespun intergenerational flickerings both sharpened my intuition and transfigured into little epiphanies. Exceeding the political conjured by the ruling classes, they helped me narrate origins, autobiographical and Mucker, in a new light, so that a possible justice could be imagined and a mysteriousness to existence sustained.

Ergo, the traces of a Mucker sentience that have come my way throughout the years guide my own *oikography* (home imprinting). I want to allow these traces to form a lifeworld, a landscape, a story. With this simple effort to pilgrim home, one more time, I hope to experience the journey differently, a bit more freely.

FIGURE 1.6. Edgar's home. Photo by Torben Eskerod.

Self: Home Imprint

I, too, was born in Kaffeeschneiss (today Picada Café), the rural settlement where my Biehl forebears first landed in the mid-1840s. Until I started first grade at the barely functional Grupo Escolar Rincão dos Ilhéus, Hunsrückisch was the language that I lived in at home. Our family, like so many others, self-deprecatingly referred to what we spoke as *Hecke* Deutsch (German from the bushes)—which was far from the Hochdeutsch (standard German) spoken by the urban elites and the clergy. In other words, we conversed in the language of potato-planting peasants, which formed an impenetrable mesh of branches that kept us enclosed in a separate field of existence, excluded, as it were, from the nation.

My mother, Noemia, was taken out of school in fourth grade to help with farming, and my father, Fernando, found his way into a tannery after finishing fifth grade. In the mid-1960s, the young couple migrated with their two little children to the periphery of the German-sounding city of Novo Hamburgo, then the epicenter of a booming national shoe industry. These were the early days of the country's decades-long military dictatorship. My parents wanted to start a small meat-processing business to pay off the debts they had inherited from their parents and to give my sister Marina and me a chance at studying—a destiny other than child labor.

Even though we saw a future for ourselves in the city, the *colônias* stayed with us. In language and homemade food for sure, since Granny Armanda and Grandpa Oscar ended up migrating too; and my other grandma, Vó Minda, lived with us after her deranged husband, Alfonso, set their house on fire. Then there were the frequent trips back to the countryside: with my father to get pork for sausages and with the whole family to the yearly Kerb (to this day, the most important festival in German-Brazilian communities). But the colonies also stayed with us in the daily bullying we experienced for being *colono grossos* (crude settlers) or *alemão batatas* (German potatoes), even though we had little sense of ourselves as German and little knowledge of that place called Germany. My kin, cornered and ashamed as they were, seemed to agree that we were *nichts*—poor white social nothings.

At school, only little Isabel was picked on more cruelly. She had the darkest skin of all and, to make matters worse, carried the German surname Bauermann. Isabel was the niece of Clelia, who helped my mother and Vó Minda

FIGURE 1.7. Making sausages on the patio of our early home in Kaffeeschneiss: Uncle Hédio (second from left), Grandpa Oscar (fourth from left), and eighteen-year-old Noemia (in the back) holding my sister Marina and expecting me. Photo from the Biehl family archive.

make sausages. Only later, during my forays into Mucker history, would I connect the dots and learn that Clelia and her kin were actually descended from enslaved Afro-Brazilians owned by the wealthy and powerfully connected immigrant Johann Georg Bauermann of the Picada 48 colony. Bauermann had his captives baptized into the Lutheran faith with his surname. Older boys would mock Isabel's looks, saying things like "Essa nunca vai ser princesa" (This one will never be a princess). This was a not-too-subtle allusion to Princesa Isabel, the heiress to the Brazilian throne, who, in 1888, signed the law that officially ended slavery but certainly not racialized domination. Mortified, Isabel and I would sit side by side under the school's stairs during recess, quietly watching the ruthless world play out.

Could this child still be me?

As I look at my first-grade school photograph, I like to think that the child appears sincere in this framed environment. I had yet to master posing naturally or smiling at the right time. Wearing the school uniform my mother had sewn, I sit in front of the Brazilian map, flanked by the flag bearing the positivistic motto *Order and Progress* and the globe of my fugitive dreams, with my hands, as the teacher ordered, resting over the Portuguese dictionary. Since my handwriting was nascent, my father, who had always been proud of his cursive, carefully signed my name on the memento, just as he used to sign his. I wonder what he saw of himself in this image. There is something the child sees and is yet to write.

In reality, in the comings and goings between our migrant home in Novo Hamburgo and the *colônias*, I found myself estranged from both worlds. I was terrified of the little violences always ready to erupt in our poor, strict household. There was so little room for play with so much order and cleanliness. I was sure from an early age that I was nobody's love and that arbitrariness ruled my little world. How I wished I belonged to another place, family, and nation, or even to none at all.

Religion, at times, did the trick, giving form to a transient locality I could find refuge in. Monthly Lutheran worship services took place in the *salão* (big saloon) that my parents had rented and that worked syncretically as our home, a bodega, a dancing hall with live music on Saturday evenings, and a church on Sunday mornings for the growing community of peri-urban *colonos*. Pastor Mertz's riveting biblical storytelling was like a movie to me, and his classical education spoke to the elsewhere of civilization I could step into,

FIGURE 1.8. School portrait. Photo from the Biehl family archive.

FIGURE 1.9. Flowers that won't perish at the Lutheran Cemetery of Linha Nova. Photo by Torben Eskerod.

right there in my own public house. This itinerant theater gave me a first glimpse of elite culture. I was left increasingly detached from my supposed origins and with the budding intuition that the house is a platform for departure and that the more invented, the more real you are.

While enveloped in my own estrangement and resolve to escape, I was still struck by things from this other space-time—things that even now rip through my forgetfulness, such as the herbal ointments my mother and grannies used to rub on our chests in the cold winter to get rid of bronchitis, and the prayers and teas of the healing lady who lived a few blocks from us and who once even fixed my broken leg.

I witnessed this human/plant caregiving from ages past applied equally to the living and the dead. I would join Vó Minda every month in her faithful pilgrimage to the grave of her beloved son Hédio—who had also once lived with us and had been hit and killed by a drunk driver. I helped her carry the flowers and wash each and every one of the little stones that adorned Hédio's grave. Time and again, as we walked back home, Granny reminded me that I had been taught the numerals at age four so that I could guide the legally blind Hédio around the neighborhood as we delivered groceries from my parents' improvised bodega.

Unbeknownst to me at the time, Vó Minda was gifting me an ancestral figure of the unwritten in the form of death—an early element of the complex home sentience that Granny Armanda would channel to me. It was the imperative to pay a return visit and to let the dead and the house "no longer there"—a "sensate conceptuality . . . out there and coming" (as Kathleen Stewart would say)—imprint you and guide you: Such are the relational and atmospheric unknowns that extend self, space-time, belonging, and historical truth.[17]

The Exile in Excrescence

It is a sunny yet cold afternoon in July 1993 when my parents and I finally take Granny Armanda to visit the site of her early life in Vila Rica. On the way, people warn us of a huge white snake roaming the ruins now swallowed by the wild flora. Unlike me, Granny does not seem to fear the creature.

The house is no more. Without the windows to behold, Vó Armanda's bent, diminutive figure walks straight to the araucaria tree she grew up with.

She is quiet as her big blue eyes tear up. That is all she wants the centennial tree to know, I tell myself. The nonhuman finding expression. An image that is enough to atone for a life almost exhausted, insignificant to history.

On the way back, we stop at Miro and Noia's farm. My parents' best friends are resting on the front lawn, along with their coworkers. We want to catch up and get vegetables and that special honey from the beehive Miro adores. Miro's older brother Egidio (known to speak his mind after a few drinks) points to me and asks my father: "Wer ist das?" (Who is this?).

Once he is told that I am a child of *colonos* born nearby—"unser Sohn" (our son)—Egidio looks straight into my eyes and addresses a third person: "Aber er ist nicht hier gewachsen" (But he did not grow up here).

In the language that (unbeknownst to Egidio) we still share, *wachsen* is used to refer to the growth of either people or plants, like potatoes out of dirt or corn for bread and for feeding the animals.

And words spill over: *Gewächs* is a distinct outgrowth on a human or animal body or on a plant, especially one that is the result of an aberration.

An excrescence—that is how I appeared to the curious farmer. Maybe he was rightly pointing to the strangeness of my dehoused existence. Of uncertain destiny: I would never really belong there. There was no earth under my fingernails. My hands were molded by words, after all.

Yet I kept returning. Apparitions and historical ethnographers like me eventually find a connection through our concern for the past and for futures marked out and gone—our own, and those of the people we came from and who remain dear to us: traces of the dead and of ways of living together, violently dismissed, that defy epistemological seizure.

I am transported by this opacity far away from the archive as characterized by the Greek *arkheion*: that home of the archive that was, as Jacques Derrida writes in *Archive Fever*, "initially a house, a domicile, an address, the superior magistrates, the archons, those who commanded."[18] In this frontier zone of seeming stagnation, and through the humanity of those dismissed as unschooled and criminal in their visions, we can ascertain forms that are unbounded and uncaptured by conventional ways of knowing.

Although cursed, this communitarian way of caring for oneself and one's loved ones *with* nature would remain alive as wandering nonknowledge, manifesting the home sentience and "plastic power" of these internally colonized folks and their offspring, including me.[19]

This became clear to me when, a few years later, I went back to the colonies to find the original of a rare picture of a Mucker family—the Fuchses—that had caught my eye while I had been perusing a local genealogy book.[20] After clashing with newly arrived German missionary Heinrich W. Hunsche, the elder Fuchs begged his family to bury him by the house and not in the Lutheran cemetery. After much probing, I found the image in the very house the Fuchses had built in 1862.

The house contained multiple records, including a box of glass negatives depicting life there in the early twentieth century and a stack of notes, receipts, and deeds, speaking to the *longue durée* of a local exchange system.

On the last page of a Lutheran family book, I found the recipe for an herbal remedy written in Hunsrückisch, which propelled Lucinda (the current owner) to take me to the garden, where she listed, one by one, the healing and poisoning properties of the intergenerational botanical assemblage she grew up caring for.

Her husband, Silvio, eagerly took me through the woods to a massive cottonweed tree and pointed to century-old carvings. "The bark helps calm sore body parts."

As I marveled at those human-plant inscriptions, Silvio added that right there, to the left of where we were standing, was the old horses' road, through which the Fuchses would have ridden to the Maurers' home.

Jacobina's Trance and the Spirit of Nature: The Mucker's Homespun Healing in Death

The oral recollection the Mucker survivor João Daniel Noé left to his offspring substantiates this elsewhere and *colono* journeying.[21] According to Noé, around 1868 several afflicted families started to coalesce around the deathlike estrangements of a pregnant Jacobina and the herbal infusions prepared by her husband, João Jorge. Noé and his wife, Catarina, who was also pregnant, took part in those early meetings, along with their small children (one had recently died) and extended kin.

"Jacobina felt that she was losing her strength and the capacity to think. There was great risk to her health during these episodes," Noé recounted.[22] This was indeed a precarious living environment, suffused with both high fertility and untimely death (particularly child and maternal mortality).[23] I

FIGURE 1.10. Healing tree. Photo by Torben Eskerod.

suspect the specter of death to have been a driving force of this Mucker story-in-the-making, as powerful a force as the cultural cataclysm that religious and secular elites were spurring in the colonies. The thought of death and the death of thought fused in the entranced Jacobina: a copresence by way of death. In this caring atmosphere, historical knowledge momentarily vanished and a new domain of perception (beyond memory making) opened up. "She said things unconsciously, and people had to repeat them to her when she came back to herself."[24] Barely audible, the sounds emanating from Jacobina's enrapt body became a shared, communal nonknowledge: the traces of possible trajectories.

The elder's recollection turned the official clock of history back from the venomous fabulation of the powerless as "false saints" and seditious Mucker and toward a whole anthropology of the sensible: the inscrutability and social intelligibility of human-nonhuman alignments in that space of refuge at the foothills of Ferrabraz Mountain. "There was enlightenment for all kind of illnesses, regardless of their names."[25]

In this extended open house, folks felt warmly welcomed and cared for. The sympathetic spirit of nature bestowed enlightenments, and the afflicted suffused themselves and their loved ones with herbs picked from the Maurers' garden. "Herbal infusions were prepared and, depending on the location of the disease, they were rubbed on the body or ingested."[26] With time, people stayed for communal meals. They sang and prayed together and, led by Jacobina, they would often recite the Beatitudes: "Blessed are the poor in spirit, for theirs is the kingdom of heaven. Blessed are those who mourn, for they will be comforted. Blessed are the meek, for they will inherit the earth."[27] Reality entered the realm of the miraculous. For some, it was an experience of the sacred or a curiosity one did not want to miss; for others, a desired affective reorientation . . . "until everything returned to normal."[28]

In his recollection, Noé portrayed his fellow pilgrims as folks who disputed what constituted enlightenment and the value of its simulations in everyday spaces, looking instead to the Maurers' home as an alternative site of belonging, healing, and truth. People wanted "to reach clarity and not go on wandering in darkness." He indicted the law as criminal, as partaking in Mucker animalization/dehumanization: "Why weren't the persons who promoted slanders and lies—they did not come from *our* house—questioned

FIGURE 1.11. On the way to Ferrabraz Mountain. Photo by Torben Eskerod.

by the law too? The answer to this question would reveal who were, in fact, the perpetrators of the cutting of the horses' tails and the slaughter of the cattle."[29]

As I see it, Noé's recollection (dictated to his son Miguel in the early 1900s) and the present-day human-plant workings of folks such as Lucinda and Silvio speak not to a local "critical fabulation" (as Saidiya Hartman would have it, given the impossibility of ancestral archival recovery) but to the surviving home sentience and healing tradition of the free-spirited "nothings" of history.[30] Through sentient traces we are given the means of opening up to such a banned language and its metamorphic power.

As Lucinda and Silvio took me for a walk in the field, I sensed glimpses of an ancestral topology of repair that included reverence for the dead nearby, the vitality of herbal gardens, forest medicinal goods, seances to access other elements of the spirit of nature, and the recalling of transmitted moralities. There it was: facing death, abandoning notions that life had hitherto accustomed us to, and embracing the unknown.

Indeed, these traces are always themselves transforming from an inchoate poetics to an insurmountable palimpsest, without ever fully becoming either and equally relinquishing neither. The ethnographer-storyteller is one among the many entities pulsating in the poetic-prismatic palimpsest of capacious traces, only to become something else: a collective of copresences that anthropological praxis can either let rot and further vanish—like a discarded Mucker way of living in an "abnormal" transient space—or allow to be reanimated by its lures.

Unknown

"Why did you close the house? Open the window!"

These words said, my father died next to my mother on July 18, 1995.

My parents had been spending a few days at the seashore when I received the call at their place in Novo Hamburgo, where I was staying for the summer, working on my Mucker war dissertation.

My mother's voice sounded oddly calm as she told me, matter-of-factly, "Puve ist tot" (Puve is dead). My father was named Fernando, but like everyone who knew him, my mother called him Puve, which is how our "German from the bushes" language renders the word *Bub* (little boy).

FIGURE 1.12. Araucaria. Photo by Torben Eskerod.

Word of my father's death put me in a state of wakefulness I had never experienced before. It was not just that he was too young (only fifty-eight years old) and that I thought I must be the next Biehl to die . . . but also, and painfully so, the sense that my father was gone and still largely unknown to me.

Truthfully, I had never seen myself in my father. And where my curiosity about him had repeatedly fallen short—from my mistaking his past drunkenness and his hard work and generosity as subservience and simplemindedness, to my lack of comprehension about what kept him going as he was being amputated by a relentless disease—a harrowing silence now stood.

And as death burst into the family, a mysterious spiritual movement started to conjure in my mind. I urgently needed any remnant that could help transform the brute void of my father into a human spirit, a ghost of mine. And that is why, I think, the first thing I asked of my mother was to retrieve a missing language: Did he say anything before he passed away?

"Why did you close the house? Open the window!"

My father sensed death approaching, and these whispers are how he treated the border between life and the world beyond—this is what I tell myself. From this border he saw a house, not locked up in fear but open to the unknown: home sentience worded.

And so one disappears.

The days that followed my father's death are a blur, with the exception of two things, or apparitions, that I know will follow me to my grave. With their mysterious multivalence, these happenstances unraveled the finality of the event. They brought me back from mournful self-deception to an altered present, and where my memory failed, they became the memorials I could turn to.

Homecoming in the Grieving Crowd

Clearly visible in my muddled recollection of the funeral is the moment when, before the pastor's eulogy, people started to gather, with their self-effacing, downcast gazes, around Puve's casket.

In hindsight, nothing was then out of time. Everyone in that transient collective had been part of a larger "talking crowd" (be it in Hunsrückisch or Hochdeutsch or Portuguese or all combined) that had preceded my father, our family, us, in the colonies and Novo Hamburgo, our migrant destination.[31] Each and every one there came from the most mundane encounters they had crafted with my father. Displaying heartfelt sorrow and in their best Sunday clothing, people like Miro, my father's best friend, simply let the tears say it all. Others found faltering words to convey the part Puve had played in their lives.

In utterance after utterance, the past physically became one with the present through these fleeting beings, ancestral and of uncertain origin, conjuring up my father's whole cosmos and his precise place in it. These flickers of life reconstituted moments of my father's existence but also a longer history of the collective that preceded us. It was a deeply moving cacophony of affects, so readily dismissed as worthless or incomprehensible by those of us who had insisted on keeping the father figure and his consciousness locked up, as it were, at home. But home always leaks out into the social. And grief made this spillage visible.

Partly real, partly imagined, the image of a social body and of living together that had always eluded me was there before my eyes, lamenting itself being ripped apart. This was not the antechamber to eternal life: Clinging to each other, the apocryphal emotions and stories intoned around Puve's dead body were a most compelling, neighborly way to pay a return visit, to shape an intimate reminiscence, to keep the spirit of the dead at one's present-day dwelling. This was death (real and imagined) as a way of sensing—a divergent means of communication, in and out of the household. And the sense of home and its people is porous and always incomplete, in the midst of being formed.

The imperative "Open" of my father's last words.

I had been awake for almost two days now, and as these emotional identifications with my dead father arrested the cognizable, they also unleashed, in flashes, a delirium of what might have been. Amid all the inner haze, I imagined that the expressions in which the memories of my father's existence were being cast had been articulated long before in the *colônias*.

I was seeing and hearing remnants of a certain way of perceiving things, ordering human relationships, and dealing with mortality and engaging the dead that had once been second nature to the peoples—let's keep them plural—whom I was trying to extract from the word *Mucker*, in which they had been inhumanly confined.

Images from my research blurred with those I was witnessing in this moment, indexing survivals and lasting flickers. Had this mode of existence been staged around Jacobina's body, which, stonelike, seemed to have lost all sensation? Had this communal stage and the herbal infusions prepared by João Jorge been a commonsensical way of addressing ailments and misfortunes in bodies old and young?

Was this their way of remembering how to live?

On a fence, somewhere between perception and consciousness, I was hallucinating connections. I could fathom this other home and banned language in which body and mind were interlaced with death, the spirit of nature, and a transient collective. For the nonhuman, gaps of comprehension, and what could have been—"the poetry it is possible not to write"—are also where one comes from.[32]

Of all the words I had hurriedly scribbled to say at the funeral on behalf of the family, the ones I have not forgotten are those I found inscribed on a tombstone from the time of the Mucker events in the Lutheran cemetery of the settlement of Linha Nova; I have yet to fully grasp their meaning:

> And the cruel word of death ripped itself from the arms of the loved one and from the children's circle. Nothing replaces for us this absence.

The Living Window Image

The most breathtaking of the apparitions following my father's death occurred a week after the funeral. I walked over to Granny Armanda to see how she was holding up and to bring her some food, as my father would have done.

"Komm herein, Joãochen" (Come in, little João).

As I knew from my mother what my father's last words had been—"Open the window!"—I wanted to know from *his* mother which words he first spoke.

Teary-eyed, she told a story, as simple as it was profound, from the time before the child could say mother (*Mutter*) and father (*Vater*) or play with gone-there (*fort-da*):

"Puve was nine months old, and he was running a high fever. I touched him, as he was restless in the cradle. And all of a sudden, he had a seizure. I screamed to Oscar," Granny continued, "'Come here quick.' Oscar came and took the child to Old Biehl, who lived next door."

Almost one hundred years had passed since Johann Karl and Maria Louisa Biehl had immigrated to those lands, and there was still no formal medical

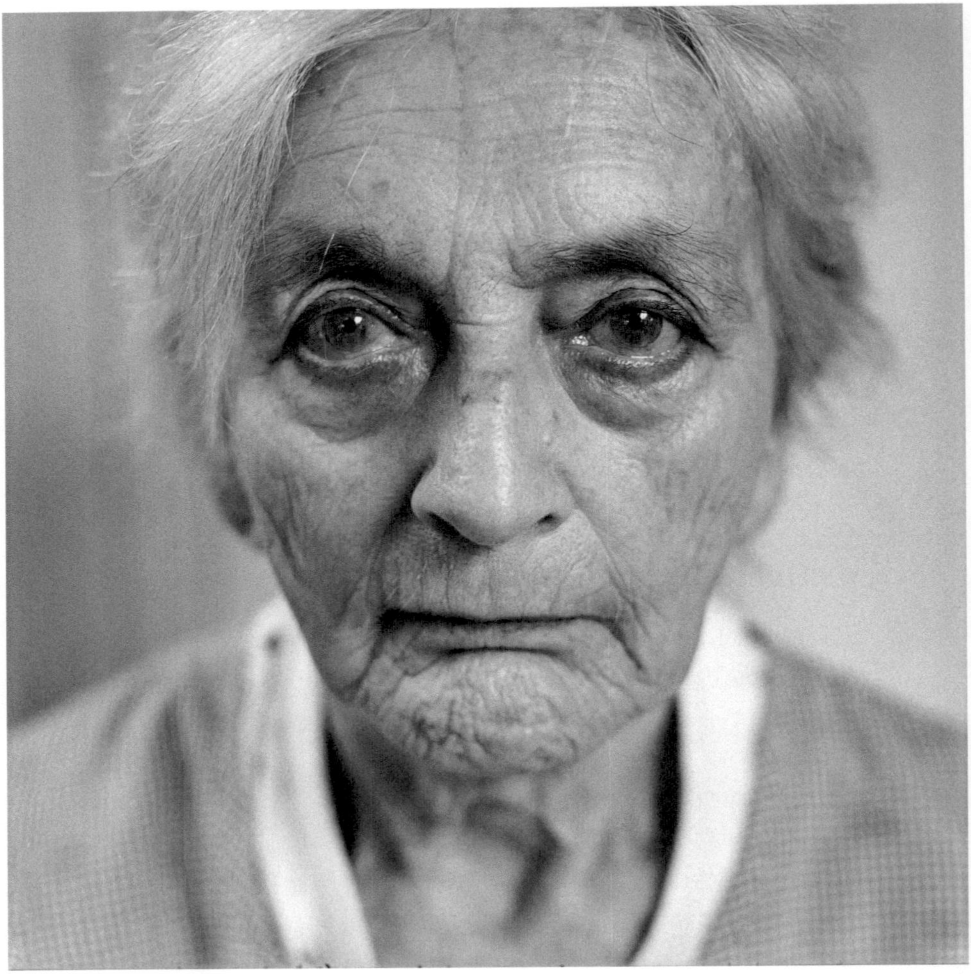

FIGURE 1.13. Vó Armanda. Photo by Torben Eskerod.

assistance or anything resembling public health in the colonies, other than people's homegrown arts of healing.

She added that "both men came back running, and Grandpa Ferdinand put Puve back in the cradle." How many feverish, convulsing, and dying children had they seen in their lifetime?

The elder of the family had some kind of therapeutic knowledge, it seemed. I could not believe what I heard next. The window image that framed Vó Armanda's dream about her dying family body (and which she had shared with me a few years earlier) reappeared in its utter materiality and breathtaking, miraculous efficacy:

"The old man pulled *a window* out of the wall and laid the glass over the child's body." This was not a delusion of the senses by the grieving. Granny was sure that the contact with the material surface of the window—both cold and reflective—had actually brought Puve back.

"Open the window!" And so one disappears. And so one comes back. An earlier time, the sense of death coming, another window.

Such was Vó Armanda's reminiscence of what language alone cannot encompass when one travels toward the unknown and healing.

A cry to revive the child in this vestigial image: "Komm herein."

To this day I keep wondering about Vó Armanda's account of Puve's seizure and the window. Most *colono* houses then had standard guillotine-style windows that were fitted into the wall. Fixed with nails, they were easily removable.[33] Was this, too, a shared modality of sensing and healing? Where had Old Ferdinand learned the window technique as a possibility of action? How did the family come to recognize its therapeutic efficacy?

Even more puzzling: Had Puve's near-death experience and the home care that revived him become imprinted in his mind? So much so that, when death approached, it was to this event-image that my father resorted to find his final words?

The truth is, the home is an energetic entity and, for my father, life and death superimposed onto each other on the surface of the window. Puve's perpetually open window, blurring the human and nonhuman, the private and public, intimacy and strangeness, contains a certain vitality itself. Indeed, when I spoke to Vó Armanda and uncovered some of the subterranean knowledge of the aperture's doubling, it transformed from a static material substrate into the site of a familial flicker between different events and possibilities and into a means of imagining through and beyond the specter of extinction (not unlike an ancestral Mucker claim to living with the spirit of nature and in proximity with one's dead).

The living window image, then, is a testament to the world's fundamental contingency and to the domestic schemes underlying the chaos of existence. It speaks to a communal figuration conjured through love against structural constraints and the work of time, a force "applying equally to the living and the dead, and which lies beyond our comprehension," as the luminous W. G. Sebald reminds us.[34]

In her mourning, Vó Armanda summoned a familiar home sentience and dragged cherished cyphers of existence from their sleep. In viva voce, she gifted me with a portal into the other side of lamentation: into how the miraculous account of a thing (along with the human aggregates in which it dwells) becomes a strange instinct that binds one to living, to a re-beginning, and to the story of a journey.

To revisit the scene of the open window in all its material, relational, and sensorial dimensions is to tap into the reciprocal process of people making houses and houses making people, thus invoking survivals that dwell in the smallest movements, reflections, and vibrations of a shared home sentience, which storytelling animates time and again.

NOTES

1. See "Araucaria angustifolia," in The Gymnosperm Database, edited by Christopher J. Earle, last modified October 29, 2025, https://www.conifers.org/ar/Araucaria_angustifolia.php.

2. The local *Hunsrückisch* language resulted from a hybridization of various ancestral German dialects with present-day sociolects and Portuguese words. See Altenhofen, "O estudo de línguas."

3. See Biehl, "Mucker War"; and Biehl, *Jammerthal, o Vale da Lamentação.*

4. Throughout this essay, I use *colono* as an emic term. In southern Brazil, it refers to immigrants who settled as small-scale farmers and their descendants, emphasizing their identity as humble, unschooled agricultural workers rather than as "colonizers" or "colonists" in the imperial sense.

5. Noé, "História do ano de 1874," 383.

6. Von Koseritz, "Der religiöse Wahnsinn." See also Biehl, "Insurgent Archivings," s2.

7. Amado, *Conflito social no Brasil.*

8. Douglas, "Idea of Home," 287.

9. Philip, "Universal Grammar," 37, 41.

10. Philip, “Testimony Stoops to Mother Tongue,” 52.
11. Bachelard, *Poetics of Space*, 17.
12. Philip, “Testimony Stoops to Mother Tongue,” 52.
13. See Biehl, “Insurgent Archivings.” For Benjamin on “flashes” and dialectical images, see “Life of Students”, 37; and *Arcades Project*, 463.
14. Benjamin, *Arcades Project*, 463.
15. Benjamin, *Arcades Project*, 591–92.
16. Eliot, “East Coker,” in *Four Quartets*.
17. Stewart, “Window,” s27.
18. Glissant, “Those Beings” and “For Opacity”; Derrida, *Archive Fever*, 2.
19. Nietzsche, *Use and Abuse of History*, 7. See also Biehl and Locke, *Unfinished*, 4.
20. Braun, *História de Linha Nova*.
21. Noé, “História do ano de 1874.”
22. Noé, “História do ano de 1874,” 383.
23. Biehl et al., “Books of the Dead.”
24. Noé, “História do ano de 1874,” 383.
25. Noé, “História do año de 1874,” 383.
26. Noé, “História do ano de 1874,” 383.
27. Matt. 5:3–5.
28. Noé, “História do ano de 1874,” 383.
29. Noé, “História do ano de 1874,” 389.
30. Hartman, “Venus in Two Acts”; Hartman and Wilderson, “Position of the Unthought.”
31. Lacan, *Four Fundamental Concepts*, 47.
32. Cabral de Melo Neto, “Psychology of Composition,” 29.
33. Weimer, *Arquitetura popular da imigração Alemã*.
34. Sebald, “Le promeneur solitaire,” 9.

ANGELA GARCIA

2

The Hostel

Mother Road

There's a canary-yellow apartment building west of Albuquerque's historic downtown. It sits in an area once known as New Town, a name meant to distinguish the neighborhood from the original Villa de Albuquerque, or "Old Town." Rather than the traditional adobes of the *villa*, which were built around a central plaza, New Town reflected the architecture and tastes of the Midwesterners who came along when the Atchison, Topeka and Santa Fe Railway arrived in 1890. The streets were linear and ran parallel to each other, and two-story single-family houses were separated by private yards. As the city grew, repeating equal-sized blocks were built in new subdivisions. What is now the yellow apartment building was once a single-family house in Raynolds Addition neighborhood, plated in 1912, the same year New Mexico was admitted as the forty-seventh US state.

The house was located on Railroad Avenue, later to be called Central Avenue. Built in the colonial revival style, it had a porch graced by segmental arches extending across the facade and casement windows grouped into horizontal bands. An early photograph of the property shows a picket fence surrounding a front yard and two young trees growing on either side of a walkway leading to a porch. The house appears solid and hospitable, a model home for a growing family.

Many of the houses in Raynolds Addition were built by real estate investors who saw Albuquerque as a Western boom town. There was a railroad and a string of sanatoriums along Railroad Avenue, nicknamed TB Avenue. The transplants from the Midwest and Northeast needed houses, each with a front yard and porch where neighbors could visit before returning to the privacy of their own homes. The new houses offered everything the burgeoning white middle class wanted and needed. They projected order, health, and morality—important since the nearby one-room adobe houses in the *villa*, most without electricity or plumbing, emphasized the foreignness of the New Mexico landscape.

During the Depression, Albuquerque declined, and the single-family house in Raynolds Addition transformed into a brothel. Some residents say the brothel's heyday was during the Prohibition era, while others point to the postwar period and recall veterans seeking solace there. Army Lieutenant Arturo Barreras was nineteen when he returned to Albuquerque from Japan. His daughter Vangie, seventy-two years old when we spoke, remembered her father's weekend binges at the brothel: "When my mother went into labor with my brother, I had to walk there and get him. Everyone called the place una casa de mala fama, but it was the nicest house I'd ever seen."

The arched doorways and spacious rooms on the house's ground floor remained intact after the transformation from house to brothel, as did the handsome staircase that led to the second floor, where the bedrooms were located. But the once-airy bedrooms were divided into smaller ones that accommodated a bed and little else. The women who worked at the brothel were mostly "Spanish" or "Mexican" and hailed from the *villa*. Some were as young as fourteen.[1] In the 1960s, many of the original buildings of New Town were demolished in an urban renewal project. It was during this period that the house-turned-brothel transformed again—this time to the Mother Road Hostel, named after Route 66, one of the first US highways. Most

FIGURE 2.1. Mother Road Hostel in Albuquerque, New Mexico.

hostels around the world charge guests for a bed, not a room. The first floor of the Mother Road operated in the same way. It also reserved private, single-occupancy rooms on the second floor for a higher nightly fee.

I lived at the Mother Road when I was sixteen and seventeen. My corner room was on the second floor and had a twin-size bed, a dresser, and a chair, all pressed tight against the narrow walls. A paint-by-numbers seascape hung on one of those walls, a beveled mirror on another. All the furnishings were the property of the hostel. My window faced Central Avenue, where a trolley car once ran, connecting New Town and the *villa*. I often sat beside it and looked out onto the street, recounting my days in a journal.

Back then, I worked as a maid at the nearby Crossroads Motel and Hiway House, both located on Central Avenue. Five days a week, I pushed a cart stacked with thin towels, cleaning solution, and deodorizing spray from room to room. I learned the rhythms of people on the road. Most departed early in the morning and headed somewhere else, while others stayed past checkout and left only when forced to. The lodgers left behind traces of themselves: a hairbrush, a sock, an earring. I cleared the rooms of their presence and readied them for someone else.

Most of the people at the Mother Road were also passing through town on their way to somewhere else. They stayed one or two nights in beds on the first floor and chatted easily as they made sandwiches in the large communal kitchen. There were European tourists, hitchhikers, bikers, and people too poor or too stingy to pay for more expensive lodging. During the day they lingered on sofas in the common room—once a "family room"—reading day-old newspapers and eating the bruised apples the hostel manager put out every morning. Then they left—for California, Colorado, Mexico, or some other place. I never learned their names.

I was one of the long-term lodgers. There were seven of us at the time. Jesús (Jessie to some) was a recovering heroin addict who walked to Presbyterian Hospital twice a week for medical treatment. Nancy was trying to get her life back together after her third divorce. Edgar worked two jobs—one to pay his own expenses, the other to send money back home to El Salvador, where a civil war was raging. William had a whirl of black tattoos that covered his muscular arms, and Marcus had two kids who visited him on Sundays. Mary sat on the porch all day, even during the cold, dry winter, knitting an endless blanket.

The lodgers on the first and second floors were separated by the fact of the road. Those on the first floor returned to it; those on the second couldn't, even if we wanted to. Money was the main reason we stayed at the Mother Road, although there were other factors at play. You could stay there for a night, a week, or years. You could pay for your lodging in pennies. You didn't need proof of identification. And the hostel resembled a traditional house, with furnishings that gave the impression of a stable home—at least on the first floor, where there was a sideboard and dining room table, a sofa and television, and a kitchen stocked with cookware. The hostel's resemblance to a single-family home offered a domestic scene where long-term lodgers could imagine being in the possession of numerous rooms and their associated furnishings and meanings. It gave the impression that one had much more than one really did.

The Mother Road was a space marked by a profound ambiguity. On the one hand, the first floor was reserved for strangers welcomed as neighbors. They were "guests" and made small talk with the hostel manager and with each other, sharing adventure stories—their hands gesticulating, their voices animated. The second floor was distant from this scene of domestic hospitality. Quiet, insular, and a little depressed, it was more like a sanatorium than a hostel.

Alone, Together

In *How to Live Together*, Roland Barthes reflects on how the rhythm of life in the sanatorium differs from that of the "outside" world. He writes, "Once the structure (the Living-Together) is established, it's everlasting; it runs on and on—like a homeostat."[2] For Barthes, who suffered from tuberculosis and experienced life in the sanatorium himself, the isolated and infinite world of the institution has something profound to say about human experience. In reading Thomas Mann's *The Magic Mountain*, Barthes writes about the sanatorium as a space of seclusion and social life, of living alone and living together, and of always being in the presence of death yet somehow feeling safe in the repetitive rhythms of daily life.

Like Mann's sanatorium in *The Magic Mountain*, the second floor of the Mother Road had its own rhythm and sociality. It was a sanatorial space with long-term lodgers who were like patients, but with no clear indication of disease. We lived alone, side by side, cohabiting with our unspoken maladies.

The atmosphere on the second floor was heavy and humming with melancholy. I saw Nancy emerge from the bathroom with red eyes and Marcus caress his bruised cheek. Edgar changed his uniform at six in the evening, swapping his blue coveralls for the green pants he wore during his night shift as a hospital orderly. Jesús's room was two doors down from mine. One afternoon, he invited me in to show me a pocket watch he found on the street. Its gold case was scratched, and the time several hours off, but the hands still moved in slow circles. I looked around Jesús's room. It was exactly like mine—bed, dresser, chair, window. Prescription bottles lined his windowsill like trinkets on a shelf.

Our affective ties were inextricably bound up with solitude and detachment. We nodded politely as we passed each other on the stairway or in the narrow hall on our way to the shared bathroom, carrying our towels and toothpaste. A brass hook, sturdy as a paper clip, kept the door closed and was never breached. When someone didn't have enough to eat, we shared our rice and cereal without making a fuss. On winter days, we warmed ourselves while sitting in the second-floor windows of our individual rooms, like convalescents taking a balcony rest cure.

There were only two occasions that I can remember when we came together as a group. On my seventeenth birthday, the lodgers on the second floor bought me sheet cake. Someone wrote "Happy Birthday Angela" on a piece of paper and pressed it into the cake's thick white frosting. That evening, I left seven slices, one for each longtime lodger, on a small table at one end of our shared hallway. When I left my room in the morning, the cake was gone and the dishes had been cleared.

When Nancy suffered what she thought was a heart attack, I accompanied her in the ambulance to the hospital. (In fact, Nancy had had a panic attack.) Once she was released, we took the bus back to the hostel. When we arrived at the Mother Road, we found the longtimers waiting for us on the second-floor landing. "Are you OK?" "What happened?" "What did the doctors say?" they asked in worried tones. Nancy responded quietly, as if embarrassed for causing such a ruckus. Within minutes we were all back in our separate rooms, our doors closed.

"What distance must I maintain between myself and others if we are to construct together a sociability without alienation, a solitude without exile?"

asks Barthes.[3] For him, the possibility of living alone yet together is tied to the question of architecture, which he describes as "both dream and function."[4] The spatial dimensions of the hostel's second floor animated the double movements of alone/together, utopia/use. We long-term lodgers lived near each other yet were enclosed in our little rooms, which felt largely detached from the hostel. There was something profoundly reassuring about this configuration in that we were both sheltered from and still in contact with the surrounding world. These margins made it possible for us to withdraw, to escape, to dream.

Back then, I carried a notebook and sat at The Frontier Restaurant, a sprawling diner that glowed amber at night. I drank coffee and drew high-rise structures with neat rows of windows, or dense cities of rooms. Mine was an architecture of nests and caves and streets like hallways. It was a model of habitation shaped by my life at the hostel.

I sketched the Mother Road too, capturing its exterior in shape and scale. So impressed with one of my drawings was the hostel manager that he pinned it to a bulletin board cluttered with posts about house rules. (No visitors, no parties, no drugs, no smoking, no sex, no gathering in the common room before six in the morning or after ten at night.) My attempts to draw single-family homes were always unsuccessful. It was too hard to imagine their interiors.

Most houses have rooms with names. Bedroom, living room, dining room, kitchen, bathroom, washroom. If the occupants are wealthy enough, the house might also have a room for recreation, another for study. The names of rooms distinguish one from the other. They divide a day's activities and whether the room is occupied by one person or more. The names of rooms structure the lives they contain.

The rooms on the second floor of the Mother Road were not known by the activities that took place inside them. Instead, they were known (at least to those on the second floor) by the names of their individual occupants: Nancy's room, Jesús's room, Edgar's room, and so on. We lived side by side in our little rooms—sleeping in them, eating in them, passing days in them. Thick cement walls prevented the spread of sound and amplified a sense of solitude. Austere and narrow, our rooms were like anchorite cells constructed within a church's walls. We left them out of need—to eat, to go to work, to use the telephone—then returned to them and closed the door.

In his book *District*, Tony Duvert describes a desolate section of a French city in vignettes of working-class sites. His description of a room in an old tenement apartment reads, "Everything in the room conveys your non-existence. A home? No, a refuge, a shadowy corner reduced to its tightest dimensions, where you've become like a fish in an aquarium, its glass bowl lined with multicolored gravel, turning around a hundred times per minute."[5]

Duvert's imagining of marginalization as reduction resonates with my experience of living on the second floor of the Mother Road. There were times when I felt stuck within the narrow room, miserable and immobilized. But the second floor also offered a vision of life that was more vivid and varied than what Duvert describes. Though alone, we lived in close relation to each other, connected by the very walls that separated us and by the worn hallway floor that ran from one end of the building to the other. Contact between us was fleeting and mostly avoided. But we communicated through our daily needs and routines. In the kitchen, I quietly asked Edgar for updates about his family in El Salvador. Entering or exiting the front door, I'd find Mary knitting on the porch and would compliment her blanket. Passing William in the hall meant brushing up against his large body. Occasionally, Nancy knocked on my door and asked if she could borrow shampoo or a dollar, and Marcus never left the second floor without asking if we needed anything from the convenience store down the street. Jesús and I left the hostel for work at the same time each morning. Our destinations were in the same direction, so we walked up Central Avenue together, cars whizzing by.

Sometimes I emerged from my room at the exact moment someone else did. We'd glance at each other and gesture for the other to pass. We approached each other with gentleness, saying excuse me or *con permiso* as we passed in the hallway. There was a rhythm to our being together, an adagio movement. Radiators hissed in unison, footsteps shuffled, floorboards creaked. Our ties to each other were unremarkable, both ordinary and discrete. We lived alone,

EXIT

FIGURE 2.2. Interior, Mother Road Hostel.

together, with our doors closed but always with the promise of opening when need be.

In *How to Live Together*, Barthes quotes a passage from Franz Kafka's diary: "I sit in my room in the very headquarters of the uproar of the entire apartment. I hear the doors slam. The house door is unlatched and screeches as though from a catarrhal throat, then opens wider with the brief singing of a woman's voice."[6] What interests Barthes is Kafka's experience with the familiar sounds that define his space—his "territory," to use Barthes's term. Kafka's room is part of a collective (apartment, street, city) where external sounds flow though him and are kept at bay. They connect and delimit his room, defining the writer's essential solitude while signaling his contact with the wider world. The space for distance and connection that is opened by sound speaks to the possibility of an idiorrhythmic community that encompasses shared life and individual rhythms.[7]

One winter afternoon, while walking up the staircase that led to the hostel's second floor, I heard the voice of a woman singing. The doors to the lodgers' rooms were closed except Mary's, whose room was farthest from my own. I walked down the hallway toward Mary's room, drawn by her melancholy tune. Mary's door was open less than halfway, perhaps signaling her desire for company, or to be left alone. I hesitated before knocking, and when I did the singing stopped. For several moments, Mary and I remained frozen on either side of the door, waiting for the other to speak or leave. Finally, I announced my name.

The door opened wider, releasing a burst of heat into the hallway. Mary stood on the threshold, her face flushed and sweating. In her hands was her long, knitted blanket, still unfinished. "Will you help me?" she asked.

She gestured for me to enter her room, which was even smaller than mine. She pointed to the cast-iron steam radiator; its valve was stuck, and she couldn't turn it off. "My hands are too tired," she said, holding out her blanket as if to explain. I took a glove out of my peacoat and put it on, hoping it would protect my hand as I tried to turn the hot valve. Mary watched silently as I struggled. Finally, the valve closed, and heat stopped releasing into the room.

I looked around. A spider plant with long wiry stems sat on her dresser drawer. On the floor beside her bed, a tower of books. I hadn't known Mary to be a reader. I caught glimpses of a few of the titles. One stood out: Marge Piercy's *Woman on the Edge of Time.*

"You have a beautiful voice," I said to Mary. Her blue eyes were flecked with gold. She looked at me despairingly and glanced at the door; it was time to go. Before I left, Mary handed me a hat she'd made—an intricate weave of brown, red, and yellow yarns. I'd seen her wear it on winter days while she sat knitting on the porch. A gift.

Mary closed the door behind me. I strained to hear her singing while walking down the hallway toward my room. But all I could hear was chatter from guests sitting in the first-floor common area, all of them sheltered together during a brewing snowstorm. I never heard Mary sing again.

The Cathedral

I walked to work, which meant crossing the I-25 underpass, a shady refuge for the down-and-out. I was always relieved when Edgar accompanied me on my walks, as he prevented the men who sat below the underpass from hollering at me. When we reached the Crossroads Motel, Edgar and I went our separate ways. We'd wish each other a good day but never "See you later" or "See you back at the Mother Road," as there was always the possibility that we might not see each other again.[8]

One day, as I walked back to the Mother Road from work, the voice of a girl rang out. "Hey!" she yelled. I stopped and watched as she crawled down the concrete slope of the overpass like a crab, her scraped knees peeking out from beneath her oily jeans. "Hey," she repeated, her voice smaller this time. Traffic passed over our heads. "Do you have some food?" She looked about my age and had short black hair and a yellow bandana tied around her neck. Her name was Kate.

Kate and I slid into a red vinyl booth at Milton's Diner. She looked like a dark-haired Jean Seberg, but more interesting, with her chipped blue fingernail polish and a backpack carrying her only belongings. From behind the tall menu, she admitted that she didn't have any money.

We split a patty melt and french fries. Kate talked excitedly while she ate, telling me stories about nights spent in cemeteries and in old cars down on Fourth Street, west of downtown. A pendant of Saint Jude, the patron saint of lost causes, dangled from her neck. "But then I found the Cathedral," she said. She wanted to take me there. I assumed the Cathedral was a church of some kind, maybe the Mormon temple that handed out free food on game night, which was also an occasion for proselytizing.

We headed southwest, down First Street, then walked along defunct railway tracks that cut through a wasteland of broken beer bottles and cigarette butts. Kate talked the whole time, her cheerful voice in sharp contrast with the depressed landscape. Eventually, I realized we were headed toward the rail yard—a ghostly complex of large structures once used to repair steam locomotives. At one point, the rail yard had been Albuquerque's main source of employment, with over a quarter of its residents working there. The shift from steam to diesel had led to its decline, and by the 1970s the rail yard was largely abandoned, except for a couple of buildings used for equipment storage.

We arrived at a cluster of buildings with towering walls of broken glass. Kate led me through a gaping passageway and into one of the old freight shops. I understood immediately why she called it the Cathedral. The deserted building was grand, with high metal beams and walls made up of small glass windows, some amber, others green, a lot of them busted out. Light filtered through them, brightening the blackened concrete floor. I looked up toward the pigeons and rooftop holes. Chandeliers made of rusted beer cans hung in the air.

In one corner of the building was a collection of rundown chairs and stained mattresses. There were about twenty teenagers there. Most of them lay around and gave me glazed looks. A couple kicked around a deflated soccer ball as if in a school gymnasium. Kate called them her "tribe." She walked over to the corner, sat on the ground, and pulled me down with her. Clothes and furniture were organized along one of the walls. The clothes were divided into piles: pants, shirts, undergarments. Chairs were grouped together. A bucket of food sat on a small, wobbly table. There were worn books and magazines, and a small, out-of-date TV, its plug leading to nowhere.

The Cathedral frightened me. It was too large and empty a space, with no private rooms to withdraw to, no individual enclosures. It felt dangerously permeable too. Shards of glass gathered along the perimeter of the communal space, and bird droppings were splattered on the floor like paint. A trapped sparrow fluttered helplessly across the length of the building, looking for a way out.

It wasn't just the space that frightened me; it was the fact that I was so close in circumstance to the people who gathered there. They were my age and already world-weary. Some of them dressed like punks, though most seemed to have given up on projecting any sort of style or attitude. Kate introduced me to them one by one. Abby, Johnnie, Lupita. Some acknowledged me; others kept their eyes closed, perhaps asleep in the heat, perhaps dreaming. A girl peeled an orange and offered me a section of it. Another lit a joint. Over time, I found myself drawn to their somber sociality, to their gentleness. ("The highest point of gentleness is its possible erasure."[9]) At the same time, I wanted to assert my distance from them. I was grateful when Kate announced that I lived at the Mother Road. They nodded knowingly. What did they know?

Kate started spending nights with me at the Mother Road. I'd sneak her in and make room for her in my narrow bed. I washed her clothes with mine in the pay-per-use machine in the back of the building and saved food for her. My room became a house for the two of us. A house within a hostel.

She got a job cleaning rooms with me at the Crossroads Motel. Within a few weeks, we earned enough money to get our own studio apartment set behind an Italian restaurant. It was a nondescript box of a place with one small, north-facing window. Kate said she felt safe there, sheltered. But she refrained from calling our apartment "home." "Let's go *back*," she'd say. Sometimes she called it a "shack," a designation that upset me, conjuring images of abandoned hovels.

Even though Kate refused to call it a home, she seemed intent on making it one. She was an expert thief, and the most beautiful objects in our apartment (crystals for healing, silk scarves for lampshades, a mid-century teapot) were treasures from her escapades. She cut flowers from the gardens of other people's houses and arranged them in glasses of water. I bought a record player from a garage sale. In the evening, I listened to scratchy records of Anne Sexton readings; Kate, The Kinks.

We visited the Cathedral on weekends. It was autumn and chilly at night, and we brought sheets and blankets we smuggled out of the motels we worked at. The Cathedral kids were grateful for our gifts and offered us joints and swigs of rum in return. We huddled together on the concrete ground, a great emptiness pressing against our backs. No one talked about our childhoods, perhaps because we were still living them.

Sometimes the Cathedral kids visited Kate and me at our apartment. They'd show up unannounced, with beers and joints or requests for them. They took long showers in our tiny bathroom, washed their clothes in our kitchen sink, and lay on our bed, updating us about romantic relationships and brushes with the police. I felt anxious when they visited. They disrupted the domesticity I was trying to establish, a daily rhythm that depended on order and routine: wake at seven, walk to the motel, clean from eight in the morning till three in the afternoon, then return to the apartment. Kate and I made dinner on our two-burner stove and ate at a café table—a hand-me-down from the restaurant—beside the window. I felt something when it was just the two of us at that table. A sense of home. The kind of home evoked by Gaston Bachelard—home as womb and shell and cradle full of dreams.[10]

I told Kate I didn't want the Cathedral kids spending so much time in our apartment. We got into an argument, taking opposing sides on what the "shack" was and who it belonged to. Was it our house or a halfway house for Kate and her friends? If it was a halfway house, what were we doing, dressing the place up like a real home? Kate wanted the door to always be open to others, whereas I saw the door as a necessary physical boundary, a demarcation of an essential solitude that I wanted to share with her alone. The rhythm of life on the second floor of the Mother Road had made me accustomed to a certain sense of enclosure, an existential and social way of being that was almost monastic. Kate couldn't bear it.

Ours was an unresolvable argument accompanied by tears and threats to *just leave*. Eventually, Kate did, returning to that dark place with the grand name. I stayed in the apartment for several weeks before returning to the Mother Road to inquire about my old room on the second floor. It was occupied by someone else.

Homecoming

Thirty years later, I found myself standing in front of the Mother Road. The building first appeared to me as if in black and white, like the photograph taken one hundred years earlier, back when it had been a single-family home. Looking more closely, I could see that the building was pocked and marred by time. Its yellow walls were dirty and chipped, revealing layers of white and gray plaster; the windows' wood frames were cracked and peeling. The weathering of the building showed the passage of time and was caught up in it.

The building manager and his graying dog sat in the front yard, watching traffic along Central Avenue. I stood on the sidewalk across from the gated entry, which carried a sign that read, "Private Property." I told him I had lived there once. He immediately warmed to me. "You know it was a brothel," he said. "And then the Mother Road," I added. He told me that it was no longer a hostel.

"The neighborhood is changing," he continued. He pointed out two new cafés and explained that a farmers' market took place every Sunday across the street in the little park where the junkies used to fix and the homeless camped. The changes in the neighborhood led to the conversion of the Mother Road hostel to private apartments. More money, less riffraff. But construction was taking longer than expected. The walls between rooms were so thick that tearing them down to create studios and one-bedroom units proved difficult. "The walls don't want to come down," the manager said. I asked if I could go inside.

The front porch was an empty stage for mismatched chairs. The manager fumbled with his keys. I couldn't remember the front door ever being locked.

The entryway was entirely different. It was small and closed off, with a locked door that opened onto what had once been the common room. "First-floor apartments," the manager said when he caught me looking. A new stairway, curved and creaky, led to the second floor. My old room was to the right of the landing. Its door was closed. The manager told me the room was the only one without a kitchenette, just a closet-sized bathroom. It was the least expensive unit.

"Who lives here?" I asked, surprised by my question.

"A guy named Jessie."

"Jesús from thirty years ago?"

The manager nodded. "He'll never leave."

We walked back downstairs and stood outside in the chilly air. The manager asked me when I had lived in the hostel. "Late '80s," I said, as I watched a young couple pass us on their way out of the building and onto the street.

I went to the Cathedral. It, too, had been transformed. Now it was The Rail Yards Market, the centerpiece of a neighborhood redevelopment plan. A plaque called it a "historic site," and a sign announced, "A Monument. A Testament. Viva Rail Yards."

I entered the same way Kate had led me in decades earlier. The broken windows had been replaced and the rafters cleared of bats and chandeliers. The atmosphere was festive, with individual vendors selling handmade pottery, jewelry, and exotic plants. Every weekend, families gathered there for art, music, and food.

I thought about Kate and the Cathedral kids as I walked around the new rail yard, remembering the winter night we had built a bonfire in the center of the vast building. We had passed around a bottle of rum and told stories like hobos on a train. Occasionally someone hollered and we listened to their voice echo. We reached our cold, chapped hands out toward the fire. When darkness fell, we sang song after song, one kid after the other, moving around the circle, passing time. "One More Night." "Rapture." When someone started singing John Denver's "Take Me Home, Country Roads," the whole group started to belt it out, laughing.

Neither the hostel nor the Cathedral was a house in the common sense of the term, but their inhabitants made homes for themselves there, nonetheless. Entangled with changing social formations, economic structures, and individual circumstances, precarious spaces such as these make concrete realities and fantasies around concepts of family, house, and home. They invite us to think about the possibilities for home making, and about the materialities and socialities that enact it. And they offer an expansive vision of living—alone and together—in the narrowest of places.

NOTES

1. "Old Town Chronicles" (no. 5), Elinor Crans, collector, 1936–1940, 5-5-52 2, Fray Angélico Chávez History Library, Santa Fe, NM.

2. Barthes, *How to Live Together*, 37.

3. Barthes, *How to Live Together*, xxv.

4. Barthes, *Eiffel Tower*, 6.

5. Duvert, *District*, 11.

6. Franz Kafka, quoted in Barthes, *How to Live Together*, 79–80.

7. Idiorrhythmy is a key concept for Barthes and refers to a mode of living where individual and community needs are pursued harmoniously.

8. Sometimes Edgar referred to the Mother Road as *el albergue*, a Spanish term that also translates to "hostel" as well as "shelter" or "refuge." Since he had fled war-torn El Salvador, Edgar's terminology points to the sanctuary-like quality of the hostel.

9. Dufourmantelle, *Power of Gentleness*, 42.

10. Bachelard, *Poetics of Space*.

PART II

Homeostasis

SUSAN HELEN ELLISON

3

The Laboring House

The material world is infused with sensations and distinct ways of knowing: rooms full of weeping, exhausted countries, a house that is only as safe as flesh. —KATHERINE MCKITTRICK, *Demonic Grounds*

Dust clouds catch in the wind with each of our shaky steps. Streams of pebbles and larger rocks slide from beneath our feet as we haltingly climb the narrow path—a tight series of switchbacks easily washed out during the rainy season. Brisa grabs her smallest child by one hand, while her six-year-old son scrambles ahead of us. My godson, Teo, brings up the rear. The ascent is both invigorating and terrifying. We are headed to Brisa's plot of land—a scrub-covered outcropping, the place where she plans to build a home. Alongside her future neighbors, Brisa helped cut the makeshift path into the rocky terrain.

FIGURE 3.1. Brisa leads two of her children up the switchbacks to her plot of land while Teo and I trail behind, 2019. Photo by the author.

Large stones that break pickaxes belie the sandy, unstable earth in this "red zone," a dangerous area for construction in La Paz, Bolivia—a capital built into a canyon where entire city blocks periodically slide off the face of the map.[1]

For several years, Brisa has eagerly updated me on the slow progress: the weekends spent cooking meals for her soon-to-be-neighbors as they forge paths to adjoining plots. Despite my words of caution, my fears of landslides and of land scams, Brisa is fully invested. This home—not yet in existence, but fully realized in her mind—is meant to be different from any other house where she has lived: not merely her own, but a home unmoored from the attachments that have caused her so much pain.[2]

Her calvary, as she often describes her life—sometimes with a laugh, sometimes with tears streaming down her face—began when she was seven.[3]

When Brisa was growing up just outside Bolivia's judicial capital, Sucre, her Quechua-speaking mother regularly brought corn to a wealthy landowner, Doña Potencia, exchanging it for sugar and flour. Doña Potencia repeatedly urged Brisa's mother to allow the girl to join her (Doña Potencia) on the homestead. Brisa's mother initially refused but eventually acquiesced.

"My mom handed me over and disappeared," Brisa remembered. "They did the paperwork with the notary in town, took along my birth certificate, and then I didn't know anything more of her until I was twenty."[4]

Throughout the Andes, practices of child circulation have allowed families to manage lean times and provide aging relatives with companionship, although these arrangements can be painful, too.[5] Children like Brisa, however, occupy a somewhat different position and were once categorized as *criadas*—a term Brisa still uses to describe her own experience.[6] *Criada*, from the verb *criar*, connotes child-rearing but is also an old-fashioned term for servant. *Criada* describes orphaned children—or those born to impoverished, frequently Indigenous families—who are raised in wealthier, often white/*mestizo* households.[7] Guardians ostensibly compensate their child laborers with clothes, housing, and schooling. Brisa's "adoption" as Potencia's *criada* occurred in a context of spatialized racial ideologies in which, Grace Young explains, "the [white or *mestizo*] patron family functions ostensibly as

a civilizing agent to transform [Indigenous domestic workers'] rural customs into appropriate urban ones."[8]

From age seven to seventeen, Brisa lived with and worked for Potencia's family as a *criada*. She received no payment for her labor and bitterly criticizes the compensation she did receive—emphasizing, always, that she only finished ninth grade and experienced the arrangement as abusive. Brisa's new *señora* quickly put her to work. She learned to cook, butcher animals, and clean. Potencia later sent Brisa to distant La Paz to serve as a companion-caregiver to her granddaughter, Anita, and, ultimately, to assume the full responsibilities of domestic labor. There, she lived with Potencia's daughter, a woman Brisa simply calls la Doctora (in reference to her status as a judge in one of Bolivia's highest courts), and little Anita. Potencia periodically swept into La Paz to torment Brisa or to bring her back to Sucre during holidays when the extended family descended on the estate and she needed extra help. When they were both adults, Brisa briefly returned to Anita's house as a paid domestic worker. Brisa's relationship with multiple generations of Potencia's family endured for decades. Indeed, every house where Brisa has lived, even during periods of her life when she sought employment elsewhere and began building kin under another roof, has been linked to her labor in her custodians' homes. The house at the center of Brisa's domestic work has never been singular. Nor have the relations built through those houses been restricted to an employer-employee dyad.

This chapter centers the reverberations of domestic labor as it is materialized in interconnected, unbounded residences—houses—and their lived effects on workers' racialized bodies and kinship ties.[9] Anthropological research on the house, particularly that in the Andes, foregrounds the centrality of building homes—through the shared labor of roof raising and experiences of codwelling—to processes of making kin, as well as the strains such codwelling produces.[10] Here, I attend to the ways specific rooms contribute to Brisa's ambivalent construction of kinship to the women who housed her as a *criada* and later employed her as a domestic worker. For Brisa, codwelling with others is not only, perhaps not even primarily, an experience of being nurtured. Unlike more cozy accounts of homemaking, Brisa does not characterize the houses where she has lived as hers or as an extension of herself, but rather regards them with a sense of unbelonging and unease.[11] Through the physical construction of a new home, however, Brisa seeks to *unmake* the same ties she has long relied on to keep herself housed. As I show, houses can be troubled sites in the relational labor of both making and *unmaking* kin.[12]

Research on domestic service has explored the fraught experiences and kinship ties of families linked by the caring labor of nannies, housekeepers, and cooks—frequently women who travel from poor neighborhoods or poor countries to wealthier ones.[13] At the center of domestic service relationships is the house. The house provides the physical location where that labor unfolds, a space in which ideological associations of intimacy, privacy, kinship, race, and sexual access shape both expectations and tensions that emerge for employer and employee alike.[14] Frequently, the spatial organization of elite homes works to reinscribe domination via its architectural design, enabling employers to cope with the uncomfortable boundary crossing wrought by the presence of domestic help.[15] As Katherine McKittrick writes, "Practices of domination . . . naturalize both identity and place, repetitively spatializing where nondominant groups 'naturally' belong."[16]

For *criadas* like Brisa, experiences of "living in" are complicated by their ambiguous position or "place" in the house, a form of codwelling that conjoins racialized social classes and produces kin-like relations even as the spatial organization of the houses where they cohabitate with guardians may reinscribe racial and class difference.[17] The blueprints of such houses frequently reveal the historical spatio-material arrangements of racialized servitude while employers, *criadas*, and paid domestic workers assert, negotiate, and even challenge those physical and ideological boundaries in the present. Brisa's experience further evinces how domestic workers' bodies provide their own kind of blueprints as they accumulate injuries from repetitive stress, heavy lifting, recurring exposure to toxic chemicals found in cleaning supplies, and sexual violence, among other hazards workers encounter "on the job."

Particular household locations play a central role in forging, fatiguing, and sometimes fracturing kinship and kin-like relations, as these are spaces where emotional and bodily intimacy veers from injurious to palliative, and always remains deeply shaped by those quarters. At the same time, Brisa draws on her ambivalent kin-like ties to secure housing beyond her guardian-employers' walls, as they act as her benefactors, facilitating and financing other housing arrangements.[18] She further sustains those ties through *compadrazgo* (fictive kinship/coparenting).

Although Brisa quite literally has kept a foot in Potencia's, the Doctora's, and Anita's *cocinas* (kitchens) for decades, those same women have managed to keep a foot in her *salas*—in her living rooms—after she left their employment. The results have not been entirely happy, but codwelling labor across these houses has forged durable financial-familial attachments. Amid the seeming fixity of a household architecture of domination—the maid's quarters, service bathrooms, and a kitchen that naturalizes the racial-sexual subordination of young women like Brisa—we also encounter the plasticity, the unfinishedness of Andean homes in all their nested multiplicity.[19]

While sharing food, sweat, and blood may have made her a *kind* of kin with her guardian-employers, as Brisa labors to build her own home, she also aims to untether herself from injurious relations. That ideal home isn't one detached from nonnuclear kin, as in so many liberal fantasies of private property ownership.[20] Rather, it is one through which she hopes to assemble less painful yet nevertheless housebound relations.

The kin connected through these various houses includes Doña Potencia, her daughter ("la Doctora"), and Anita—Brisa's childhood companion, charge, and, eventually, her *comadre* (comother, or godmother, of Brisa's son) and employer. While Brisa often speaks warmly of Anita and the Doctora, she harbors no tender feelings toward Doña Potencia. These kin also include Potencia's adult sons, two of whom played a violent role in Brisa's childhood, and a third who later provided refuge. This family further includes Brisa's first partner, who fathered two of her daughters. In Brisa's assessment of their relationship, he served as a portal through which she could walk out on domestic service and Doña Potencia . . . at least for a while. Brisa met her second husband, Miguel, while renting an apartment from his parents high on one of La Paz's steep *ladera* neighborhoods.[21] Brisa still dreams of escaping Miguel's parents, her former landlords-turned-in-laws, by building a home of her own.

Let me turn, then, to the spatial dimensions of those enduring, ambivalent, and often injurious attachments and the many ways household labor scores Brisa's body.

The Roof, the Bathroom, the Pig Pen, the Kitchen

Brisa periodically reflected on the physical boundaries built into the houses where she worked.[22] Take, for example, the tiny maid's quarters where Brisa slept in the Doctora's La Paz house. Like many elite Bolivian houses, this one included a windowless room adjacent to the kitchen that could serve as a broom closet or a maid's bedroom—as it did for Brisa.[23] To add insult to this partitioning, Doña Potencia would dump her suitcases on Brisa's bed when she visited from Sucre, reasserting Brisa's status as a servant (despite often casting her as a daughter-like ward) whose small space was not truly hers.

More often, however, Brisa foregrounded other dimensions of the La Paz house and locations on Potencia's larger Sucre compound, linking them to the injuries she suffered within them. One incident made Brisa laugh despite the punishment it included. Although Potencia promised her schooling, Brisa wasn't yet enrolled and couldn't read. One early morning she pulled a bottle of black liquid from the refrigerator that she presumed was concentrated coffee ready to be diluted in a mug of hot water.[24] It was soy sauce. Brisa hooted gleefully when recounting Potencia's disgust and winced at the memory of the beating that ensued—a memory that linked Brisa's bruised body to the kitchen where she prepared Potencia's breakfasts.

Usually Brisa's "shortcomings" were more mundane: failing to make dinner on time, forgetting to clean a particular room. "Beatings, beatings, it was always beatings," Brisa sighed. After years of abuse and unhappiness, Brisa decided to run away. In fact, she tried three times—the first time taking Potencia's granddaughter, Anita, along with her. They didn't make it far. Potencia beat the bottom of Brisa's feet with the iron's cord until they bled, punishing, with one of the tools of Brisa's labor, the part of her body that dared to escape.[25]

Years later, Brisa's soles bled again. Potencia flew into a rage over Brisa's failure to hang the laundry to dry. Frantically, Brisa climbed onto the roof of the family's La Paz home, hoping to speed drying in the hard, Andean sun. She slipped. As she fell, her feet caught on the metal of the corrugated roof. The metal sliced her feet open but stopped her slide, possibly saving her life. Her feet, however, haven't quite been the same since, she explained, absentmindedly reaching down to squeeze her heel as she spoke.

With these and other injuries, Brisa traced her experiences spatially, linking particular locations in the houses where she labored with scars left on her body and in painfully engraved memories.

Some of those stories also involved men. Brisa recalled,

They had this young chauffer, and I thought, "What if I run away with him?" . . . Well, we [domestic staff] weren't allowed to use the bathroom in the house. So the Doctora built this bathroom for the workers [where] we had to cross the patio. And that's where I met up with this boy. I think Doña Potencia suspected something, because she came looking for me. Maybe you've seen these leather straps they have in Santa Cruz? To tie up cattle? She started to beat me with one. And Anita tried to climb up onto her, crying out "No, Grandma, don't hit her!" [Potencia] left me in the bathroom all night long. She made me sleep in the bathtub.

In recounting her flirtations with the chauffer, Brisa situated herself firmly as a household worker, a person denied access to the interior bathroom. That external servants' bathroom reinforced the racial-class distance between Brisa, Potencia, and the Doctora, and yet it was also a place where little Anita tried to come to her rescue, attempting, in her child's way, to show Brisa care.

As Brisa reflected on her childhood, she traced physical abuse along paths she traversed across Potencia's former hacienda house and the rooms where she was punished for the sins of Potencia's sons. As many domestic workers report, Brisa was sexually assaulted by men in the family. More than once.

On one occasion, the family had returned to Potencia's estate to celebrate the patron festival of Saint Mauro. Brisa remembered, "There was this plaza a block from the Señora's house. And [Potencia] sent me to bring *chicha* in a bucket [from the plaza].[26] But her middle son, Ángel, called out, 'Bring me a glass of water.' So, I went upstairs [where he was waiting], and he tossed the glass of water and threw me on the bed. I was shouting and screaming, 'No!' Doña Potencia heard and came in and told me, 'Brisa, get dressed,' and used terrible words I won't repeat. I told her what happened, crying. She didn't believe me."

Brisa continued, imitating the conversation between mother and son: "'What happened, Ángel?' 'This girl, I caught her in my room stealing.' Ay no! I got the beating of my life. And [Doña Potencia] threw me in the pigsty. I slept there all night."

Covered in open wounds, Brisa soon discovered that "some kind of pig louse had burrowed into me." What she went on to describe suggests botflies had laid eggs in her lacerations. Later, when the Doctora arrived, the woman questioned her mother about what happened. She also confronted her brother, Brisa remembered, saying, "Listen Ángel, the girl is fourteen years old and she's strong but . . . what's going on with you?"

The Doctora took Brisa to a bathroom, bathed her, and dressed her wounds properly. Another bathroom, yet this time one where the Doctora showed Brisa care by challenging her mother and brother—suggesting she believed Brisa—while tending to her physical injuries. Later, the Doctora used tweezers to extract the maggot larvae the flies had deposited in Brisa's gashes: "I've got three holes in my back where she pulled them out," Brisa explained, her hand groping along her shoulder as she spoke. But the Doctora's concern did not prevent Brisa from suffering further. When Potencia's other son, Alonso, arrived from Cochabamba, Brisa woke at four in the morning to let him into the house, only to face more unwanted touching in the kitchen.

Research on the embodied experience of domestic service finds widespread reports of sexual violence and patterns of women employers blaming domestic workers for men's sexual advances. In the Latin American context, Valeria Ribeiro Corossacz explains, the "historical fact" that Brazilian slave owners forced enslaved women to initiate slaveholding sons into sexual relations "has been naturalized and incorporated into Brazilian common knowledge, spread through expressions such as 'ter um pé na cozinha' (to have one foot in the kitchen), indicating that someone considered white is actually related to a black slave woman or domestic worker that cooks."[27] Here the linkages between bodies, rooms, and blood kinship are made explicit through such idiomatic phrases. As Ribeiro Corossacz writes, "This imaginary invokes a cultural idea of the 'sexual availability' of domestic workers who, like objects, are 'inside the house' and available for taking."[28] In these expressions, *blood* kinship, produced through rape or unequal sexual relations, yokes apparently white bodies to the rooms occupied by laboring brown ones.

So, too, Brisa's assaults underscore how codwelling produced injurious intimacy reinforced by particular spatial arrangements within houses. Brisa experienced sexual assault in a kitchen and in a master bedroom, where Potencia's sons treated her as a household object available for their taking. Although she bore no children from those attacks, the possibility of kinship born of violence lingers in those rooms. Indeed, Bolivian history, like the Brazilian history recounted by Ribeiro Corossacz, is crowded with such children.[29] Sociologist Silvia Rivera Cusicanqui argues that Bolivian discussions of domestic violence have largely ignored the "symbolic and physical violence which is exerted within the home but outside of familial ties—specifically against domestic workers."[30] For Rivera Cusicanqui, these "interstitial" spaces fraught with violence are crucially "responsible for linking indigenous societies with the rest of the country."[31] As Brisa's experience reveals, however, the borders between waged and unwaged care work, like those between kin-like ward and employee, are like thresholds: permeable, yet also the site of violent boundary work.

In Bolivia, the assimilationist, nation-building project of *mestizaje* worked through institutions like schooling and such family and housing arrangements as Brisa knew, including the sexual violence that occurred within them. Indigenous *criadas* were reared, educated, and urbanized but remained, nevertheless, subordinate to *mestiza* patrons. These intimate relations may reflect another dimension of what Bolivian political scientist René Zavaleta Mercado dubs Bolivia's "señorial paradox," with *señorial* here referring to the positions of lords/masters.[32] The señorial class of women like Doña Potencia enacted ideologies of Indigenous assimilation and "social betterment" by housing wards such as Brisa. Yet, Potencia's position as an elite *mestiza señora* also depended on the persistence of Indigenous subordination (rather than full assimilation according to ideologies of *mestizaje*). Brisa's experience underscores the metonymic quality of house and nation in colonial processes of intimately addressing the so-called Indian problem as it pervades the present.[33] The residue of that "señorial paradox" thus shapes a variety of laboring relations beyond those established under Bolivia's former hacienda system.

In Brisa's narrative, the house itself often acts as a proxy for the injuries she received. Its rooms materialized her fraught status as Potencia's *criada*, while Brisa viscerally remembered those same spaces as locations where she forged ambivalent attachments with the Doctora and Anita—through her housekeeping and caregiving labor and the care she received in turn when the house and people within it did her harm. Yet these attachments followed Brisa to *other* houses and the rooms within them—further binding her to Potencia's family, even after she left their guardianship.

Anticréticos, Affines, and Ambivalent Attachments

When Brisa was in her twenties and settled in with her first partner, the Doctora—a well-placed judge—used her contacts to help the family's former *criada* get a job providing tea and coffee service to bureaucrats in one of the capital's many government ministries. Brisa would later rely on family connections to find work as a secretary at a gym in an arty La Paz neighborhood, where I would meet her soon after. Brisa eventually broke up with her first partner and began looking for a new place to stay with their two daughters. She turned to the Doctora, who loaned Brisa money to rent an *anticrético* (described below). Brisa interpreted the money as compensation for the years she had worked as a *criada* without pay: The Doctora was, in her view, reimbursing overdue wages. That *anticrético* payment proved consequential for years to come—for Brisa and for a whole host of unequal kin relations produced through it. Thus, the *anticrético* provides further insight into how houses can serve to make, affirm, and, as we shall see later, unmake kin. But to understand how, it is necessary to understand something of Bolivia's unusual *anticrético* system.

Anticrético payments provide informal credit to homeowners needing a quick and substantial infusion of cash. Rather than paying monthly, tenants "renting" through *anticrético* supply a large sum of money up front to their landlords, who repay the "loan" when the tenant departs. This lending system emerged in a context where, historically, many Bolivians couldn't access credit through formal banking institutions and where monthly rental payments are usually very low. Both parties, ostensibly, win. A tenant essentially lives rent-free (because they will be repaid when they depart), while the landlord can invest that large lump sum in income-generating projects or use it toward other urgent purposes. Of course, repayment is not always ensured—and many people find themselves unable to recover their investment. The Doctora agreed to help Brisa make a lump sum *anticrético* payment on an apartment after Brisa was no longer providing unpaid, live-in domestic service as a *criada*. With the *anticrético*, Brisa effectively loaned US$2,500 to her new landlords. The expectation, of course, was that her landlords would return that sum at the end of her stay. It didn't work out that way.

Brisa rented the *anticrético* apartment from an older couple who lived in one section of a larger property owned by their adult son, Miguel. That household compound, located high on one of La Paz's *laderas*, is organized like many such homes in Bolivia: Behind brick or adobe walls, several rooms or multiroom households center around a shared courtyard. Such compounds are built into the canyonsides leading down into the city center—a thousand-foot descent bursting with brick and adobe structures balanced precipitously on shifting terrain, their exposed rebar jutting into the sky.

Miguel built the multistory compound to accommodate his parents and siblings. "Miguel always had this vision that the whole family would live together for mutual support. But nobody else really put the work in like he and his parents did," Brisa lamented. In so doing, she gestured toward members of Miguel's family who, she believed, failed to fully enact their kin obligations by helping construct the new home, even as they benefited from it—codwelling without the requisite labor.[34] Brisa continued, "They whined, 'Why would you buy land so high up on the mountain?'" She pulled out an old photo album and flipped through it. "You remember what it was like back then?" she asked, pointing to the once-empty lots surrounding the house I had been visiting since 2004. "It was just an old trash dump."

Although Miguel's parents rented the room to Brisa, Brisa and Miguel soon met each other and, to the dismay of his parents, embarked on a romantic relationship. "From then on, it was a calvary," Brisa remembered, invoking the injurious journey to becoming second-class kin. After only a few months with Miguel, Brisa found herself pregnant with Teo. Brisa and I had, by then, become close friends, and she invited me to be a witness to her small wedding in a notary's office, where I served as both photographer and legal signatory for her marriage to Miguel.

Miguel's parents were irate. They accused Brisa of getting pregnant by another man. They called her a whore, a painful reminder of the sexual assaults she had suffered in Potencia's house. They derided her with racial epithets and generally made her life miserable. Miguel condemned his parents for their mistreatment, but it continued, unrelenting, after they wed.

"I've been dealt a bad hand," Brisa told me, reflecting on the abuse she had suffered both as a *criada* and as a daughter-in-law. What is striking about that trajectory, however, is how the Doctora's intervention unwittingly helped create a whole new set of kin relationships for Brisa—both happy and cruel. Brisa eventually returned to Potencia's family after Teo was born—doing *paid* domestic work in the now-adult Anita's cavernous home. Brisa then recruited Anita into another kind of long-term relationship, naming her *madrina* (godmother) of infant Teo. Brisa named me as Teo's other *madrina*, giving him two godmothers for good measure: one *mestiza*, one white.[35]

After hearing about the in-laws' verbal tirades for several years, the Doctora arranged for Brisa to move to a one-room cement structure sitting empty on a plot of land owned by her brother—Potencia's one son who had *not* assaulted Brisa. That sort of tiny house, too, is a familiar one in Bolivia: Landowners frequently erect simple structures to mark property before the titleholder takes up residence in a finished house. Owners of land and homes may "hire" an individual or family to live there, rent free, as *cuidadores* (caretakers) in exchange for protecting the property from those who might try to usurp it without a title—whether landless peasants or urban squatters. Brisa, Miguel, Teo, and Brisa's two young daughters from her first relationship moved to the dusty plot—situated by a small river that separated the nearly windowless rectangle from wealthier mansions in La Paz's South Zone—to "care" for it.

Although it was a dark, cramped space, it would become, for Brisa, a sanctuary: a home free from her in-laws.[36] The housing arrangement, however, lasted only five years. The Doctora's brother sold the property, and so Brisa, Miguel, and their children returned to the compound Miguel had built and shared with his parents. And Brisa's calvary continued.

Debts, Deeds, and Disentanglement

From a loan to cover Brisa's *anticrético* to a simple structure meant to assert proprietorship, the Doctora and Anita sustained their intimate entanglements with Brisa through this series of houses. Although men were also a part of this story, women were the center of houses that materialized those unequal yet enduring bonds—ties further woven into Brisa's strained relationship with her in-laws.

When Brisa married Miguel, her former landlords refused to return her *anticrético* deposit, "as if I had bought my husband with it." In fact, they *couldn't* repay Brisa. Her in-laws had gone into disastrous debt to build new rooms atop the old—as many families do in La Paz, building upward as resources allow and as a means of investment.[37] They used the house—owned by Miguel—as collateral on a bank loan. They defaulted, and then everyone living there was facing eviction.

In a brilliant move orchestrated by the Doctora, Miguel and his family subdivided the plot, with his parents claiming ownership under Bolivia's laws of *usucapión*, wresting half the compound from the grip of the bank.[38] Brisa's in-laws, responsible for the foreclosure, continued to occupy the property liberated from the bank. They promised the Doctora that Brisa, Miguel, and their children could live in one of the small apartments in the salvaged property. Miguel obtained his own informal loans so they could build a private bathroom—a whopping US$3,000 to pay a plumber and bricklayers.

At that time, Brisa walked me around the still-empty rooms, excitedly planning their renovations. And then, one day, Brisa and Miguel returned from work to find their belongings strewn on the packed dirt patio. His parents had reoccupied their rooms, forcing Brisa and Miguel to settle into the foreclosed section of the property—waiting, uneasily, for the day the bank might evict them.

Even as they waited, they built additions. For years, Miguel and Brisa had supplemented their incomes by doing piecework in their living room for a boot company, breathing in glue fumes that seeped into their bedrooms and worsened Miguel's asthma. So, they constructed a separate workshop to separate their living quarters from that toxic effluvium. One of Brisa's daughters also needed a private room to share with her boyfriend. Thus, Brisa and Miguel continued to build their home as if it weren't owned by the bank and amid abuse hurled from Miguel's parents across a shared courtyard. The gamble proved worthwhile: Their lender, Mutual de la Paz, went bankrupt, transferring debts and foreclosures to other institutions. But no bank official showed up to evict them.

Yet familial debts and defaults menaced Brisa and Miguel once more, as his parents' unpaid loans threw *their* ownership of the once-salvaged property into jeopardy.[39] While the Doctora had previously saved half the compound from foreclosure, Brisa suddenly faced the renewed spatial incursions of her in-laws as they pled to occupy parts of the foreclosed half in which she dwelled—the house miraculously spared by a bank in crisis.

However fraught the relations within, that housing had enabled Brisa to make kin through her close codwelling with Miguel's siblings and parents, through the physical labor of expanding and redesigning their shared—yet contested—quarters, and through the birth of three children. But her in-laws' financial (mis)dealings also prompted Brisa to sustain and call on her kin-like ties with the Doctora and Anita through their continued patronage of her housing, their legal counsel, and their persistent affective entanglements.

When Teo was five years old and the family was still living in the *cuidador* house, Anita invited me to visit while Brisa was working in her home. We were, after all, co-godmothers to the little boy, both *comadres* to Brisa. Rather than joining us for tea as I had naively expected, Brisa set to work prepping meals. Strikingly, Anita didn't invite me to sit in her pristine living room. Instead, we perched on stools in the steaming kitchen. Anita hovered over Brisa as she worked, pointedly asking questions about her relationship with Miguel, urging her to find a better man with less difficult parents.

In effect, Anita inserted herself figuratively into Brisa's bedroom and living room, counseling her to abandon ungrateful yet housebound kin. Brisa quietly continued chopping carrots, although she rolled her eyes at Anita's suggestions once we left and could talk openly about the dynamic. Brisa's actions, however, spoke. She has remained with Miguel amid the disastrous dealings of her in-laws, ignoring Anita and the Doctora's advice and choosing his kinship over theirs. As a consequence, Brisa now characterizes the Doctora as estranged kin. Fed up with the financial mismanagement of Brisa's in-laws, the *anticrético* money gone, the rescued house once again facing foreclosure, the Doctora now refuses to speak to her, while Brisa's relationship with Anita grew distant.

In this context, Brisa's pursuit of a new home high on the hillside provides her with a means to unmake kin bonds by uncoupling herself from the houses where codwelling, labor, and lending have left her feeling ensnared by the kin ties that once housed her. Unable to take out loans from the bank due to being blacklisted for credit—thanks to the financial misdealing of his parents—Miguel nevertheless contributed money from his piecemeal boot work to help Brisa buy the plot, although his asthma made him less enthusiastic about the strenuous ascent.

Brisa articulated her aspirations for her elevated plot, saying, "I want a home even if it's only a room." Her appeal to a home "even if only a room" invokes a common refrain in La Paz: *casa aunque en la punta del cerro*—a home/house "even if only at the top of the hill."[40] Those heights don't index luxury condos with spectacular vistas as they might, say, in California, but rather the steep, knee-busting climbs of La Paz's precipitous, auto-constructed neighborhoods.

Echoing Virginia Woolf's classic, *A Room of One's Own*, Julia Pauli found that, in Mexico, women who remained behind as their husbands migrated north mobilized remittances to escape the control of their mothers-in-law, constructing "alternative and autonomous social spaces: houses of their own."[41] For Brisa, however, homeownership—her "home, even if it's just a room"—is not only about finding a space apart from meddling mothers-in-law. Rather, she aims to fully disconnect her experience *of home* from the ambivalent attachments, debts, and violence she has experienced in every one of her housing arrangements thus far. Her previous attempts at unmaking or refashioning those bonds—from running away as a *criada* to finding employment outside of domestic service—were thwarted repeatedly as she both relied on and felt trapped by the relationships she forged through houses she shared with Potencia and her children. Brisa's account of her own life and housing arrangements pivots around "close but unequal" bonds produced and reinforced through the very "care" that kept her housed.[42] In this regard, building a home, for Brisa, is not about making kin of caretakers, compadres, and codwelling in-laws, but rather about breaking house-made attachments in which she has always occupied a place of intimate subservience.

Conclusion

While research on domestic work often reveals how employers organize space to reinforce racial and class difference, Brisa is reorganizing her own space to disentangle herself from the housing and relationships she has often experienced as injurious—even when she called upon her guardian-employers' moral and financial debts to manage *other* painful housing situations (such as living with her in-laws). Driven to build a home high on unstable and ambiguously legal terrain—the only place she can afford—she runs the risk that this house, too, may do her harm. Yet as Brisa shares her excitement over her soaring plot "where the condors nest," she often emphasizes the construction process itself and the new relationships being cemented through it: a kinship born of building homes.

When COVID-19 struck, it claimed the lives of both Anita and one of Brisa's beloved daughters. Brisa and Teo nearly lost their lives at the beginning of the pandemic, too, although both eventually recovered after lengthy hospital stays. The adjoining room that Brisa and Miguel had constructed especially for her daughter remained empty for a long time after her death, a constant reminder of a beloved child lost to COVID-19—and of Anita, whose

FIGURE 3.2. Brisa's friend and neighbor, Ximena, stands atop a pile of rocks where Brisa intends to build her new home and surveys the La Paz neighborhoods below, 2019. Photo by the author.

relationship to Brisa had always been bound up with her many houses. While she actively sought to untether her experience of home from Potencia and, eventually, the Doctora, COVID-19 severed Brisa's still-tender relationship with Anita in a way that Brisa did not want and could not control.

But just months before the pandemic hit, on that blindingly bright day in 2019 that opened this chapter, we climbed the rough terrain leading to her plot, looking toward a future not yet wracked by so much loss. Brisa pointed to the small structures dotting the bluff, rattled off the names of their owners, and recounted what she had learned about their lives and the difficulties that had brought them to their precarious plots. We made our way vertically to the one-room home built by a new friend, Ximena, who would be her immediate neighbor—a single mother who had carried each brick up the mountainside in sack loads on her back. The woman gingerly walked us around the property, which was littered with stones and grassy patches burned from outdoor cooking. She gestured: here, a kitchen; there, a bathroom. And then Brisa did the same on her plot—pointing to walls and doorways that existed only in her mind.

The wear and tear of domestic labor still scores Brisa's body, yet she does not experience all such household injuries as violent. That knee-busting climb, its own kind of calvary, becomes an incarnation of her perseverance. The calloused labor of construction, though physically punishing, allows her to dream of and work toward a future home, one she imagines disentangled from a lifetime of asymmetric affinities that both kept her housed and prevented her from feeling truly *at* home. She harbors no illusions about the uncertainty that remains before her—a reality the pandemic has only reinforced. But Brisa carries on, forging new bonds of relatedness, raising roads, and eventually, she hopes, raising roofs, carving a neighborhood, carving a home, out of a cliffside.

Agradecimientos

Para Brisa, mi querida comadre y fiel amiga. Gracias por todo tu cariño y apoyo a lo largo de los años y por compartir tu historia conmigo, primero como amiga y luego como antropóloga. Con amor para tus hijxs—mis ahijadxs—y en memoria de tu querida hija, tu hermana, y nuestra comadre, las tres perdidas en la pandemia.

SUSAN HELEN ELLISON

NOTES

1. Bolivia has two capitals: its seat of government, La Paz, and its judicial capital, Sucre.

2. The Spanish term for a house, *casa*, can be translated as either *house* or *home*. Research on the Andes (below) frequently casts homes as meaning-laden spaces of deep social embeddedness produced through the material construction process itself and experiences of codwelling. Yet such social embeddedness can also be crosscut by steep status inequalities and violence. Throughout this chapter I use the English words *home* and *house* intentionally to underscore how specific living arrangements and spaces—which might otherwise simply be glossed by the Spanish word *casa*—have different affective registers for Brisa. Home speaks to domiciles where Brisa feels she has greater control over the form those arrangements—the physical space and the relations produced and sustained within it—might take.

3. *Calvary* refers to the physical suffering of Jesus during his crucifixion and denotes mental or emotional anguish. For Brisa, it also evokes her capacity to endure in the face of unrelenting hardship. For further reflection on endurance in late liberalism, see Povinelli, *Economies*.

4. Brisa lived as a ward of Potencia's family from the mid-1980s through the mid-1990s.

5. See Leinaweaver, *Circulation of Children*.

6. L. Gill, "Painted Faces"; Zamora, "Acerca de las discusiones."

7. *Mestizo* is a racial category for people of mixed Spanish/European and Indigenous descent, but *mestizaje* also operates as a racial ideology that understands such "mixture" as a mechanism of Indigenous assimilation and nation building.

8. Young, "Myth of Being," 369.

9. For research on Bolivian domestic workers' own organizing efforts and advocacy for expanded legal protections, see Cabezas Fernández, "Diecinueve años de lucha"; and Peredo and Mayta, *Perspectivas en la lucha*.

10. See Colloredo-Mansfeld, "Architectural Conspicuous Consumption"; Leinaweaver, "Raising the Roof"; Skrabut, "Housing the Contingent Life Course"; and Van Vleet, *Performing Kinship*.

11. Carsten and Hugh-Jones, *About the House*. As Yael Navaro-Yashin argues in *The Make-Believe Space*, affect is born not only of intersubjective relations but also of "space and entanglements in materialities," in this case with the spatial and material dimensions of rooms where Brisa has worked (134).

12. I have explored some of these themes in Ellison, *Domesticating Democracy*.

13. See Ally, *From Servants to Workers*; Constable, "At Home but Not at Home"; Ehrenreich, Hochschild, and Kay, *Global Woman*; Goldstein, *Laughter Out of Place*; Hondagneu-Sotelo, *Doméstica*; and Rosenbaum, *Domestic Economies*.

14. Constable, "Sexuality and Discipline"; Dickey, "Permeable Homes"; Landes, "Further Thoughts"; Lugones, "Heterosexualism"; Peñaranda et al., *Se necesita empleada doméstica*; Ribeiro Corossacz, "Sexual Harassment"; Stephenson, *Gender and Modernity*; Stoler, *Carnal Knowledge*; Young, "Myth of Being."

15. Dickey, "Permeable Homes"; L. Gill, *Precarious Dependencies*; Peñaranda et al., *Se necesita empleada doméstica*; Parreñas and Boris, *Intimate Labors*; Ara Wilson, "Intimacy"; Winchell, *After Servitude*.

16. McKittrick, *Demonic Grounds*, xv. In the introduction to *Demonic Grounds*, Katherine McKittrick considers the poetry of Dionne Brand, whose writing, for McKittrick, reveals not only how "existing cartographic rules unjustly organize human hierarchies in place and reify uneven geographies in familiar, seemingly natural ways" but also how "these rules are alterable and there exists a terrain through which different geographic stories can be and are told" (ix–x). While McKittrick is particularly interested in diasporic Black women's geographies, I invoke her—and Brand's—insights here and in the epigraph of this chapter because of their relevance to thinking about both the spatial dimensions of domination in the context of domestic labor and the possibilities of imaginative reconfiguration, or what McKittrick calls the "meaningful struggle for freedom *in place*" (x).

17. Grace Young argues that, in the Andes, the tendency of employers to cast domestic workers as daughter-like "is part of the effort to secure her dependence and continual devotion to the family," while obscuring the material and status benefits she provides to them, particularly to her *señora*. Young, "Myth of Being," 370. See also L. Gill, *Precarious Dependencies*. Peñaranda, Flores, and Arandia (*Se necesita empleada doméstica*, 77) found that although some Bolivian domestic workers speak scathingly of employers who deploy such familiar rhetoric, others characterize the best employers as treating them *like* kin and describe their own efforts to "earn" their care. "From this perspective," the authors write, "improving working conditions doesn't depend on legal or economic factors . . . but rather on affective and paternalistic aspects whose origin is rooted in the colonial era" (translation mine). By contrast, Mareike Winchell argues that in Cochabamba's valleys, the hacienda system produced a complex form of shared dependency between the children of former hacienda masters and once-bonded Indigenous laborers. While the children of former masters brought their fathers' out-of-wedlock children and former servants into sponsorship and formalized kin relations out of a sense of obligation and "inherited shame or guilt," former laborers and other residents, too, "summoned kinship as an idiom and a relational structure for demanding Mestizo accountability to a violent labor past and the structures of racial hierarchy it left in its wake." Winchell, *After Servitude*, 60, 12. See also Leinaweaver, *Circulation of Children*; Zamora, *Acerca de las discusiones*.

18. For an account of similarly complex affective-material attachments in Bolivia's posthacienda valleys, see Winchell, *After Servitude*.

19. Here I am thinking with Biehl and Locke, "Anthropology of Becoming," and with Millar, *Reclaiming the Discarded*, as these "unfinished," "plastic" ways of life take on material form in the house.

20. Castellanos, *Indigenous Dispossession*; Cattelino, *High Stakes*; Stout, *Dispossessed*.

21. *Ladera* refers to the steep walls of the canyon where La Paz nests. Historically, the auto-constructed neighborhoods on the *ladera* have been home to the capital's Indigenous, working-class, and poor residents.

22. Dickey, “Permeable Homes.”

23. L. Gill, “Painted Faces”; Cabezas Fernández “Diecinueve años de lucha”; Peredo and Mayta, *Perspectivas en la lucha.*

24. A common coffee-making practice in Bolivia.

25. On yet another occasion, Brisa fled and ended up spending a stretch of time at a La Paz orphanage before eventually being “recovered” by the Doctora.

26. *Chicha* is a fermented drink.

27. Ribeiro Corossacz, “Sexual Harassment,” 393.

28. Ribeiro Corossacz, “Sexual Harassment,” 393. Commenting on Black women’s experience of the transatlantic slave trade and its aftermath, Katherine McKittrick writes, “Once the racial-sexual body is territorialized, it is marked as decipherable and knowable—as subordinate, inhuman, rape-able, deviant, procreative, placeless.” McKittrick, *Demonic Grounds*, 45.

29. See Winchell (*After Servitude*, 58) on the “opacity” of asymmetrical sexual relations and rape on former haciendas. See also L. Gill, *Precarious Dependencies*; Smith, “Pitfalls of Home.”

30. Rivera Cusicanqui, “Violence and Interculturality,” 283; Stephenson, *Gender and Modernity*, 15–17. See Zamora (“Acerca de las discusiones”) on eighteenth-century efforts to provide legal protection for *criadas* subjected to abuse.

31. Rivera Cusicanqui, “Violence and Interculturality,” 284.

32. Zavaleta Mercado, *Lo nacional-popular.* See also Winchell, *After Servitude.*

33. Barragán Romano, *Indios, mujeres y ciudadanos*; Larson, “Redeemed Indians”; Soliz, *Fields of Revolution.*

34. Brisa’s complaint invokes widespread expectations around the shared labor of house building/roof raising and kin making in the Andes. See Colloredo-Mansfeld, “Architectural Conspicuous Consumption”; Leinaweaver, “Raising the Roof.”

35. Over sushi, *comida chifa* (Chinese buffets), and Cuban sandwiches during her lunch breaks at the gym where she worked for one of the Doctora’s relatives, Brisa and I would talk about the dynamics of that arrangement and the expectations of *compadrazgo* as a kin-making practice that is often racialized and classed—particularly in the context of our relationship and that of hers with Anita. When another friend asked if Brisa harbored any expectations about me taking Teo into my own home or back to the United States when I returned for graduate school, Brisa guffawed loudly, explaining that she had no intention of sending her own child off to live with another person as her mother had done with her. “Care about him and be in his life,” she told me. “That’s all I want.”

36. Only later would Brisa realize that, although the terrain was flat, the structure was located on precarious land. A year into their stay, a terrifying flash flood filled the house, sweeping away belongings and clogging what remained with mud. This house, one she had hoped would be a refuge, nearly cost her children their lives. Luckily, Brisa’s teenage daughter managed to save Teo and herself from the floodwaters, scrambling to higher ground while their parents were away at work. The high-water mark staining the interior walls testified to the destruction and danger they escaped.

37. D'Avella, "Ecologies of Investment"; Skrabut, "Housing the Contingent Life Course."

38. Laws of *usucapión* allow people who have occupied a property for extended periods to take possession of it as their own.

39. Such financial-familial tensions are commonly attached to housing and take many forms. Noelle Stout's research on the financial burdens of pursuing the American dream reveals how people become so invested in the ideological centrality of homeownership that they refuse to walk away from underwater mortgages even as foreclosure looms (Stout, *Dispossessed*). In India, Lamia Karim found that microfinance institutions mobilized rural "housebreaking" practices to recover outstanding loans (Karim, *Microfinance and Its Discontents*). And my own work on loan recovery practices in Bolivia shows how lenders utilize "defaulting debtor" graffiti to humiliate a broader constellation of kin relations connected through the physical structure of multigenerational houses, leveraging public shame and the family conflict it produces to mobilize repayment (Ellison, "Painted by Default").

40. Chuquimia et al., *Casa*; Torrico Foronda, *Emergencia urbana*.

41. Pauli, "House of One's Own," 173. Such homes, including their design and construction material, reveal the manifold ways women find creative expression through house building and freedom from family dynamics they find stifling. See also Skrabut ("Housing the Contingent Life Course," 278) on houses as "flexible containers that not only reflect family growth but also the constant reassemblage of kinship."

42. L. Gill, *Precarious Dependencies*, 70.

EUGÊNIA MOTTA

4

The Dying Home

. . . Oh, pedaço de mim
Oh, metade arrancada de mim
Leva o vulto teu
Que a saudade é o revés de um parto
A saudade é arrumar o quarto
Do filho que já morreu
. . . Oh, pedaço de mim
Oh, metade adorada de mim
Lava os olhos meus
Que a saudade é o pior castigo
E eu não quero levar comigo
A mortalha do amor
Adeus

. . . Oh, piece of me
Oh, half ripped from me

Take your figure away
That *saudade* is the reverse of a birth
Saudade is tidying the room
Of the son who has already died
. . . Oh, piece of me
Oh, beloved half of me
Wash my eyes
That *saudade* is the worst punishment
And I don't want to take it with me
The shroud of love
Farewell
—CHICO BUARQUE, *Pedaço de mim* (author's translation)

As Always, but for the Last Time

I realized it was already dark when I pulled aside the heavy curtain and saw the black patch of sky visible from the living room window. For some time now, the house had always been in the dark, making it hard to tell whether it was day or night outside. Although it wasn't cold, Maria was lying on the sofa under thick blankets. When I announced my departure, she asked me to make her a bowl of porridge before I left, the only thing she had recently been in the mood for. She gave precise instructions about the consistency and the right amount of sugar. The extraordinariness of the request moved me.

Maria had been a vigorous woman, talkative and full of appetite. In her house, there were usually lots of people and pots of rice and beans waiting on the stove for visitors. My friendship with Maria had been largely cultivated in that kitchen, where my role was to cut, peel, and wash. She never allowed me to cook, let alone asked me to prepare anything for her. Not only did she think that only she could make good food, but she also thought of me as not very good at housework. But everything had changed in recent months. She tasted the porridge and was surprised, as she was whenever I had done a good job in the kitchen. She squeezed my hand and we hugged goodbye, as always, but for the last time.

Walking down the hill of the Alliance favela that day, I remembered a conversation Maria and I had had a long time before. It hadn't caught my attention at the moment, but in recent months it had come back to me again and again. Maria and I, when we weren't in the kitchen preparing something, would talk, leaning back on the double bed in one of the bedrooms. She would talk loudly, gesticulate a lot, pat me, and squeeze my arms and legs to emphasize some part of a story she was telling or an argument she considered important. One ordinary afternoon, long before she fell ill, we were chatting animatedly in her room, when suddenly a shadow appeared in her eyes and she said to me: "I'm sure I'm going to die early. I'm not going to get old." She was around fifty and seemed perfectly healthy, just as the house she lived in looked nice and airy to me, but Maria also saw the specter of death in it. Several times, when I noticed that objects and furniture had been moved, she would tell me that it was a bad house and that she didn't feel well there.

I went back to Maria's house a few days after I had prepared the porridge, following her funeral. Everything was lit up by the spring sun, and lots of people were circulating between the living room, the kitchen, and a long table set out in the street and ornamented with many colorful decorations. It was a Children's Day party, organized in honor of my friend, who had celebrated the occasion every year by inviting infants from all over the community to eat, play, and receive presents. In the corner of the living room was a piece of furniture with a picture of a smiling Maria dressed in white, a rosary that had belonged to her, and a picture of an angel. This small altar stood next to a huge photo of Wellington, cut out and applied to a background with an image of a blue sky full of white clouds. Below the smiling portrait of the boy was the word *Saudade*. Wellington had been Maria's youngest son, shot in the back by a policeman a few years earlier. The hum of the party, the preparation of the hot dogs, and the decoration of the huge cake were interrupted a few times by silence, crying, and long hugs. On the day of that sad party, I was inside that house for the last time.

Humans and Houses: Their Lives and Deaths

This text is about Maria's death, about what happened before and after what I've just recounted. But I write about death to think about what life is, and about how living—keeping yourself and your loved ones alive, and living a valuable life—requires a constant commitment to keeping things circulating and flowing. Many of these are actual things—objects and material substances such as food, furniture, and banknotes—with which affections circulate and through which relationships are made and maintained. Work is constant because life is always at risk of ending or losing its value. Living is not a state, but a composite process of many other processes that need to

FIGURE 4.1. Complexo do Alemão, Rio de Janeiro. Photo by the author.

take place for life not only to be maintained in the present but to continue to be oriented toward continuity in time, toward the future.

The gradual and unstoppable perishing of Maria's biological body was accompanied by the emptying of her place as a cook, mother, grandmother, friend, godmother, and community leader. She fought against this emptying obsessively, believing that she would be cured when she moved to a different house and continuing to make plans to build a place of her own for her social project.

At the same time that she tried to challenge the fate Maria had declared to me about her death, she knew that she would never get rid of the feeling that she had failed in her role as a mother by not getting her son to stay away from "bad company." The "bad" house she lived in had been bought in a hurry, in a desperate attempt to save Wellington from the common fate of young people who work in the drug trade: violent and premature death at the hands of rival gangs or the police.

These are always considered bad deaths because they interrupt the desired destiny of people living long, healthy, and honorable lives. They have a characteristic that is felt in families but also in entire communities, such as the favelas of Rio de Janeiro, where these deaths are recurrent: Bad deaths spread through lasting mourning, marked by the guilt felt by those who think they could have prevented the death from happening and by revolt against the perpetrators. This mourning materializes in houses through explicit signs of loss—such as photos of those who have died or graffiti on the walls facing the street—but also through the production of diffuse negative feelings and sensations, the consequences of which can be fatal, as Maria's account of her illness proves.

It is said that the word *saudade* in Portuguese has no translation into any other language. It is unique.[1] It refers to the sense of loss and lament for a person or a thing distant in time or space. This is the word that is printed on the T-shirts of bereaved families who bury murdered young people and that adorns small domestic memorials like the one in Maria's house. It is printed on the walls of Rio's favelas with the names of those who bled in their streets and alleys. The materialized *saudade* inside and outside houses shows the long duration and collective dimension of bad deaths at the same time that it demonstrates how houses participate in long-lasting mourning. The song by Chico Buarque that serves as the epigraph to this text was written in honor of Zuzu Angel, a Brazilian fashion designer and activist whose son was kidnapped and murdered in 1971 by agents of political repression. *Saudade* also historically connects the military dictatorship (1964–85) to the contemporary faces of police brutality.

In the following pages, I show the relationship between the deaths of people and houses to talk about the intertwining of their lives and what bad deaths say about what a good life is. Living and dying are moral, collective, and material processes. Being and keeping others alive—humans, houses, families—require intense and constant engagement. Life, if one considers the lives of humans and houses (and their progressive extinction, or dying), has two dimensions—one that is extensive and another intensive. These are inseparable and completely interdependent dimensions, but to consider them as distinct aspects helps us to understand the processes that I observed. The extensive dimension concerns duration. The intensive character of life concerns the processes that maintain it and steer it toward the future. I find it useful to borrow the idea of homeostasis from biology to think about what these forces or capacities are. Being alive is more than a momentary status. It implies a series of (internal) processes, most of them having to do with flows—and thus relationship with surroundings and other beings—that are necessary to the maintenance of a living state and to the possibility of sustaining life in the future.

The intensive character of life, the drive for continuity—both immediate and over time—expresses itself in the world through the capacity of beings to act morally and to attribute moral value to the acts of others. At the core of this morality is the drive to remain alive—with *as much life as possible*—for oneself and one's people, and to maintain the possibility of envisioning a *good* future.[2] The recognition of the presence of this capacity is the condition and the result of entities having personhood: that is, besides acting morally, having a biography—an autonomous and coherent existence in time—and existing in relation to the world.

Materiality is a central aspect of the processes I describe. But it presents itself in various ways. In the vital relationships between houses and people, the processes of *house-ing*, matter, and materiality may exist as things one can touch and see, but also as internal images of such things.[3] Materiality here doesn't oppose symbolism, abstraction, or imagination. It refers to the quality of entities having a discernible volume and shape and occupying or constituting a space.

A Bad House and a Failed Mother

Before she became ill, Maria would frequently move furniture around. She justified this by saying, with a melancholic air, "This house isn't good for me. It's a bad house." I did not quite understand what she meant until I discovered the "good house." It stood a few dozen meters from the bad house. It had two floors and a tall yellow wall in front, and it was close to two houses where Maria's two daughters had lived. This had been the first house in Rio de Janeiro that Maria could call her own after deciding to leave Pernambuco—the Brazilian state where her husband, Antonio, had grown up—with him and her baby girl, Andrea. She had previously lived in the house of her brother-in-law in Rio, "as a favor." This allowed Maria and her husband to save money they earned, he by working in local factories, she by cleaning houses or selling food on the beach. After some time, they could buy the land where they built the house little by little, as they were able to secure the resources to expand and make improvements.

This is a common story among the residents of Rio's favelas. Many of them are immigrants, mainly from the northeast of Brazil, who came to the rich southeast, primarily Rio de Janeiro and São Paulo, in search of work, especially during the middle of the twentieth century. Families already settled there welcomed the newcomers, sheltering them in their homes until they could build their own. Three of Maria and Antonio's children were raised in the house. To prosper through their work, raise the children to become good people, and keep the adult daughters—as well as the grandchildren who arrived—close to home constituted an arrangement that Maria presented positively. She considered the house to be good because it was the result of honoring behavior and the conditions under which she and her people could imagine themselves as part of a positive trajectory, all of which was inscribed in the beautiful windows, thick walls, and nice tiles in the kitchen that Maria described to me. The morality that informed her judgment about the good house made the one where she lived when I met her a bad house.

When Maria's youngest son began to work in the business of illegal drugs, she tried to steer him away. Moving from the good house was part of her effort. Involvement in what is perceived as the world of crime is nearly always interpreted by people who do not see themselves as part of that world as a taint on the family of those so implicated, and this stain especially affects mothers. Although the two houses were not far from each other, the new one was on a wide street not so close to the drug-selling point. Most of all, establishing this physical distance was a public sign of disapproval of the son's behavior and therefore an attempt to preserve a good name in the community. But Maria saw Wellington's killing as a complete failure to avoid the family's disgrace. She considered the acquisition of the bad house not only as an error but as a morally wrong reason to get a place to live. She told me several times that it would have been better to "get back" to the northeast with the boy, and she regretted greatly not having done so. Maria and some friends said that she was not the same after her son died and attributed her illness to his death.

The house where she lived acted on her by producing physical sensations, which she claimed were caused by "the air that does not circulate well" or by "the furniture that does not fit." Sometimes she interrupted a nice conversation, looked around, and just said, "This house does not do me no good."

Both houses had personhoods that were understood to be the condition and result of participating in the possibility of a good future (the good house) and the threatening of these aspirations (the bad one). Their biographies were intertwined with the way they acted on people. The bad house connected Maria's and Wellington's bad deaths.

Living in the Hospital

Maria was first hospitalized at an emergency ward at the beginning of 2014, more than five years after Wellington's death. She was then transferred to a private hospital that serves the public health care system.[4] She shared a room and adjoining bathroom with another patient. In the first days, friends and relatives brought her objects such as forks and spoons, cups, knives, and pillows. Maria requested more items to increase her comfort. She asked me for a blanket, which I brought from my house at my next visit.

The hospital space, which—by principle and through the effort of many people—should be impersonal and aseptic, was transformed over the weeks through the composition of objects from different homes. Over time, the room became increasingly inhabited by familiar objects, more comfortable, and—as some people mentioned—cleaner. Women close to Maria would come in and immediately check the entire space, looking for anything that might be out of place or dirty. Many came with food specially chosen and prepared to "make her stronger" or tasty dishes that would comfort her. Maria made an effort to behave as a true host, trying to ensure that people felt welcome, maintaining conversation about pleasant issues, and avoiding speaking of the disease.

At the same time, the flow of people and objects coming from other houses and being "shifted" to the hospital room caused the home back in the favela to become, in Maria's words, "abandoned." She clearly did not believe that her husband, who continued to live there, was able to take care of the home on his own. The stove was barely used, there was no food, and dust accumulated. Some women friends, including me, took turns going there to tidy up the space.

The dynamic of these flows between many homes and the hospital room suggests that a house's quality of being proper can be increased or decreased. Buildings and places can be drained off or completed by their "houseness"—that is, by their combined characteristics as places to sleep, eat (preferentially), store personal belongings, host, and offer care.[5] These latter two actions, hosting and caring, are the ways that people become and remain close. Some people are considered family—when they are recognized as sharing ties considered corporeal and transmitted by corporal substances—others "like family," and still others as friends, colleagues, and neighbors.[6] By contrast, spaces and places may be "housified" by the mobilization of objects and substances.

Maria was responsible for the care of her home, which involved cooking, planning the shopping, managing the money of the house, cleaning spaces and clothes, and hosting her people. These activities simultaneously made Maria the center not only of the maintenance of her home but of a configuration of houses, a wide arrangement made of several houses.[7] And, because of the many people who depended on her in various ways, these activities made her a good mother, a good neighbor, and a good relative. Most of what she did for other people involved caring, cooking, and cleaning, gendered activities that made her a good (and complete) woman.[8]

The idea of houseness that I propose here seeks to call attention, first of all, to the moral aspect of *house-ing* and of houses as processes and to the daily efforts and investment that allow a proper house and a good woman to make each other.[9] By bringing houseness to the hospital through the—literal—mobilization of objects from various houses, Maria remained at the center of flows that, at the time, ran in the opposite direction than they had formerly. But her tension with her abandoned house was constant. It reveals the homeostatic efforts to maintain and redirect flows of people and things to keep her house alive and herself as a true and valuable woman.

The observation of this process allows us to think of how, in different ethnographic universes, different degrees of houseness may connect to the diverse status of places that are residences (where people dwell) but that do not come to be considered complete houses, such as prisons and temporary lodgings for workers.[10] These spaces have lower moral value than "family houses." These living spaces that are not called or considered houses (or that may have lost their houseness) are nearly always connected to proper houses in a significant manner, very commonly and most firmly with a mother's home. Mothers are very frequently considered the most complete incarnation of feminine personhood, often referred to as "queens."

Proper houses are *spaces* in which houseness is presented in an accentuated and relatively stable manner, and they are connected to the value of people and the intense character of life. Other places can possess houseness, but not enough for them to be considered complete houses. In any case, as Mary Douglas formulated well, the house is always a "where," a situated entity, whose materiality is implied, be it incarnated in tangible substance or imagined.[11] But, as it is always defined and thought of as the situated point where specific flows converge—of people, objects, and food—it is always material. The observation of processes of house-ing and dehouse-ing places matter and materiality into another analytical space. A house is never complete; it is always in the making, and its properness is always at risk.

Dying at Home

After months of hospitalization, Maria returned to her community. Her health was deteriorating; her mobility was increasingly reduced. This time, her house was transformed from an "abandoned" state into the house of a dying person. Once again, the furniture was moved or changed function.

When she returned home, Antonio had placed a new sofa in front of the old one in the living room. The table was placed in a corner, and the rack had a new television. The curtains, which had always been open, were now closed all day long. The new sofa would guarantee that Maria could watch television lying down and still have space for other people to sit. The new television was considered a necessity, given that Maria could do increasingly fewer tasks and rarely left the house.[12] The proximity of the new sofa to the door that led to the hall allowed Maria to support herself when she walked from one room to another. The distance between furniture was adjusted to allow two people to circulate side by side: Maria and someone supporting her.

In the kitchen, the cabinet that also served as a bench was cleared of jars and food containers, and two boxes holding medicine were placed on top of it. The utensils were gradually changing places, stored in a spot Maria did not approve of. She was giving up cooking, and other women came to prepare meals since her husband went to work every day as a doorman. A windowless bedroom that had once been used by Wellington and then for storage was emptied, and the cabinet in that room was sold. The bed from Maria and Antonio's room was placed there, and a new one was purchased to replace it. This arrangement would both provide more comfort for Maria and give her caretakers a place to rest during the day or to spend the night.

Maria was upset that she could no longer conduct simple tasks, but her greatest source of discontent, the theme of most of our conversations, was being left out of meal preparation. To cook, serve meals, and purchase food was fundamental to making Maria the center of a configuration of houses. The transformations of her house were an especially painful aspect of her dying. She was a young grandmother, had a social project, and was recognized as a leader in her community. Not being able to maintain a proper house diminished her morally as a person, because it conflicted with what was considered natural and desirable for a woman her age. The material transformations were necessary, and at the same time they were a constant reminder of her changing position from one who cared (for many) to one who must be cared for.

The Death of the House

The little altar placed in the living room right next to Wellington's memorial materialized the connection between the two deaths in yet another way. The personal objects and the written words indicated the type of struggle mourners engaged in to deal with this sad departure. Maria's death, like Wellington's, required more material and symbolic investments, distinguishing it from a good death.

A long process was then concluded, one that had shattered the chance of a decent future for Maria's family. To have a son involved with drug sales can represent the moral disgrace of a large group of people linked to him, especially the mother, who is considered the main source of education for her children, the guide responsible for them becoming either "workers" or "bandits." A deeper, prolonged mourning always falls on the progenitrix, given that the connection through pregnancy and nursing is considered the most significant of all the relations among people.

A week after Maria's death, conversation began among her daughters, her husband, and some relatives about what to do with her belongings. The oldest daughter, Andrea, said with anger that some people were behaving "like vultures," wanting to take clothes and other objects of the deceased. The issue was also raised of what would be done with the furniture that belonged to Maria and her husband, the (bad) house, and two kitchenettes that she owned (residences with only one room, a bathroom, and a kitchen).

Close to one month after the burial, I met with Andrea. She was indignant. She had discovered that her father was dating a woman who lived in another state. Andrea believed that dating a man who was recently widowed was a sign of unequivocal immorality and was concerned that the woman's objective was to take the family properties. She wondered if the two had begun seeing each other before Maria's death. Weeks later, the widower announced the new relationship, which many friends and neighbors saw as a scandal. They thought it was too early and demonstrated disrespect for the deceased and her family. He was not mourning as he was expected to.

Andrea stopped speaking to her father. In his absence, she rushed to find objects, documents, and photos that she understood belonged to her mother. When the youngest daughter discovered that the new girlfriend would come live with Antonio, she also stopped speaking with him. Andrea warned all the friends she shared with her mother that they were prohibited from speaking with the father's new girlfriend when she came to the community. She said, "This is my mother's house!"

I did not dare to disobey Andrea's order. I watched from afar, a few times, the woman who was considered by many to be dishonorable and dishonest. From the little I could see from the outside, she quickly moved the furniture and redecorated the house. She took down an enormous photo of the family together at Antonio's birthday and also the image of Maria's youngest son. The couple did not resist for long the ill will expressed toward them by neighbors and family. Everyone still referred to the house where they lived as "Maria's house," and lamented its destiny when they passed by. Within a short time, the widower and his new girlfriend went to live in another state.

The house in which Maria had spent her final years was sold less than a year after her death and was transformed into a storage space for the beverage store next door. Little was left of the residence that I knew. Maria's two daughters, who had lived in the same favela, moved to other neighborhoods. Thus, the house—this arrangement composed of the material structure, the objects stored in it, the people, and the possibility of a good collective future—also died. The collective of people and things that belonged to it was completely undone. The entire network in which Maria's house had occupied a central place disintegrated, not only ceasing to have a possible *good* future but failing to have one altogether. The joint plans and the vision of a collective future gave way to resentment—dispersing relatives, even spatially. The house was no longer bad or good; it was not exactly Maria's, but it also did not belong to Antonio's girlfriend. It lost its connection with the other houses. The bad deaths of the mother and son announced the crisis of the house, but it was the final violation of its honor, caused by disrespect for mourning, that traced its destiny to the end.

Bad deaths spread out: from the death of one person to that of others, from people to homes, and from within the home to the streets and alleys. This diffusion also occurs in terms of the subjective experience of a loss that is transformed into a deep existential disturbance. The events, emotions, experiences, and materializations of these deaths—from altars to graffiti—reveal a world in which humans, homes, and places combine and constitute each other.

Afterword: Afterlife and Presence in Ethnography

When Maria died, her eldest daughter told me right away and asked me to go to the hospital. I met her, along with her sister and Maria's husband, in a small structure that was separate from the main building. Maria's body rested on a marble platform and was completely covered with a sheet. As we waited for the hearse, I sat next to Antonio, who had always treated me very well, but even in the months when his wife had been ill, he had never spoken about

FIGURE 4.2. Graffiti on a house conveys messages about bereavement and longing. Photo by the author.

his feelings. He asked if I would attend the funeral. He was worried and explained why it was so important that there be a large crowd at the wake.

He told me about going with Maria to the cemetery to have his son's body exhumed. As they walked back to the exit, they came across a procession accompanying a coffin toward the grave. Maria had been moved and concerned because only two people were accompanying the dead man. She took her husband by the arm and they joined the pair, following the burial until the end and talking to the strangers afterward. She commented to him then, as he was telling me now in front of his wife's dead body, that there was nothing sadder than a funeral with few people. I said that, yes, I would be present at my friend's funeral and burial. He was crying in a way I'd never seen before. He got up and called me over to the marble table, lifting the sheet and asking me to look at her with him and touch her face and hand. Maria was present and kept asking for our presence. The next day, there were so many people at the funeral that they couldn't fit into the hall where the coffin was displayed with her body exposed for the final farewell.

I was able to write about Maria's death only after a long time. A bad death is hard to take. It asks for meaning, for an explanation, for a story. Maria found her own story, a place for her son's death through her illness and the house that she saw as an expression of her failure as a mother. This saddened me and made me wonder what meaning I could give to her death and my participation in her dying. I, too, couldn't wrap my mind around losing her in such a painful way. As Norbert Elias wrote, life has no meaning (*Sinn*) in itself; what there can be is the meaning (*Bedeutung*) that other people give to someone's life.[13] Here is yet another sign of my attempt to give meaning through the renewal of your intense presence in this world, Maria. *Saudade* of you, my friend.

NOTES

1. In the words of Fernando Pessoa: "Saudades, só portugueses / Conseguem senti-las bem, / Porque têm essa palavra / Para dizer que as têm" (Only the Portuguese feel *saudades* / Are able to feel them well, / Because they have this word / To say that they feel them). Pessoa, *Quadras ao gosto popular*, 301.

2. Part of the Brazilian anthropological literature about Haiti calls attention to the native term *moun mwen* (my person). Flavia Dalmaso, Felipe Andrade, and Pedro Braum all show that it expresses proximity and mutual obligation. See Andrade,

"Comércio, Mobilidade e Dinheiro"; Braum, "Rat pa Kaka"; and Dalmaso, "Kijan moun yo ye?" My use of "one's people" here is inspired by the Haitian expression, as presented and interpreted by my colleagues, as a way of treating relations perceived and lived as those of connection, belonging, and mutual constitution with the vocabulary of kinship used, or not, according to the situation.

3. Biehl and Neiburg, "Oikography."

4. Brazil's Unified Healthcare System (SUS) is public, universal, and free of charge. It was created by the constitution of 1988, within the redemocratization process after the end of the military dictatorship of two decades that lasted until 1984. Private hospitals can contract with SUS and reserve beds without any cost to the patients, as they are financed by the state.

5. I refer to those objects that are called "my things," as in the expression, "That is where I store my things." People refer in this way to objects considered valuable and closely related to them as persons (to their identity, their biography, and their relationship with the world), such as documents, clothes, photographs, and family relics.

6. I refer not to people who are related by corporal ties, so-called blood relatives, but to those whom people refer to in approximation to these terms. This is the case of expressions such as *like a brother* or *like a mother*. Their use is very common, and the use of the term of kinship alluded to in each treatment is different. In other words, to say someone is "like a mother" or "like a sister" not only denotes proximity but also refers to distinct hierarchies and obligations, similar to relationships between mothers and children and between siblings, respectively, in these cases.

7. Marcelin, "A invenção da família afro-americana"; Motta, "Houses and Economy."

8. I discuss the idea of the completeness of womanhood in another text, describing why and how Maria and her friends did not consider me a complete woman. I "had studied," was white, and lived in a neighborhood of "rich people." All these characteristics were associated with the image of a "madame," the kind of woman in whose houses Maria and her friends used to do all the domestic work. Besides, I was older than thirty and had no children. See Motta, "Uma casa boa."

9. Carsten and Hugh-Jones, "Introduction."

10. Guedes, "Narrando, comparando e maldizendo."

11. Douglas, "Idea of a Home."

12. I heard various mothers in the neighborhood talk about television as a necessity, as well as a subscription to cable TV. Both were seen as important resources for keeping children "at home," "under watch" of the mother, and thus protected from the bad company "of the street."

13. Elias, *Über die Einsamkeit der Sterbenden.*

PART III

Afterlife of Slavery and War

AYLUONNE TXAI TERESZKIEWICZ

5

The Prayer House

for the embattled
there is no place
that *cannot be*
home
nor is.
—AUDRE LORDE, "School Note" (italics added)

At dusk—from the floor of a modest, one-room rental in San Francisco's Chinatown—my father would reach for his steel guitar and play us the blues. Leaning against one wall, his feet nearly brushing the other, index and ring fingers ensconced in brass to the knuckles, eyes half-closed. As strings warped under a measured pressure learned by ear, he would bend time and space in an intangible manner, shifting our small, far-flung, diasporic node of the

Great Migration into a liminal space, an intimate proximity to a near-mythic Southern origin. At seven years old, I sat spellbound. This *beginning* was one in which the two of us were always imbricated—a temporal and spatial continuum indexed in our embodied story. Yet it remained just this, a story at the outermost edge of language. Our self-narration was *felt*. The reality of belonging, however, proved enigmatic.

Other evenings, my father would craft an instrument from carved gourds and foraged relics of metal, using carpentry tools he nested into jigsaw puzzles within the constraints of our room. He built the kalimba, a westernized version of the mbira instrument, originally from Zimbabwe; its distinct melodic sound has spiritual resonance, meant to conjure the ancestors, spirits, and homelands of its player. Music escaped under the door, as did our imaginings.

Outside we weathered the frictions of daily life as the occupants of a building known for its small, unfit rooms in a neighborhood—and increasingly a city—in which we were both racially distinct. Throughout my childhood, my father and I moved frequently across various landscapes. Each new home we created became de facto pedagogical, due to the constant need to position our bodies in time and space and the effort to critically contemplate our otherness within disparate milieus. As I grew older, I intellectualized the context for why my father and I needed to move through countless living spaces: his disabilities and struggle with sobriety, and the larger specters of race and intergenerational poverty that positioned us both in the world. Decades later, this experience still drives my academic life into the ever-complex intersections of race, place, and belonging.

My father's coming-of-age exodus delivered him from the East Coast to California's counterculture milieu of the 1960s. He never once spoke of home. Through initial ancestry research, I learned that his family was historically from North Carolina, descended from enslaved peoples who forged lives across Bertie County before fleeing from farmland in the South to Washington, DC, and, at last, to Metuchen, New Jersey. These were devout members of the African Methodist Episcopal Church and dozens in number. Constrained in my knowledge of this genealogy, I entered ethnographic research through the Southern landscape to, in part, reckon with my own familial ties to the broader story of the American Southeast. The location of my fieldwork lies three hours south of my paternal origins.

Entering Brunswick, North Carolina

As I drove for the first time toward the small and historically Gullah Geechee town of Brunswick, North Carolina, over the banks of the Lower Cape Fear River, the valleys of former rice fields were first to come into view. What I did not initially see were the remnants of extensive tidal irrigation systems—wooden trusses, built by enslaved people—that harnessed the Atlantic Ocean and filled the marshes of local rice plantations. Damp soils and pine trees occlude any evidence of their formations.

What I also did not see were the pools (with depths up to one hundred feet) of a dark, tar-like substance: blooms of creosote, the carcinogenic chemical that the region's agricultural industries used to treat and preserve wood in the twentieth century. These blooms spread through the same deep depressions the plantation irrigation systems created.

The town of Brunswick is situated both in the shadow of these plantations and on land declared hazardous by the Environmental Protection Agency (EPA), a Superfund remediation site. This legal designation allows federal governmental resources to be spent to "clean up" this toxic land and its legacies. Once I understood this context, the entangled landscape appeared antagonistic—in need of remedy.

And yet, an ethnographic attunement complicated this tableau. Looking toward the river's edge, past the ghost rice fields and salinated, bone-dry trees to what stands just beyond, at the horizon, there is a prayer house—a small, white, one-room chapel built in vernacular architecture, with two stained glass windows from the turn of the twentieth century casting ochre and cobalt light onto a bare wooden floor. This one-thousand-square-foot structure, built of longleaf pine, was transported to its current location in 1910 on the backs of oxen by formerly enslaved Gullah Geechee men. Since 2019, local community leaders, scientists, and scholars have gathered here to discern its fragile anatomy and to analyze how they can restore this symbol of Gullah life and heritage through historical restoration practices.

The Prayer House

By definition, this Gullah Geechee prayer house is a chapel, not a church. Built on plantation land, it bears the vernacular traces of "the praise house"—cabin-like hallowed spaces fashioned by enslaved laborers as

FIGURE 5.1. The prayer house at dusk, December 2023. Photo by the author.

subversive sites of worship on plantation grounds. Within the community, this prayer house is known by many names: the house of worship, God's house, the ancestral house, the spiritual anchor, the sacred home. For 150 years, it stood as a gathering place for congregants until its doors closed in the early 2000s and time ushered it into "disrepair." In 2019, a local land trust joined with a community organization to purchase and restore the structure and enable it to reclaim its foothold in the landscape.

This prayer house endures as a vessel of historical world making, one of the last remaining structures of its kind in the region. In Brunswick, as across the state of North Carolina, enslaved persons' cabins and scores of "lesser" plantation houses are ambient, yet invisible—nearly all having returned to the earth in some capacity. For this community in particular, ancestral homes were demolished, either as the outcome of the construction of the fertilizer and creosote factories, new housing developments, and interstate highways, or because preservation was simply not possible, and the bones of structures ceded to rain, rot, and gravity. Many of these cabins, it is believed, are now soil in the landscapes surrounding and rooting the prayer house, absent but never gone.[1]

The prayer house's deep significance and influence vastly exceed the domain of its four walls and seem to generate a type of spatial and temporal continuum. The sacred structure appears to fold into the larger environs of the community, its characteristics and attendant ethos revealed in the ways residents articulate the past, present, and future of belonging in Brunswick and, more broadly, in the American Southeast.

Under chattel slavery, traditional domestic spaces were relentlessly threatened, and the domestic sphere and its claims to protection were routinely and violently disavowed.[2] Thus, being-at-home—and generating homeplace—in Brunswick took form, in part, in the malleable yet unassailable realm of a faithful congregation and reached far beyond the bounds of an explicitly domestic space.

The prayer house mirrors the figure of the "home," and the community's relationship to it reflects acts of "home making," precisely because both demonstrate the capacity to entwine and alchemize between spatial and temporal scales, stretching from the private prayers and cultural identities of one town to the vast diasporic network of the transatlantic slave trade, and from local genealogy and individual ancestral stories to a collective anticipation of

God's judgment. Like a prism, the dimensions of the prayer house's influence at once expand and contract depending on the vantage point.

Attuning to this critical elasticity, my theoretical framework figures the prayer house as an anchoring heuristic and situates it at the charged intersection of two processes: a six-year historical restoration and an ongoing Superfund remediation, which unfold within the same three-square-mile landscape. Both of these processes cast the prayer house and its value as a site of homemaking into greater relief. For this chapter, I will focus on two characteristics—or intensities—made visible here in Brunswick: home as flight and home as divine attribution.

Flight(s)—Home as Elsewhere and In-Between

ELSEWHERE

Tucked away on the banks of the Cape Fear River, the prayer house nearly exceeded the farthest, marshy edge of the plantation property line. Built by fathers and sons during fugitive moments of time, the structure balanced across four foundation stones and sheltered a community of enslaved Gullah laborers as they nurtured, crafted, and enacted alternate realities—reorienting toward God, deities, spirits, and Africa while in the "New World." When inside, they could braid together new social and cultural lives in the immediate aftershocks of the Middle Passage.[3] This is often where they came when they were not in the fields or their cabins.

Existing at the margins of a hostile land, this prayer house became a central atlas of survivals and possibilities. Each gathering, religious or otherwise, ensured a protected and private space in which to make claims to one's sensorial body, chosen kin, and social status and provided modes of political address that were distinct from the world in its current enunciation. Despite being a nondomestic space, the prayer house was an act of dwelling that provided a sacred, interpolating relationship to the landscape as *home*: a place cultivated in "the slave plot" as a counterforce to the more violent and sociopolitical relationships with the land forged by the plantation as an economic, political, and world-making episteme.[4]

In cases where Christian churches were viewed by the planter class as a pacifying instrument for control, and thus permitted and "respected" as Christian institutions, a barrier of safety emerged. This bestowed a level of protection that enslaved persons' cabins were not permitted to provide. These churches also emerged as sites for retooling Christian thought into an abolitionist campaign, instructing and articulating paths to liberation. The prayer house, too, became a site of shelter for this resistance.[5]

By positing this prayer house as a self-governed and autonomous space, congregants created the possibility for a protective subjectivity.[6] According to bell hooks, this particular understanding of a dwelling is the titular "homeplace." She argues that "homeplace"—the affective or architectural site of "home"—is central to the survival, recuperation, and liberatory praxis of Black people and others at the margins.[7]

For most of the twentieth century, the prayer house provided a nurturing space where children came of age as religious and ethical subjects through Sunday school, after-laboring-the-land Bible studies, and what several interlocutors have referred to as the Easter speech on a social issue of importance. Speeches detailed, defined, and often defended a budding moral compass vis-à-vis the community and the "outside." Beyond religious services, the prayer house provided social services in the absence of state-created, safe, and reliable institutions across the Lower Cape Fear River in Jim Crow Wilmington. Similar to the role of juke joints in historically Black communities, the prayer house provided professional networking for local economic opportunities in addition to familial care such as the provision of food and the sharing of health remedies for common illnesses.[8]

The congregation created a safety net for the community before there was any safety net for Black communities; the church bell would ring for emergencies to tell residents to gather or take shelter from storms, both meteorological and political. Some interlocutors believe that in the wake of the Emancipation Proclamation, watch nights were hosted inside the prayer house, a Gullah tradition of late-night religious services to honor the very moment enslaved persons technically became "free," at midnight on January 1, 1863. In effect, the prayer house was the backbone and anchor of a growing and rooting social world.[9]

This sanctuary also symbolized, and physically facilitated, the dualities seen at the heart of diasporic Black identity in the American Southeast: the understanding of oneself as "African"—and, if known, within a specific ethnic group—and as "American." It is through this twoness that I interpret this concept of home as flight: a perpetual effort to grasp the edges of two continents and origins.

Within the church's walls, the congregants forged together these two geographic worlds. Individuals still harbored the embodied knowledge of the African Rice Coast, the rhythms of language, the intricacies of agricultural expertise, and the bonds of resonant cultural practices that remained steadfast even within the categorical violence of enslavement. As Queen Quet (Marquetta Goodwine), leader of the Gullah Geechee nation, details in *The Legacy of Ibo Landing: Gullah Roots of African American Culture*, the coastal plains, thick with heat and the hum of mosquitoes, became an unintended refuge for cultural endurance. Here, in the master's absence, memory endured—not only in words but in the body, in practice. The land itself conspired in its preservation and allowed fragments of a distant elsewhere, a constellation of West African homelands, to root and remain on the shorelines of mass disembarkation, such as those of southeastern North Carolina.[10]

The physical attributes of the chapel's architecture and grounds also entwine African and Christian traditions. On either side of the restored main pulpit are diamond-shaped carvings—an African Americanism that I tended to unknowingly while cleaning the aged wood. During a presentation at the site, I learned that the diamond is one of the few shapes capable of fully enclosing a Christian cross while also reflecting an African understanding of the soul's cyclical journey—sunrise, afternoon, evening, and night—as an ancestral path in eternal motion. In the cemetery, shards of pottery, seashells, and children's games lie buried, and the prayer house cemetery sits proximate to the riverbank, a quiet testament to a Gullah *homegoing* tradition: the belief that the same waters that carried individuals to the New World would at last return them "home" after their death.

Here, my own oikographic sensibility flared: After venturing through various spiritual practices, my father had clung fast to the Christian Bible, its songs and parables. And when the time came, he requested a hospice nurse—an older man from Ghana who had been a reverend—to pray with him for his final homegoing.

IN-BETWEEN

The community's relationship to the prayer house was—and remains—an act of flight: Suspended between Audre Lorde's "cannot be" and "nor is," from the epigraph that began this chapter, this relationship reflects a search for freedom and homegoing shaded by the indelible threat of impossibility and irreconcilability. The prayer house concretely signified a temporary safe space for enslaved people, a *freedom from*. Inside, the prayer house was a speculative world of people imagining and seeking alternate, redemptive forms of being-in-the-world: the chapel's doors the ambulatory to the liminal space between nonfreedom and freedom and between freedom *from* and freedom *to*.

Outside, however, there remained ever-present dangers. Standing near the confluence of the Brunswick and Cape Fear Rivers, the prayer house bore witness to the volatile social and economic history of the region, from the post–Civil War period to the birth of the New South. After the fall of the Confederacy, it witnessed the burgeoning rise of the self-governed Black city of Wilmington, North Carolina, and the first and only fusion government during the post–Civil War period. The prayer house was also mere miles from the site of the subsequent 1898 Wilmington Massacre, the only completed coup d'état on US soil, which saw the deaths of countless Black residents and an upheaval of Black political power. Thousands were forced to flee; some escaped across the Lower Cape Fear River to this town of Brunswick and the sanctuary of this structure.[11]

Even when, in 1910, parishioners lifted the prayer house, moved it onto the land of a recently freed man—renaming it in his honor—and installed an iron bell that tolled births, deaths, and calls to worship for nearly a century, the sanctuary was never fully beyond the reach of harm. Through Jim Crow and the upheavals of the civil rights era, physical violence, legal injustice, and the relentless incursions of industrial, environmental, and speculative exploitation pressed closer as unyielding mutations and recursions of an original harm, at times tearing asunder the very site of sacred safety itself.[12]

Nevertheless, the framework I use—of "elsewhere" and "in-betweenness"—does not seek to equate liminality with precarity. Instead, it reflects the active and necessary practice of creating and re-creating home against and beyond the imminent foreclosures of the antebellum and Jim Crow South. Home was and is a verb, a continual becoming. As one resident made clear: "The [prayer house] is a testament to the fact that we are *here*; we are not going anywhere."

FIGURE 5.2. The edge of a home's yard before the woodlands, February 2024. Photo by the author.

Childhood Roads

On our first tour of the acreage surrounding the prayer house, Thomas, a community leader, led me and a staff member at the land trust through the back roads of his childhood. We wound through vines and underbrush a quarter mile from the Superfund site and at the forested edges of the former Oak Plantation. With one eye on the dirt road, Thomas picked dark, charcoal-colored berries off rogue branches to hand to us, all while carefully detailing and condemning the project management of incoming developers. As a child, he had called these berries sparkleberries. Playing around these backroads was to be "hidden," "free," and "safe." To walk these roads was to re-traverse the same path of the chapel 110 years ago, as it was moved from the land of enslavers to that of a freedman. It was to imagine a world that mirrored this felt sensation of possibility.

Two weeks after the tour, I was cleaning the chapel's cemetery with a group of volunteers to help make its boundary edge clear to outsiders—to protect it from trespassers and the developers who inched closer to the property each week, with looming Cat tractors and unfocused eyes. Peeking from the top of the debris pile of branches, mulch, and discarded plastics was a limb of a sparkleberry bush. This childhood road no longer belongs to the community; it was speculated on and purchased by private developers.[13]

Alongside being a powerful, speculative, world-making practice, Black geographies are, in part, a project of memory and archiving. I wondered about the cartographic quality and material significance of these berries sprouting around the cemetery and along the road that had led to the chapel, invoking ineffable attachments to this land as home*place*. Gullah Geechee communities are simultaneously the foundation of critical cultural worldings in the American South and of the political and economic marrow of the early United States *as well as* active keepers and carriers of global elsewheres that have evaded surveillance, an amalgam of "indigenous" Black American identities and West African carryovers.[14] At the same time, Gullah Geechee communities face continued inequities directly tied to their lands—namely, rapid dispossession through development, climate change, and the environmental violence of decaying

Superfund sites signaling ticking time bombs along the coastlines of the American Southeast.[15]

One lens for grasping this duality of safety/harm is to approach narrativization and emplacement of this Gullah house of prayer as a tangible past, present, and future heritage forged through the long afterlives of the plantation and enslavement. This represents what Sharon Fuller describes as autonomous Gullah lifeworlds beyond "subsistence," a distinct form of dwelling that activates in the in-between of acknowledging the *nor is* and embodying, with a singular power, the *cannot be*.[16] Beyond subsistence, in Fuller's formulation, is the transformation of sensorial and intimate day-to-day practices of being-at-home as Gullah into an emplaced liberation. These ongoing acts of living meaningfully and well evolved into a subject position not through explicit proclamations or words per se but rather through the granular realities of how people live, take root, and create community at the quotidian level, across generations.

At the North Carolina Rice Festival in March 2023, I heard North Carolina's commissioner for the Gullah Geechee Cultural Heritage Corridor, Michelle Lanier, conjure the ubiquitous bright green longleaf pine—the material anatomy of the prayer house—as emblematic of this fertile in-between. Through careful and evocative phrasing, she stated, "The longleaf pine was witness to the arrival of Black people, and the longleaf pine was extracted, just like our ancestors. It was bled . . . and this blood was used to make ships watertight so they may again cross the sea and bring more laborers here. And so, the longleaf pine is a kindred ecological species to the Gullah; it is an ecosystem of witness, most present in this part of the region."[17]

Lanier described this tree not only as a material arbitrator in the landscape of ghost rice fields and industrial remnants, its very own resin transmuting into toxic creosote, but also as a local idiom for ethical actors. She offered a conceptual vantage point from which to interpolate the tensions between the indelible horrors of slavery within the North Carolinian landscapes and the emergence of Gullah identities and worldings. In effect, the same pine forests that once bore witness to the terror of the enslaved—the site of punitive violence, or the very threshold that disappeared those running to freedom—also offered the wood that built their sanctuary, their prayer house.[18] This tree has become a living allegory, binding together legacies of violence, toxicity, and sacred survival. Its very form is a testament to the endurance and entanglement shaping acts of being-at-home in Brunswick.

Restoring the Prayer House

The goal of the land trust is to restore the chapel to as close to the original architecture as possible; upon successful restoration, the town then plans to transfer ownership of the prayer house to the state of North Carolina as a state historic site.[19]

The National Register of Historic Places has strict rules for how to measure and evaluate the historical authenticity of a structure and requires detailed—and evidential—responses to complex questions in survey form, a bureaucratic interpolation of the relationships between people, land, and critical historical events: What is the (related) story of your people, this landscape, and the materiality of this structure? Can you prove the validity of these stories? Can you argue for their relevance to the social and political history of the United States?

Often, this specific regulation disproportionately impacts Black communities, who might have fewer preservation resources and access to the highly expensive materials needed to be "historically accurate"; the urgent concern is often whether their ancestral house or culturally meaningful structure can survive any more time passing.[20] The town hopes to build a congressional case highlighting the inequity of these standards in an effort to update the criteria for federal historical registration to account for "intangibles"—the "ecologies of witness" such as cultural spirits, hauntings, and afterlives of peoples—that become tangible and elemental within structures like the prayer house and are fundamental to its historical significance.[21] As one resident stated, "You may look inside the structure, and it is *new*, but it is still our [prayer house], spiritually."[22]

Fundraising for the restoration of the prayer house cued negotiations of individual, familial, and communal history to leverage philanthropic capital. The cyclical and seasonal process of grant writing allowed for rehearsals and revisions of these ancestral, anecdotal, and familial stories—shared at bedtimes, hidden in spoken recipes for slow-stewed greens and rice, scratched on papers placed in dresser drawers—to contour the present-day collective identity of Brunswick as a Gullah community. As a grant writer, I witnessed this powerful, iterative storytelling and self-narration. In my first conversation with the mayor of Brunswick, I was struck by his closing call to action: "Now that we know who we are, we must plan to preserve everything we can."

As a physical and epistemic practice, the historical restoration of the prayer house enacted a form of critical nostalgia: an act of return to ecologies and materialities of the antebellum South for community self-possession, becoming, and *re*-membering of this twoness and the claims to belonging it affords and complicates.[23]

Divine Attribution(s)—Home as Sacred Witness and Judge

I see the sign
Sign of the Judgement
Sign in the Fig Tree
Loose horse in the Valley
Tell me what you're gonna do.
Your hiding place,
No hiding place.
Hail O the Time Draws Nigh
—From "Sign of the Judgement," ring shout song (Black spiritual)

A mile from the town's community center is the border of the Superfund site and the morass of toxic creosote. At its heart are two acres of land annexed for the original plantation trustees, still occupied by descendants who, it is whispered, have all fallen ill from blood-borne diseases. The prayer house is within a quarter mile of this.

Gil, the emcee of the 2023 North Carolina Rice Festival and a leader in the community—always seen smiling out at the crowd, a beat after the joke, nodding at nearly everyone in acknowledgment of some relation—would pass away in the time between that event and the following year's festival. I would attend his memorial in January 2024. His brother, Thomas, a beloved leader in his own right, spearheading the prayer house's restoration, would fall ill with the same disease that claimed Gil's life. Their extended family, known across the county as respected elders with local roots that trace back many generations, are descendants of enslaved Gullah laborers in Brunswick.

As part of the Superfund remediation, the EPA hosted quarterly town halls to update the community. Each of these community meetings

FIGURE 5.3. Pines near the boundary of the Superfund site, August 2023. Photo by the author.

concerning the remediation has adhered, almost to a *Groundhog Day* effect, to the same script, for over fifteen years. Approximately the same measure of progress has been presented each time. The same maps of land parcels are explained; the same images are presented of orange-vested field scientists "hard at work"; explanations of "what's next" sit on PowerPoint slides and nudge looming frustrations within the audience. There is always the same ambiguous reference to an awaited green light. At every town hall, the same binders are arranged on a folding table near the entrance. Each contains selections from the 165 legal and scientific documents pertaining to this site—nearly two thousand pages spanning sixty years.[24] Each document's purpose hinges on uncertainty. There are tense internal debates over the urgency of the remediation, the precise location of toxic pools, how the chemicals corrode local bodies, how the viscous substance moves through sediment over decades, whether contamination has reached groundwater wells serving children at three public schools, and if this toxicity can ever be fully removed. Systemic delays are made legible through these stacks of written evidence hedged in legal prudence.[25] "We simply need all the information we can get before we proceed with appropriate action," the remedial specialist explained to a silent audience in December 2024.

One of the meeting attendees, a key stakeholder, turned to me at a town hall gathering and said, "I need to leave; would you mind taking notes? Sorry, I have been going to this same meeting for over ten years; they are never any closer to clarity." Repair for past damage is deflected again and again out of the parameters of the perceivable and tangible present to an almost hall-of-mirrors futurity.

Even this region's map-making history reflects a time-stretching ethos of deferral, etched and re-etched into the landscape as a palimpsestic precursor to contemporary barriers to environmental justice. The historic landscape surrounding the prayer house is both figuratively and literally enclosed within concentric rings of containment: first, the speculative maps drawn by Britain's colonial surveyors in the mid- to late eighteenth century, designed to extract the most resource capital from the land; second, the borders of nine successive rice plantations, each adopting the precise contours of those colonial cartographies; and third, the property lines of chemical factories that replaced abandoned plantations in the post–Civil War era.[26] These exacting, layered regimes of enclosure, at once historic and futurity-oriented, now define the boundaries of the EPA Superfund site.

In other words, these inherited land-use boundaries are what determined (precisely, down to the foot) where the EPA could legally draw the Superfund site in 2006 and, thus, the parameters of future remediation and repair. Technically, not even a house across the street from the *map-turned-plantation-turned-factory-deed-turned-Superfund-boundary* can count as a site for examination and treatment. These borders vibrate their own temporalities and generate new ones: recursive refractions of an initial colonial encounter that delineated what is owned, protected, and in need of "justice"—and what is not.

Town residents are actively navigating this constant deferral of action and the overt and collateral manipulation of indeterminacies affecting their homes, pushing against these obstacles when and where possible. More often than not, though, residents remain suspended in a vacuum of waiting, one that appears to carve away at the affect of hope and binds the community to a space of forced endurance. Deborah Thomas's work is pertinent here, specifically on the simultaneity of time(s) within entangled frameworks of Blackness: how some people's lives seem to be progressing while "for others, time seems to stand still."[27] For Brunswick, this is experienced both at the affective register and as the concrete material outcome of systemic, deeply historicized propensities for *delay*. The EPA attorney for the site would frequently proclaim, as if on cue: "Remediations are rarely ever complete."

"God-Willing"

And yet, for some, this waiting transformed into something sacred, even demiurgic. Rather than a *postponement* of life, it became the creation of a world otherwise, one more livable. To wait in this way, under God's witness, was perhaps to speak of being-at-home in the deepest sense—to address the morphing, recursive constant in the landscape. This transformation emerged in an unexpected space: a meeting hall of EPA scientists.

The following quotes are from the March 8, 2023, quarterly community meeting in Brunswick, hosted by the EPA, which I attended. Carl Dixon, an EPA representative, began with the statement, "Our goal is to take care of this soil, [and] provide Brunswick the cleanest slate possible. . . . We want future development to unfold here that will benefit this long-standing community."

Resident and community leader Mr. Tillman responded, "After all the damage that's been done here, what is justice? Is it justice to receive acres of our own land that we should have always had?" He later stated, "I am focused on repairing our [prayer house]."

Mr. Tillman is looking past the dominant ethos for "clean" environmental futures that—when, and if, it ever comes to fruition—will prioritize repurposing toxic land at the risk of effacing cultural heritage and historicity: evidence of lifeworlds made viable and deeply meaningful despite the toxic threat, as Ryo Morimoto argues in his chapter in this volume. This grassroots historical restoration of the Southern prayer house appears to be an act of communal agency, to resist—and subvert—the EPA's futurity-oriented strategies of environmental cleanup and to *reclaim* futurity within the very act of waiting.

Another community member, Richard, speaking directly to the remedial manager and site attorney during a particularly tense meeting, echoed this sentiment, stating,

> I listened to Carl about environmental justice, and certainly I agree: We all have had environmental injustice and the health of people and so forth. But I have to question how you want to keep people healthy, but no one is talking about how poor we are. I don't see a lot of things about economic equality—about us growing, staying in the fight, not just *surviving*. . . . I think that is a cold gesture.
>
> You know, the Jericho Road of life is a winding road, and I don't want to see you guys be that thief that left that fellow half-dead. You can refocus yourself to be a good Samaritan. I think that is what it is all about, helping each other on *the ride home*. [Italics added.]

Notably, Richard offered the EPA representatives a chance at redemption through an act of kindness framed not as personal autonomy but as alignment with God's vision, invoking the Jericho Road as a moral terrain distinct from bureaucratic obligation.[28]

These were not the first times a community member wove religious references into moral assessments when speaking about the Superfund remediation. A refrain I heard nearly every meeting, from the mayor or another attendee, was an almost incredulous "God-willing." Verbal and conceptual appeals to God emerged as a type of refusal of the spatial and temporal tenets underpinning environmental justice. The mayor, the most vocal and pressing in meetings, would share with me that it felt as though he had been waiting his whole life for this moment, and that "God's hand was at careful work."

The Jericho reference gestures toward residents' quiet, discerning, and grounded realization that environmental justice, in its fullest form, may never arrive. It reflects a clear-sighted capacity to look elsewhere, to an *otherwise*. The indefinite wait for the EPA was replaced with another kind of endurance: a patience for an equally indefinite resolution that was marked not by passivity, but by a steadfast affective charge, shaping the encounters between Brunswick and the EPA.

The reality that this community has lost faith in the EPA remediation's promises exposes the unmet ethical and moral obligations underpinning "environmental justice" as well as clear-sighted allusions to an otherwise. Members of the community may be resolved that although they have to wait longer to receive full environmental justice for the toxins underneath their homes, they have faith that God is the ultimate moral witness.

Two legacies cross wires in this context: the fast and slow violences of Brunswick's extractive rice plantation industry leading to toxic corporate negligence, and the insurgent poetics of Gullah heritage—physical and affective labors to lay claim to land and collective identity forged in part through spiritual and sacred vigilance. While historically the prayer house effectively bulwarked against the fast violences, more than a century later, the prayer house, and the faith its form nurtures, serves as both a moral compass and an instrument against the *slow* violences from industry's lingering chemical toxicity on the repurposed plantation and the deep uncertainty surrounding the EPA's remediation decisions.

By focusing on their divine attachment to God and the prayer house, residents, it seems, tactically channel their earthly concerns into the level of the demiurgic—the power of creation, the capacity to turn "could be" to "what is," and the poetics of the spiritual sphere.[29] The faith of community members in the healing capacity of this paradigmatic shift points to what recent scholarship has articulated as Black freedom and repair "beyond injury"—an effort to look at fated protection as an already arrived and active source of

FIGURE 5.4. Photo sent by George, shortly after the alligator's emergence, October 2023.

life, joy, and power.[30] Here, Richard's call for not just environmental justice (which can, perhaps unexpectedly, read as staunchly reactive or even passive) but economic justice (which centers the community's proactive ability to grow what already exists, to live meaningfully *beyond subsistence*) signals a paradigmatic shift in how the repair of home is defined.

The community's confident, colloquial appeals to God suggest that, unlike the EPA's bounded notion of repair within property lines, justice—environmental and otherwise—is imagined as expansive, radiating from a modest four-walled structure that just barely contains all the aspirations it holds and yet sustains a sacred vigilance. As Jean Toomer scribes in *Cane*, "the pines whisper to Jesus" and the spirits, and as the gospel song refrains, in the end, there is no place to hide.[31] Their home will soon be on earth as it is in heaven.

Conclusion

At 5 p.m., while I rested in a small rented room across the Lower Cape Fear River, George, a local resident, sent a text as he wove through the back roads toward home.

"Just Now."

Moments later, I received a video of the pond near Richmond Plantation, the most immaculately conserved and historically significant plantation estate in southeastern North Carolina. Southern rock music played in the background of the video (a gruff, moody song from the old stereo of George's truck). Its dirge-like qualities sharpened my instinctive feeling of suspense, even discomfort. George shook his phone—blurring the shot—and I caught on: This was an alligator sighting, or would be. The creature had yet to show its head. Given that only an image of water flickered across my screen, I paused, but George texted, as if he could see me, "Wait for it."

Then, a large head surfaced—and stayed.

This jagged head, frozen mid-emergence, cleaved my thoughts. And I still wonder about its significance to me as an analytic. I could figure the subaquatic and sharp-toothed creature as Southern history, broadly speaking: an

archive of profound cultural worldings and violent dispossessions serving as the nation's source code, particularly as it surges—at once, and invariably—into present perception.[32] Or, I could view it as the many diverse claims Southerners make to this archive as heritage, claims that reveal implications at scales both small and large.[33] How does one live within vexed historical locations with physical, affective, and genealogical intimacy? To make a home, for example, beneath street signs bearing the names of your neighbors, knowing their ancestors orchestrated the Wilmington Massacre of 1898?

I interpret this creature's staggering presence as the political, sensory, and embodied paradox at the heart of making "home" in this Southern landscape. Viscerally, I *sense* it as a juxtaposition in ever-braided emergence here: a web of past and future harms (fast and slow violences in lockstep) beside the constant and interstitial choreographies of repair, even justice, in the *now*—an alloy of deaths, triumphs, joys, rages, and restitutions always just around the bend, hidden in the marshes.[34]

In March 2025, we stood with our heads bowed on the morning of the ceremony dedicating the restored prayer house back to the community. Descendants of its original congregants rang the bell for the first time in over twenty years, embracing afterward in tears. Just two weeks before the reopening, Thomas had passed. We offered a benediction in gratitude for his steadfast dedication; we acknowledged his ancestors in silence. His portrait rested at the foot of the main pulpit.

Standing within this small, one-thousand-square-foot prayer house in Brunswick, North Carolina, I felt it was an unfinished protagonist.[35] It reached beyond the confining parameters of any cartography; if properly mapped, it might "swallow the page whole."[36] I imagined the pine frame stretching on multiple axes—from its anchor on the Southeastern coastline across the lengths of the Atlantic, at once tethering itself to distant shores, an elsewhere home stowed away in the psyche, embodying the arcs of durative and cyclical time and symbolizing the boundless witness at the helm of world-making justice.

I now find myself at the threshold of a new vantage—one from which to glimpse this elusive, intricate, and kindred place, and to lay claim to this corner of the American Southeast as embattled yet fertile ground in our shared ancestral quest to be *at home* in this world.

NOTES

1. The family of an interlocutor and fellow researcher is intimately entangled in the history of the area. His childhood home stood on a former plantation, and while one of his ancestors potentially participated in the Wilmington Massacre of 1898, another hid Black neighbors for their safety. He shared with me, "I am from here, way back." "[The remnants] are everywhere," he said, "but it's invisible; you need to remind yourself again, and again." He framed the landscape as a quiet but constant resurfacing of evidence that elicits moral engagement. See also Catherine Fennell's chapter in this volume, "The House Underfoot."

2. Davis, "Legacies of Slavery," in *Women, Race, and Class*; Spillers, "Mama's Baby, Papa's Maybe."

3. Sharpe, *In the Wake*.

4. See Sylvia Wynter's figuration of the domestic space of the slave plot as containing forms of shelter and pharmacopoeia-filled gardens; as an emplaced cosmos that enacts striking insurgencies against the market logics of the plantation; as place, chronotope, and world-making episteme (Wynter, "Novel and History").

5. See Hopkins, *Down, Up, and Over*; Sambol-Tosco, "Slave Experience"; and Warnock, *Divided Mind*.

6. Dwelling through the spiritual, God, and religious ties in the antebellum South emerges as an act of reclaiming your beingness and ability to be at home in a world foreclosing on you. See Hopkins, *Down, Up, and Over*; Warnock, *Divided Mind*.

7. See hooks's essays "Homeplace" in *Yearning* and "Black Vernacular" in *Art on My Mind*.

8. The storage unit behind the chapel still shows evidence of this informal safety net in material form, through old job pamphlets, medicinal books, and school supplies.

9. Mary, the woman who lives right across the property line, who has dancing brown eyes and a discerning laugh and whose grandma attended the church, joined us one day as we landscaped the small daylily garden out front and marked trees for clearing. She acted out being in the pews, saying her grandma sat in the front left pew, as viewed from the altar. She rose to the front of the altar to give the beginnings of a mock Easter speech. Smiling, she stated, "Yes, this was our place."

10. Goodwine, *Legacy of Ibo Landing*. See also Campbell, *Gullah Cultural Legacies*.

11. Bellamy, *Moving Forward Together*; Brunson et al., *Interracial Communication*; Prather, *We Have Taken a City*; Umfleet, *Day of Blood*; Zucchino, *Wilmington's Lie*. See also Umfleet, *1898 Wilmington Race Riot Report*.

12. See the history of the Sixteenth Street Baptist Church bombing in Birmingham, Alabama, on September 15, 1963, by white supremacists and anti-integrationists.

13. Thomas denied this in the form of nondisclosure, never confirming nor denying the purchase with others if asked, and I was not certain if this "sin of omission" was a form of subjunctive thinking, an "otherwise."

14. Campbell, *Gullah Cultural Legacies*; Fuller, "Don't Know Nothin' 'bout Subsistence" and "Indigenous Ontologies"; Goodwine, *Legacy of Ibo Landing*; Lanier, "Rooted."

15. See coverage of land grabs down the southeastern coast, particularly in Hilton Head, South Carolina.

16. Fuller, "Don't Know Nothin' 'bout Subsistence," 102.

17. Lanier, "Gullah Geechee Cultural Corridor."

18. Dungy, *Black Nature*; Finney, *Black Faces, White Spaces*. See also J. Drew Lanham's work on the affective and semiotic cacophony of the "Black outdoors" in *The Home Place*.

19. The formalization of historical restoration as heritage preservation in the United States is regulated by the secretary of the US Department of the Interior—namely, the staff of the National Register for Historic Places and their manual, *Standards for the Treatment of Historic Properties*. Within this lengthy document, which I read while supporting the writing of a grant to the National Trust for Historic Preservation's African American Cultural Heritage Action Fund for the prayer house, restoration is defined as, quite simply, "treatment": an act of vigilant, thorough, and esteemed care for a structure guided by the "expressed goal of mak[ing] the building appear as it did at a particular—and at its most significant—time in its history" (Grimmer, *Secretary of the Interior's Standards*, 50).

20. As may be expected, the majority of the most preserved structures and cultural landscapes in the American South are the plantation estates of founding fathers, planter-class elites, and Northern industrialists who made their fortunes, in part, on the labor down South: Mount Vernon, Monticello, Biltmore Estate, and Bellamy Mansion. For more on this topic, see Melnick et al., "Integrity as Process and Feature."

21. A leader at the land trust stated: "In areas where it wasn't strong enough, they built around it, to hold it up, instead of removing and replacing. So the bones, the stories, and the energy, and the spirit of the church is still a part of it, even though it all looks new."

22. Examples of material conduits for this potential interpolation and connection to history lie within the bones of the prayer house and include square-headed nails shaped by the hands of grandfathers and great-grandfathers continuing to shore the shelter up, the ancestral iron bell, wood salvaged from timber leftovers for the vernacular structure, and the bespoke stained-glass windows.

23. Boym, *Future of Nostalgia*; hooks, *Yearning*.

24. The EPA maintains an archive for every Superfund remediation, made public under federal law, CERCLA's Section 103(c) Hazardous Substance Release Notification mandate.

25. To protect the community's identity, I do not cite the specific administrative record. Records for all Superfund sites are publicly accessible at US Environmental Protection Agency, "Search Superfund Site Information," Superfund Enterprise Management System (SEMS), https://cumulis.epa.gov/supercpad/cursites/srchsites.cfm (accessed January 16, 2026).

26. The overarching precedent rooted in these parameters enforced the goal of economic speculation—i.e., what extractable value exists in the land and what future profits the land could yield when heeding to prospective capitalist criteria. See Bartram, *Travels*; and the annual reports of the North Carolina Agricultural Experiment

Station, beginning as early as the 1877–79 report, *Annual Report of the North Carolina Agricultural Experiment Station, 1877–1879* (Raleigh: Board of Agriculture, 1879), North Carolina Digital Collections, https://digital.ncdcr.gov/Documents/Detail/annual-report-of-the-north-carolina-agricultural-experiment-station-1877-1879/4238535. Subsequent annual reports from 1879 to 1944 can be accessed in the North Carolina Agricultural Experiment Station collection hosted online by North Carolina Digital Collections.

27. Thomas argues that "situations in which pressure (in this case, catastrophic violence) produces the potentiality of simultaneous time" can help to expand our "understandings of the relationship between causality and temporality" (*Exceptional Violence*, 185).

28. This is a reference to the biblical story told by Jesus in the Gospel of Luke: "A man was going down from Jerusalem to Jericho, and fell into the hands of robbers, who stripped him, beat him, and went away, leaving him half dead" (Luke 10:35–37). This man was saved by a "good Samaritan," an individual from the group normally believed responsible for such robberies.

29. The spiritual foundation of environmental justice in the American South, in particular, is a rich but potentially underreferenced field of knowledge. Garrett Graddy-Lovelace's essay "Scales of Reference and Reckoning," developed as part of an Antipode Foundation–supported workshop, is instructive, as are companion essays published by Antipode in May 2019, particularly as they pertain to understanding the scale, planes, and registers of defining justice and reckoning, and the sacred affect of Black ecologies and "healing." See "'Let Justice Roll Down.'"

30. Lewis, "Black Life Beyond Injury"; McKittrick, "Mathematics Black Life" and "Plantation Futures"; Thomas, "Refusal (and Repair)." See also Lanham, "Joy Is the Justice."

31. Toomer, *Cane*, 11.

32. Benjamin, "Theses on the Philosophy of History," 253–64; Perry, *South to America*; Toomer, *Cane*.

33. Lowenthal, *Heritage Crusade*.

34. Nixon, *Slow Violence*.

35. Biehl and Locke, *Unfinished*.

36. Broom, *Yellow House*, 5. Broom writes about the historically Black neighborhood of New Orleans East that was her first home.

SEBASTIÁN RAMÍREZ

6

Home Under Threat

Mercedes had been stuck inside her home for a week. At her bedroom window, she sat behind a lace curtain through which she peered into the street and its seemingly unending dangers. Her friends would bring over a few groceries during the first days of her confinement, but as time wore on, fewer would risk being seen approaching her door. Guillermo, her son and the target of the death threat that now cloistered them, paced the house incessantly, only to suddenly settle in front of a telenovela, still as a statue. He cocooned himself in sweaters and blankets, rubbing his hands, drinking *tinto*, and smoking prodigiously in an effort to ward off the anxious cold that stirred deep within him. He, too, looked at the street, but he kept his distance from windows and doors. Instead, he held close a folded copy of the *panfleto*—the leaflet that announced this death threat—studying it with the same assiduous terror that now drew his mother's gaze to the streets.

Mercedes saw the *panfleto* first. "It was a day like any other. Normal," she recalled when we first spoke in 2017. On her way to the market, in her neighborhood of Cazuca high in the hills of Soacha, a city just south of Bogotá, she suddenly felt the eyes of her neighbors on her.

"They looked at me like a strange bug. They stepped away from me. I saw leaflets on the light posts, but that was normal. I didn't pay attention. But then, when I got back home, I saw it, the *panfleto*, on the door. Without reading it, I knew." On the door of the house she had built over the course of a decade and a half, a poorly printed leaflet announced the latest targets of a social cleanse. She took it down and brought it inside where she could study it with Guillermo, away from their neighbors' prying eyes. Yet that precaution came too late. Their house was now marked as a target by a violence whose provenance was both mysterious and intimate. That the leaflet hung from her door was an unmistakable sign that her son's name figured among the targets of the social cleanse.

The *panfleto* announcing Guillermo's death threat was, in many respects, a classic example of what has become a veritable genre. The leaflet's header announced its authors as the Black Eagles, a criminal organization of national reach widely understood to be a remnant of the former paramilitaries. It vies for control over marginalized areas of the country, and in particular of their drug trade. The name of the organization was adorned by the iconography of war: assault weapons, a coffin, a skull and crossbones. The body of the text announced its intentions at the outset—"DEATH, CLEANSE, AND TIME TO SCRAM"—and continued,

> Curfew owing to the multiple complaints from the community. The following are declared military objectives: any persons we find outside after 10 p.m.; death to fucking *basuqueros* [coca paste smokers], *sidosas* [AIDS-positive females], thieves, street dwellers, and young drug users. WE HAVE THEM IDENTIFIED. This is a necessary cleanse. Parents care for your children; we will straighten the crooked with lead or knife. You are either with us or you'll disappear. We know there will be widows and mourning mothers, but this is for a better life and a unified neighborhood. The following names are in our lists.

A list of twelve names followed. "Guillermo *alias el mono*" was sixth on the list.

THE BLACK EAGLES

DEATH, CLEANSING AND DEADLINE FOR YOU TO LEAVE

curfew, due to multiple community complaints we declare every person we see from 10pm onwards a military target, death to drug dealers, weapons dealers, ammunition dealers, activists and gays, thieves, snitches, rapists, homeless, and other gonorrhea sons of bitches who believe the city is theirs. The names of those persecuted are below.

Hans Didier Sanabria
Nicolas the aid-carrier
Camilo the aid-carrier
Juan Carlos Amaya
Andrés camilo
Tayron Daniel
Johan Sebastián Guzman
Esteban torres
Milena lesbian
Carlos garex "la vieja garex"
Milo peñarandá "la mila"
Ferney parraga "shimul the aid-carrier"
Douglas Leonardo "La ballarina"
Andrés the hairdresser
Marcos alias Paola transvestite
Amartz transvestite
Julián David
Jory Nicolás

***Giovanni alias el fosforo**
***The twins**
***Jhon Edison Gomez**
***Chiqui Gomes alias ratón**
***Alexis el Pollo**
***Carlos gatas**
***El negro alias tetris**
***La flaca**
***Brayan aliar el fiero**
***Ferney Calceda alias el paisa**
***alias ratón**
***Diego la mera rata**

We won't stop here, there are names to be confirmed, but we know that along the way we will find them. WELL BEHAVED CHILDREN GO TO BED EARLY, AND THE DISOBEDIENT CHILDREN WILL BE FORCED TO SLEEP, inhabitants of Soacha do not worry that we are here to stay to always give you support, security and control of the area so that you can live in peace from these criminals already mentioned.

You have been warned, you have 15 days to leave the city and do not believe that this is a prank or a game, do not expose yourselves more than you already are!...
Bars, hair salons and whorehouses where HIV (AIDS) is spreading),
robberies, rapes etc ... Because of some faggots already mentioned in the above lists, its better if you leave so you won't continue to inflict harm on society.

FIGURE 6.1. A typical *panfleto* that circulated in Soacha in 2017.

Printed at an almost industrial scale, the *panfletos* are posted under the cover of darkness and circulated in public spaces, demarcating not just targets of the cleanse but the reach and breadth of the authority that issues them. Like the official edicts that they ape, these pamphlets claim to represent a political community from which the authority to declare targets of execution springs forth. The apparent response to "complaints from the community" in the pamphlet issued by the Black Eagles defines an ethical commons on which the legitimacy of their rule hinges. The language they employ simultaneously parrots the cumbersome paper language of officialdom alongside colloquial idioms and obscenities. "Military targets" are invoked alongside "fucking *basuqueros*," coiling references of legal and illegal forms of subjection in a heteroglossia of violent rule.

While each *panfleto* outlines a vision of sociality that is structured around the ordering of its particular brand of governance, commerce, and the configuration of particular ethical modes of life, broadly, its accusations revolve around concerns for purity and consumption. Drug users, and in particular those who smoke coca paste, are invariably lumped with thieves, rapists, and LGBTQ+ folk in an encompassing category of deviance that is at once infectious and irredeemable. Though the threats posed by each of these groups run a seemingly ample gamut, there is an insistence on impurity that locates the subjects of the cleanse as dangerous to communal organization through the potential they pose to disregard the binds of neighborly life. Order, productivity, and heteronormativity are conflated within the text of the *panfletos* that then locate the killings of their subjects less as punishment for perceived infractions and more as anticipatory sacrifices of less-than-human objects.

The reference to *sidosas* (AIDS-positive females), for example, is meant to generally stand in for gay men, irrespective of their seropositive status. Allusions in the feminine conflate queerness with a loss of masculinity, while the insistence on the possibility of infection locates sexual desire as a threatening and violent force to be repressed. Heteronormativity is central to the pseudomilitaristic schema of neoparamilitary groups and has further proven to be a powerful mobilizing principle in political discourse in the country more generally, yet within the context of social cleanse campaigns, queerness is construed as an infectious threat.[1] According to Uriel, who participated in social cleansing campaigns in his youth, "They gays you have to kill because they are disgusting. A faggot is not born, it's made." There is another danger, of course: that other men are also vulnerable to the possibility of queer desire, and that heteronormativity can be secured only through the death of difference.

Drug use, the crime Guillermo was accused of, similarly operates within the logic of generalized threat; yet biological corrosion of morality is more closely associated with a potential economic loss. According to Rogelio, a man who lived in Cazuca and who, despite never participating in social cleansing campaigns, supported them, "We have a little problem: thieves and vice. Vice is screwing us over because [drug users] only live for their dealer, and the dealer fills his pockets with our money. So, I'm all for dropping them [i.e., killing the drug users], because the Bible says, 'a tree that bears no fruit should be cut down.'"[2] Arguments for the murder of drug users are often based in the quasi-sociological readings that connect job precarity, drug addiction, and criminality. Not only is the lure of drug use seen as particularly potent for youth in neighborhoods such as Cazuca, with extremely limited economic opportunities outside the drug trade, but the sustenance of their drug use is imagined to necessarily drive them toward theft and violent crime. But there is another, apparently more profound, danger posed by drug users and coca paste smokers in particular. Often described as "zombies," "degenerates," and "disposable," youths who consume coca paste are often presented as individuals who have relinquished their agency and their humanity and who have then been consumed by their addiction. When I spoke with José, a neighbor of Mercedes, he worried about what drug users "turn into": "These kids, they are lost; you never know what they'll do. They just need their fix, and they don't care." Much like LGBTQ+ folk, drug users are made out to be overwhelmed by antisocial desires. Furthermore, this desire precludes the possibility of economic and social contributions beyond its own fulfillment. To be a drug addict within this logic is to forsake the bonds of both productivity and empathy that connect members of the community and to therefore become a threat to these very bonds.

Every year, hundreds are selectively killed, and thousands displaced, in what are known as social cleansing campaigns around the country.[3] Many of the killings are announced in *panfletos* like the one that featured Guillermo. They are often perpetrated by neighbors under the auspices of criminal gangs and with the complicity—or even the participation—of local police who tout these threats and murders as the necessary procedures of order in places official justice cannot reach. The groups that claim responsibility for social cleansing campaigns are often the heirs to paramilitary groups that—though they nominally disbanded more than a decade ago—have flourished in the many aftermaths of Colombia's war. The killings target groups identified as social dangers: drug users, petty criminals, LGBTQ+ folk, and especially trans women. The label of social danger is porous, however, and is often extended to include those who resist the para-official rule of criminal gangs, such as activists, informants, and political agitators.

Those targeted by the social cleanse enjoy a curious recourse: The killers seldom, if ever, venture into homes in search of their victims.[4] Colombian political scientist Carlos Perea Restrepo frames this prohibition as an exercise in jurisdictional delineation: "The social killing does not intrude in the private ambit of the family, it does so on the very conviviality of the public sphere: the street its preferred camp of action."[5] When I asked Armando, a social leader in Soacha and a private advocate of social cleansing campaigns, why those threatened were not killed in their homes, he explained: "It's just not done. It must be a public thing. The crimes are in the street, so the justice has to be there too." Armando's logic couples the exercise of justice with its visibility. His concern is with the spectacle of jurisdiction, with rendering sovereign claims legible. The emergent sovereign claims of the social cleanse demand hiding the victims: their concealment into homes, their disappearance, their erasure from communal sight. The home of the threatened is here a space of safety and entrapment. Yet it is a space that has been marked, that stands out in its extraction. The *panfleto* affixed to the door signals a spectacular retreat into the home, if not exactly into the domestic. There are no guarantees that this prohibition of entering the home will be respected, of course, but in the absence of official protection or support, retreat is often the best option available. For folks like Guillermo and his mother, the home becomes both a sanctuary and a prison.

Displacement

A few days after Guillermo found the *panfleto* threatening him, I went to check on him and his mother. I hunched in the back of a repurposed jeep (buses did not make the journey up the steep dirt trails) as the elegant colonial homes of solid stucco walls in the city's historic downtown quickly gave way to tall brick buildings that went right up to the main avenue. Farther up the mountain, along the narrow streets, the buildings got shorter. Fourth, third, and second stories remained unfinished, rebar sticking out of rooftops in the optimistic expectation of future construction. Still higher up, the roads turned to dust and mud, scabrous with holes and stones. The houses were now single story, assembled from sundry and even ramshackle materials: bricks, metallic sheets, plastic fencing, rocks. Some had yards in which even more material accumulated, waiting for a critical mass of stuff and neighbors to allow for additions and expansions.

Mercedes and Guillermo's house stood halfway up an unpaved alley, alongside other homes of bare brick and reclaimed corrugated metal. Some of the houses on their street were painted in shades of yellow, blue, and orange, part of a development project by a European NGO that had visited almost a decade back and thought to brighten a seemingly blighted neighborhood. Over the years the colors have faded, yet the paint now offers a canvas for graffiti artists who populate the walls with animals, dinosaurs, mythical creatures, team emblems, names, and phrases. Mercedes and Guillermo's house featured a stylized signature in white and a message: "Tati, I love you." Neither the owners of the home nor their neighbors knew Tati. The street narrowed toward the end of the block, giving way to bare slopes of sand and rock, a sweeping vista of the dried-up lake below, and the undulating orange waves of homes etched into the mountain face beyond.

I was welcomed inside through a barely opened door and found mother and son sitting practically in darkness. The house had only a few windows, all draped in drawn curtains. The small sounds of a television drama played from the single room in the back, next to the kitchen. A door leading to the yard and the bathroom outside was bolted shut. Mercedes and I huddled in the main room, at our feet a mattress where Guillermo slept at night. We balanced on precarious wooden chairs that sat against a wall adorned with baby pictures of Guillermo, rosary beads, and old Christmas cards. Some of these, I noticed, were drawn by hand, by Guillermo no doubt, many years ago. The rest of the place was devoid of most furniture or appliances. Shelves and armoires stood empty. Geometric stains and rumpled crocheted doilies traced, ghostlike, the erstwhile presence of a television, a stereo, a toaster oven. Mercedes handed me some *tinto*, and when we were done sipping, I put the mug on the floor. There was no table. She had sold the good TV and the dining set

FIGURE 6.2. Homes on the *loma* are built on steep hills, often through communal effort and over the course of years. Photo by the author.

in the past few weeks, Mercedes explained, as her already strained savings had quickly dwindled now that she was not working. She avoided looking at her son, who was in the bedroom half watching a staticky romance playing on the small TV, a gift from a neighbor given shortly before the *panfleto* appeared. Guillermo also avoided her gaze. "They are things, no more," she sighed. Mercedes was obviously withholding parts of the story, and I would later piece together that it had been Guillermo who had sold most of the home goods in the previous months in desperate efforts to satisfy his need for *basuco*, the drug based on coca paste that held dominion over much of his life. However, if the disappeared furnishings had been a source of guilt and resentment before, it felt as though confinement had tempered the outward expression of these passions, leaving only exhaustion and fear. The emptiness itself was theirs to inhabit.

Still, understanding that the story of the furniture was a touchy one, I tried changing the subject to what I imagined to be happier times. I asked if Mercedes missed her life in the campo. She had grown up in the northeastern plains of Arauca, a land close to the Venezuelan border, home to some of the country's richest cattle ranchers and its most destitute peasants. She left her parents' home when she was fourteen and had met Guillermo's father. She followed him as he moved from place to place, caring for cattle and crops, and she cooked and cleaned for the men who worked the fields. "There was never much money," she recalled. "He liked his drink and the jobs never lasted. Well, with him nothing lasted."

After he left her and Guillermo, making ends meet became even more difficult for Mercedes. "I had to do everything by myself, and no one cared how or why I did it." She recalled without nostalgia the backbreaking chores afforded to her, a woman alone with her child. "I woke up at dawn to cook. Cook, clean, cook, work. That was it. When he [Guillermo's father] was around, we pulled together. He worked in the field, and I did my thing. But alone, I worked and worked, and I didn't even make enough to buy eggs. Not bread! Nothing! We cooked from the *sagú* we picked by the road." Farm owners tend to reserve the best and most stable jobs for couples, and often she was offered only the lowest paying seasonal jobs. A few times she managed to secure more permanent employment as part of the landowner's staff, but she was inevitably fired to make room for the wife of an incoming farmhand. And so she continued to move from farm to farm, searching for fleeting opportunities wherever she could find them. "There was never much of a home," she said when I asked her if she missed the tranquility of a life away from the city. "We just moved with the few things we owned. Not much. Barely anything. Sometimes not even that."

In 1998, Mercedes was working on a cattle farm, tending after the day laborers. "La Fortuna, it was called," she remembered. "It was a *finquita*, a nothing sort of place. But things were getting hot all around it." For about forty years, the war had been heating up. What had begun as the reshuffling of self-defense groups in the aftermath of a partisan civil war had grown into a conflict between guerrillas, paramilitaries, and drug cartels that mobilized tens of thousands of soldiers and mired the country's hinterlands in spectacular violence. The leftist guerrillas of the Revolutionary Armed Forces of Colombia—FARC—enjoyed years of military success against a shambolic, corrupt, and poorly funded national army.[6] For working people like Mercedes living in the rural areas of the country, the guerrillas had become a feature of daily life, demanding occasional tribute and offering unfulfilled promises of reform.

"They would come by," she recalled, "and ask us to kill a chicken, or to cook, or something. They would sleep in the grounds, but not in the house, and then leave. They said they were bringing change, but I didn't see that." Landowners were the true targets of extraction, often enduring extortion and kidnapping for ransoms that would support the war effort. "They were the law, but they left you alone, for the most part."

By the end of the twentieth century, the war was picking up all around the country and, thanks in large part to an enormous infusion of cash from the US government, this corner of Colombia was the stage of a new phase in the fighting.[7] At some point in 1999, a new group of armed men strolled into town. Some looked and acted like members of the army, wearing fatigues and armed to the teeth, but others wore civilian clothes, blending into the crowds, keeping a watchful eye on what happened in the streets. They identified themselves as parts of so-called self-defense groups, independent from the national army, there to liberate the area from the guerrillas' incursions. Everyone knew their story.

As guerrillas had expanded their operations across the nation's farmlands, seizing control over country roads and local economies, they had funded their rise through drug trafficking, illegal taxes, extortion, and kidnapping, mainly targeting farmers and ranchers. These grew tired of living under guerrilla control and, emboldened by the economic and logistical support extended by US and Colombian governments, created "self-defense groups" to wage their own war against "the insurgents."[8] The groups grew into full-fledged paramilitary operations, seized control over the country's flourishing drug trade, and began a vicious campaign against the guerrillas, unfettered by the (albeit extremely weak) legal constraints faced by the regular army.[9] These groups presented their campaigns as attempts to "reassume" state presence through the appropriation and extension of violence. The state often recognized this role, tolerating or even collaborating with paramilitary groups.[10]

The paramilitaries quickly settled into Mercedes's town, using pamphlets and murders to proclaim their renewed claim to rule. "They made announcements that they were now the law," she remembered, "and then they killed a bunch of people." In addition to the sporadic direct confrontation in the jungles, guerrillas and paramilitaries would pursue each other through proxies, punishing supposed enemies picked from among the townsfolk. Mercedes's work in La Fortuna put her squarely in the middle of an increasingly violent yet underhanded conflict. Even the modest and involuntary encounters she had had with guerrilla fighters marked her as a potential collaborator. "But," she quickly pointed out to me, "uno ni pa'alla ni pa'aca. I wasn't taking sides." When the murders began, they were touted as the imposition of a new order, the extermination of the contagion of guerrillas and their ideologies. The killings cemented the newcomers as authorities in the area, successfully cowing any rebuke from the locals.

Paramilitaries espoused far-right policies and inflicted violent punishment on civilian populations they considered enemy collaborators.[11] The category of collaborator was broad indeed. Often those who had been extorted by guerrillas into providing housing, food, or other logistical support became targets of paramilitaries.[12] Along the way, leftist political actors, those who refused to pay their extortion fees, or simply those whose lands they could steal, were labeled enemies and targeted with threats, displacement, and assassination. In his 2005 book *Law in a Lawless Land*, Michael Taussig describes the paramilitaries as the "black hand" of the state, and according to Medina Gallego and Téllez Ardila, these groups allowed the Colombian state to wage a nonconventional war against "civilian populations who were conceived as the enemy's social and political base."[13] Paramilitary groups around the country routinely relied on the practice of social cleansing in their efforts to wrest territory from guerrilla control and impose their own domination over civilian populations.[14] These campaigns targeted so-called dangerous elements within the community and focused specifically on those who refused or rejected the structures of control imposed by armed groups. Social leaders and human rights activists, LGBTQ+ folk, Indigenous leaders, thieves, and out-of-work youth were often publicly accused of endangering society at large and were killed with impunity. These murders, as with much paramilitary activity, were carried out with the tacit consent, or even active participation, of official forces.[15] These death threats and selective killings worked to symbolically mark the imposition of a changing juridical order. Critics of the war have shown that displacement works to capture inefficiently exploited capital by "clearing the territory of inefficient and leftover people" so that their land and resources can be integrated into international markets.[16] The social cleanse sought a different clearing of the territory that focused instead on those labeled socially and politically leftover. Their deaths and displacements were sacrifices meant to sustain emergent claims to sovereignty and novel arrangements of expropriation and legitimacy.

When Mercedes learned that the owner of the next farm over had been killed, she knew it was time to go. "That guy was one of God's souls," she remembered. "And they killed him like he was nothing. After that it was a massacre." Years of itinerant work had taught mother and son the value of packing light and moving quickly. Mercedes was tired of her life in *el campo*, anyway, and decided to try her luck closer to the capital, where she had heard not only that work was abundant but that help for displaced people was easy to secure. She and Guillermo hitched rides on buses and trucks and, along the way, joined the more than eight million Colombians who have been forced to leave their homes to escape the war.

Soon after their arrival at Soacha, they were pointed toward *la loma*, the unincorporated neighborhoods in the surrounding hills, where they rented a small one-room house built on taken land. "When we moved in," Mercedes said, taking inventory of her half-empty home, "it was a *ranchito* of tin and wire. We didn't have a bathroom; that's all you have to know." Back then, the neighborhood was still new. The mountain had served as a quarry for years, and when the deposits were exhausted, the mine owners subdivided their land illegally and sold it to the waves of newcomers desperate for a place to call home. Since then, the barrio has stood at a carefully managed distance from Soacha's centers of official power. For years, officials in the local administration refused to recognize the neighborhoods on the hill or extend to them the basic infrastructural investment afforded to the city's more established settlements. "To offer legalization to these zones," I was told by a functionary in the mayor's office, "is to incentivize future illegality." For a long time, these settlements lacked running water and electricity; their sewage systems were built by neighbors and continue to deposit organic waste on the mountainside today. There are no hospitals and just a few schools, and police are present only through the intermittent patrols of motorcycles whizzing by like dust storms through the unpaved streets.

After years of working as a maid and a cook in the capital, Mercedes was eventually able to purchase the plot of land on which her *ranchito* stood. In the years that followed, she entered the circuits of exchange common in impoverished neighborhoods across Colombia, relying on friends and neighbors to slowly make improvements to the home. One of her neighbors down the street worked at a brick factory and would bring home "excess inventory" to sell for cheap. Tin roofs were often recycled from older construction or bequeathed from neighbors upgrading their own.[17] Together, neighbors strung long cables from utility poles to surreptitiously light their homes at night. Groups of neighbors dug sewage canals, widened paths into roads, and lobbied local politicians so that water tankers would climb up the hill three times a week. The barrios closer to the foot of the hill provided a model of urban development to those high up the mountains. The neighbors down where the roads were a bit more even, some even paved, and where the buildings were tall and made of solid brick had arrived decades before and had also settled on taken land. Over the years, they had organized to demand that basic services and infrastructure be extended to their neighborhoods. And as electricity and sewage pipes reached their homes, so did local politicians eager to capture emergent political support from the newcomers. The swelling population of forced migrants transformed the urban landscape and, as James Holston explains regarding the urban peripheries of São Paulo, collectively wrestled a semblance of political and infrastructural belonging to the unincorporated urban peripheries.[18] The insurgent forms of citizenship built personal attachments and a shared sense of struggle against neglect and poverty. Mercedes fondly remembered the early morning pilgrimages to the water tanker and the budding friendships she struck up while carrying water pails and sharing the toils of building new lives at the city's edge.

As Mercedes recounted the story of how her rancho became a home, a different sort of sadness engulfed us. The memories of home building, of the sort of insurgencies that transformed a space through collective action and affection, now ran against the violence of neighbors turned against each other. "I try not to think about that," she said of the threats at her door and of those who issued them. The bricks that once offered security, hope, and even opportunity now testified to the sudden turning back, a betrayal born from that same intimacy that had built homes as a reprieve from war. The house, empty and dark, was scarcely a refuge. It was, rather, an unhomely reminder of the turn things had taken, of the outsideness creeping in.

Stillness pervaded the home. Mercedes at the window, Guillermo at the TV. In the recently emptied corners of the home, dust and hair and grime accumulated. Dishes stacked without being washed, food still uneaten. The *panfleto* had interrupted the innocuous rhythms of the home, the miniscule routines that kept the domestic alive. Gaston Bachelard writes of the unremarked tasks of home maintenance and care that they "keep vigilant watch over the house, they link its immediate past to its immediate future, they are what maintains it in the security of being."[19] But in the face of an existential threat, of social intimacies turned into wellsprings of danger, the mundane labors of living were interrupted, the intimate motions of care and living replaced by motionlessness. The temporality of house making, with its investments in futurity and continuity, came unmade often in the life histories shared by Guillermo and Mercedes. This ongoing process of making and unmaking home had finally been punctuated by this novel, most immediate threat. As the *panfleto* announced Guillermo's unmooring from the bonds of community—his status as ex-human—even the mundane efforts to maintain a security of being were put aside. Vigilance within was replaced by a vigilance toward an encroaching threat from outside so that only the immediacy of catastrophe as a temporal frame remained, and in its face only stillness.

Dismissals

Mercedes made the trek down the mountain and across the road that bisects Soacha, connecting Bogotá with the south of the country, to see if she could file a report with the police and, perhaps, be granted some official protection. The police, however, argued that they could not start an investigation on their own as the threat against Guillermo was "not specific," and that the official procedure for such things would begin with an intervention from the mayor's Government Secretariat. So, Mercedes headed to the city's main administrative building, where she was made to wait. She sat in the worn-out plastic chairs in front of the bustling offices, gazing up expectantly at the well-coiffed functionaries who came through their doors, always with other business to attend to. A few minutes before five in the afternoon, she was seen by a young woman who had been sitting across from her for most of the day and who now hurried to close out the office. She used her phone to take photos of Mercedes's and Guillermo's ID cards and the *panfleto* and heard the narrative of the threat with obvious disinterest. She called Mercedes *mamita* and suggested she go home and calm down. Two days later, the young woman called to let Mercedes know that no aid would be forthcoming, as the threat was deemed to exist between individuals and not organized groups.

"The lady from the mayor's office told me that giving the protection is difficult," Mercedes said to me while shakily sipping her *tinto*, "because they say the Black Eagles don't exist here. That people use the name but that there is no organized crime here. Can you imagine? They close their eyes not to see!"

"And Guillermo?" I asked.

"He left the other day," Mercedes said, her body now convulsing in sobs. "He couldn't hold it together anymore and he left. And now, he doesn't answer me!"

Official dismissals of the violence posed by social cleansing campaigns remain the order of the day. Despite numerous reports that chronicle the campaigns' murders, the specificity of their strategies and intentions, and the scores of victims and families attesting to the reality of their threat, there are no official responses dedicated to the issue.[20] At the national level, there is no mention of social cleansing in Colombia's penal code, and there is no strategy to confront the practice. Locally, the very existence of organizations that carry out these killings, and that do so in part as a gambit for control over a territory and its drug trade, is denied by both police and most political institutions. According to most police and local administration representatives I've spoken to, there is an unofficial acknowledgment of the existence of these groups, of the violent techniques of repression they deploy, and of the

FIGURE 6.3. When Mercedes first moved to Soacha, she lived in a modest home in the *loma*. “It was a *ranchito* of tin and wire,” she recalls. “We didn’t have a bathroom; that’s all you have to know.” Photo by the author.

terror they inspire in the populations over which they rule. Yet officially, both the police and the mayor's office ascribe the rise in murders in Soacha's poorest neighborhoods to "alcohol and prohibited drugs that give rise to fights, which can then trigger personal injuries and homicides."[21] According to Soacha's then–Police Commander William Javier Lara, the groups responsible for the threatening leaflets don't exist anymore, as they have been disbanded, and the *panfletos* "don't come from any criminal group and are mostly a joke people play."[22] In effect, this denial means that the folks living up in the hills of Soacha (and thousands of others living in marginal neighborhoods in Colombia) who have been threatened by *panfletos* have no recourse to official protection.

If the social cleanse sustains paralegal claims to sovereignty and the entrepreneurial illicit economies that support them, the denial of the social cleanse by government institutions likewise sustains state political projects. In *closing their eyes not to see*, the state security apparatus enshrines official fictions of order through a willful blindness to a species of vulnerability produced in the maelstrom of ongoing war, violence, and dispossession. The state retains its claim to sovereignty over the economic subjects of its administration and leaves the management of the bodies of the poor and the marginal to the para-state apparatus and its regime of terror. The polymorphous and fluid bands carrying out social cleansing campaigns would seem to raise troubling claims of sovereignty counter to those of the state. Instead, their coexistence and contiguity to state institutions, and the disavowal of their very reality despite obvious evidence of their existence, point to a tacit acceptance of the methods and objectives of the cleanse and the fungibility of sovereignty claims at the boundaries of life and terror. As Achille Mbembe writes of contemporary necropolitical regimes, "A patchwork of overlapping and incomplete rights to rule emerges, inextricably superimposed and tangled, in which different de facto juridical instances are geographically interwoven and plural allegiances, asymmetrical suzerainties, and enclaves abound."[23] Paramilitaries, neoparamilitary organizations, local police, national armies, and the diffuse alliances they form to police and terrorize civilian populations demarcate a shared horizon of expendability to "define who matters and who does not, who is disposable and who is not."[24]

The *para* becomes the sovereignty that shadows official sovereignty, adopting, adapting, and wielding cruder versions of state power: a law that speaks in a voice of the street, that authorizes a violence that is not adorned in deliberative politics or international agreements, that goes uncounted and unaccounted for. The *panfleto* offers the material link tethering the sovereignty claims of neoparamilitaries to those of the state. Official disregard and para-official vigilance are bound together in the chimeric language of *panfletos*, in their mixture of legalese and vulgarity, threat, and edict. And alongside official policies of disregard—such as the refusal to recognize neighborhoods as part of the city—they demarcate social spaces, bounding not just those worthy of living but also the sites in which life and nonlife can unfold.

Here, then, let us return to the cloistered home, alongside Mercedes and Guillermo. If the necropolitical regime devised by the *para* organizes marginalized neighborhoods under the oversight of the cleanse, the home as a site of sanctuary stands as a sort of absence in this social order. The *panfleto* hanging from Mercedes's door marked the house as a nonspace, a gap in the cleanse's para-law, a wound to the social order. The death threat reconfigured the spectacular and the mundane, bringing the domestic into the realm of spectacle, making its absent presence palpable. *Panfletos* thus turn domestic confinement into a spectacular display of sovereign power. The excluded home stands out, reifying an ordered whole, a docile population, a normalized *loma*. The house is disappeared from the neighborhood. People avoid it; it is rendered blank. The disappeared homes and bodies become, paradoxically, the backbone of the community. They demarcate the boundaries of social being through their undoing.

Sacrificed

Guillermo was killed on July 13, 2018, three blocks from where his mother had dozed off on a chair, waiting for him. "He couldn't help himself," Mercedes would later tell me. "The vice had a strong hold on him. Had him fucked. He told me that he needed a hit and he'd come back. But he stayed there. They found him on the street at night and they shot him. I was asleep, but I heard the gunshots in my sleep. I felt a cold sweat. I felt him leave."

The night Guillermo was gunned down, two others were killed with him. Two more survived, running through the houses and alleys of the neighborhood and down the steep slopes of the barren mountain. Despite my best efforts, I was never able to find them again.

The murders are often carried out in the dead of night. Dark trucks with dark windows creep through the neighborhood's unpaved streets, patrolling for the threatened. The cars are known by many names—phantom cars, caravans of death, *gatos*—and their circulation, together with the reach of the *panfletos*, demarcates the boundaries of the authority claimed by the men who carry out the killings. The killers move together, their faces hidden under hoods or beneath the heavy wool ponchos known as ruanas. The identities of the killers are seldom revealed, even if membership in neoparamilitary bands is a public secret.[25] Collaboration between local leaders, plainclothes police officers, and aspiring gang members during the distribution of the *panfletos* and the actual killings means that the mechanisms of surveillance are ill-defined and the potential to be "identified" by the social cleanse, ubiquitous.

Pamphlets occupy these neighborhoods, outlining the jurisdiction claimed by violent actors: the streets and hills that they command as well as the relationships that figure under their regulating gaze. The announcement of the sentenced also fixes into focus the apparent visibility endured by those living under the Black Eagles' gaze. Intimate knowledge is identified as the site of governance, an announcement to those not named that they, too, live under the panopticon of the cleanse. The pamphlets proliferate among businesses and houses, entering quotidian spaces that are then made pure through the sacrifice of those marked by the black hand. Those spared enjoy the security of being the community. At least temporarily.

The bands that issue the threatening *panfletos* and that carry out the killings operate within the strict bounds of territorial control, and the boundaries between their authorities are jealously policed. Movement beyond these invisible frontiers is verboten—a prohibition that extends to residents of these neighborhoods, who seldom dare to cross them, especially at night. Newcomers are often questioned about their business in the neighborhood, and their movements are surveilled by inquisitive neighbors. The one place in which movement is relatively free is at the foot of the mountain, in an area known as El Lago. The water in the lake dried up long ago, yet the swamp that remains has become a well-known open grave. When the dead are wrapped in plastic bags and thrown into El Lago, they become known as *cocodrilos*.

Cocodrilos, zombies, *sidosas, basuqueros*. The cleanse summons a veritable bestiary, transfiguring and deforming neighbors, sons, children, women, and men into beings somehow different from humans, somehow polluted, marked for eradication. *Gatos,* phantoms. The cleanse likewise populates the social world with beings of violence shrouded in the shadows of terror, lurking, waiting, hunting for those marked. *Panfletos* did not just announce the arrival of the cleanse; they revealed the streets of *la loma* to be a stage on which these transformations unfold, where folks can be pulled into a dreaded limelight or down into the inky depths—lost at a moment's notice.

In reproducing the particularities of the lexicon used in these murderous campaigns and the experiences of fear they elicit, I want to highlight the ways in which the violence that they deploy extends well beyond the bodily harm of bullets and knives. Rather, death threats are the most visible implement in the ample arsenal criminal organizations use to exert control over urban populations by transforming their denizens into beings who appear less than human. Starting with the *panfletos* and ending with the names given to murdered bodies, the work of defining a person as outside the realm of sociability coincides with an effort to deprive them of their humanity. In cutting certain individuals from the bounds of "the community," whose complaints are addressed by the authority of murderous gangs, and by then deploying a language through which drug consumption, gender identity, and criminality are conflated as threats to a shared biopolitical order, the gangs index the threatened as contaminants of a body politic that therefore demands purification.

This lexicon of violence also transforms the lived geography of the barrio into one of suspicion and fear. The announcement of death threats via publicly posted leaflets demarcates a jurisdiction of terror, one in which claims to social order and legitimate rule are backed by clandestine killings often condoned even by lifelong neighbors of the accused. The shoddily copied papers circulate freely in public spaces such as grocery stores and parks and are often taped to people's front doors, marking them publicly as threatened. Passersby rarely venture to touch them, much less remove them. I once saw one tumbling down the street in a rush of dust and debris and get caught underfoot. The stomper recognized what it was and quickly lifted her foot as if she had stepped on a squirming, living thing, releasing it once again into the tumult of the road. I thought of picking it up but, suddenly feeling watched, thought better of it and left it be. Yet the leaflets' portent of violence marked me. In the weeks that followed I began to arrange my visits through the mountain carefully, so that they would be done by dusk. Leaving Mercedes and Guillermo's home in the afternoons, the sun setting orange over the mountains, I felt watched. I would catch the sideways glimpses of neighbors who wordlessly marked my arrivals and departures and wondered who else was keeping tabs on me. Standing uncomfortably visible on the road's edge, waiting for the jeep to skip its way around the corner, I yearned to be packed tight against others descending *la loma*, to take their bags on my own knees, to make room for babies and backpacks, to be lost amid the small crowd. Getting on the jeep, relief washing over me (*I made it out*), I realized that I, too, was being transformed by the cleanse, by the way it trains eyes and ears onto public spaces. I was a vigilant, crepuscular creature, afraid of the dark, a bit paranoid. The *panfletos* also bring those not named into the fray, binding the seen and the unseen through the threat of violence.

Mercedes obviously recognized the potential violence that was inscribed onto her home the moment she saw the *panfleto* and decided to remove it from her front door. Despite her best efforts, her neighbors both recognized the paper hanging from her entrance and the names on the copies posted around the barrio. If at first a few brave and caring friends made their way to Mercedes and Guillermo's house to offer food and support, soon visitors stopped coming. "They were afraid," she told me later. "They don't want to be identified as coming here." To be marked by the black hand, then, did not mean that only those whose infractions were recognized and listed in a leaflet were the objects of surveillance. Rather, these individuals and social categories came to function as indexes of a ubiquitous scrutiny and therefore as nodes through which wider social relations were controlled. By propagating a logic of potential contamination, the threat of violence demanded the isolation not only of those identified by *panfletos*, but also of those who were in contact with them, their families and their friends.

Within this construction of shared spaces, certain locations became marked as under particular claims of authority, particular subjectivities of danger, and particular registers of unpredictability. *Panfletos* identified streets and homes as sites of surveillance and also as potential vectors in which accusations of degeneracy could spread. As streets and homes were singled out by the leaflets, so too were movements through the city rearranged by the authority the notices signaled. To approach certain sites denoted as under the control of the gang, or to be near the site of a congregation of coca paste smokers, or to approach a home that had been leafleted was to stand out and make oneself available to the violent authority that issued the threats. In this constricting and constricted social milieu, the threatened were left with little recourse beyond isolation, displacement, or death.

In thinking of the nature of contemporary violence, of the phenomenology of being rendered helpless, Adriana Cavarero coins the term *horrorism*. She describes horrorism as "a particular form of violence that exceeds death itself."[26] Disfiguration, torture, and mass death, she argues, present existential questions to all those enmeshed in the spectacle of horror. "What is at stake," she writes, "is not the end of human life but the human condition itself, as incarnated in the singularity of vulnerable bodies."[27] We can think here of the transformations brought forth by *panfletos* and social cleanses—of *cocodrilos* and zombies whose physical and symbolic deformations unfold over days, months, years, and decades, locating their vulnerability in the fabric of social bonds and sovereign powers. Those who witness the cleanse—who, in seeing the *panfleto*, know that its targets become entrapped participants of the social death it announces—are party to its horrorism by spectating the vulnerable and recognizing the potential of vulnerability in themselves.

Mercedes and Guillermo's home—marked, empty, dark, still—offered the stage for this scene of horrorism. The cleanse reflected and magnified the many horrors of Colombia's ill-defined war, domesticating uprooted histories of dispossession, gathering the remnants cobbled from destroyed homes and battered but enduring life projects. As a negative space, this home stood out, becoming a site of prohibition and fascination around which an entire social field took shape. Within the home, the vulnerability realized by *panfletos* brought domestic existence to a standstill. To live amid the horrorism of the cleanse is to inhabit overlapping paradoxes: to be seen only to be dismissed, to be named only to be erased, to be fixed so as to be disappeared.

Guillermo's body lay on the street where he was shot for hours before he was recovered by the police. Neighbors looked on from a distance, neither surprised nor indifferent, yet unwilling to approach the dead man they had known for years. "Guillermo was such a sweet boy," his mother recalled. "When we first came to the barrio he liked the mountains at night. He would stare at the city lights below and would say no one had a view like ours. The drugs took him. I couldn't save him from those. And I couldn't come to see his body. He lay there in the street alone. I was too afraid to come to him."

NOTES

1. For a discussion of political debates around gender ideology and its role in the political campaigns against the ratification of the peace agreement with the FARC-EP in 2016, see Muelle, "Cómo hacer necropolíticas en casa."

2. Perea Restrepo, *Limpieza social*, 42.

3. Perea Restrepo, *Limpieza social.*

4. This is in contrast to the selective killings of paramilitaries in the country's hinterlands, where forcibly removing people from their homes and executing them publicly was the preferred modus operandi (Centro Nacional de Memoria Histórica, "*Limpieza social*").

5. Perea Restrepo, *Limpieza social*, 55.

6. Palacios, *Between Legitimacy and Violence.*

7. Lindsay-Poland, *Plan Colombia.*

8. Civico, *The Para-State.*

9. Palacios, *Between Legitimacy and Violence.*

10. Human Rights Watch, "Paramilitaries' Heirs."

11. Ramírez, "Maintaining Democracy in Colombia."

12. Civico, *The Para-State.*

13. Medina Gallego and Téllez Ardila, *La violencia parainstitucional*, 64.

14. Centro Nacional de Memoria Histórica, "*Limpieza social.*"

15. Velásquez Rivera, "Historia del paramilitarismo en Colombia." Although paramilitary groups were not founded Colombia until the 1980s, the use of nonstate armed groups to combat perceived threats and the recourse to selective killings of civilians date back to the 1950s and 1960s and have been linked to colonial and neocolonial ambitions. The use of terror to seek the acquiescence of civilian populations was imported to Colombia via the repressive strategies developed by the French in their war against independence movements in Indochina and Algeria and through the training offered by American forces in the School of the Americas. For a review of this history, see Velásquez Rivera, "Historia del paramilitarismo en Colombia."

16. Mondragón, "La economía rural." For a thorough analysis of the relationship between the war in Colombia, developmentalist theories, and peasant displacement and dispossession, see Valderrama and Mondragón, *Desarrollo y equidad con campesinos.*

17. D'Avella, "Ecologies of Investment."

18. Holston, *Insurgent Citizenship*, 113.

19. Bachelard, *Poetics of Space*, 67.

20. I cite many of these reports in the body of this text. However, the most systematic accounting of the practice of social cleansing in Colombia is compiled by the Center for Research and Popular Education (CINEP), which publishes *Noche y niebla* (Night and fog), an annual magazine enumerating human rights abuses in the country. The annals meticulously recite each instance of human rights violations, providing a snapshot of political violence in Colombia that invariably features social cleansing campaigns prominently.

21. *Periodismo Público*, "La incertidumbre sobre la presencia."

22. *La Silla Vacía*, "Con la alerta por bacrim."

23. Mbembe, "Necropolitics," 31.
24. Mbembe, "Necropolitics," 27.
25. Taussig, *Law in a Lawless Land*.
26. Cavarero, *Horrorism*, 32.
27. Cavarero, *Horrorism*, 8.

PART IV

Disasters and Displacements

FEDERICO NEIBURG

7

House-ing on the Move

I met Daphney in the tent where she had found shelter, next to the place on Macajou Street, downtown Port-au-Prince, where she had been born and where she had lived at various times throughout her life. It was May 2010. A couple of months earlier, on January 12, a massive earthquake had struck the city and reduced the houses of hundreds of thousands of people to rubble. Daphney and her four-year-old son spent almost two days immobilized under the debris of their house, separated by the remains of collapsed walls, hearing each other's voices. Relatives and neighbors managed to open a hole through which they passed them water and finally rescued them.

As Macajou Street had become a dangerous place, Daphney was relieved to have found a refuge for her child in a tent on the grounds of an NGO for which she had occasionally worked. Apart from all her human and material losses, what tormented her most, she told me, was the immobility that aggravated her sense of dispossession and further imperiled her financial situation. The catastrophe had interrupted her movements between Port-au-Prince and Miami, a circuit she traveled to engage in small commerce of clothing and beauty products. Regular visits to the United States also allowed her to earn some money as a singer, nurturing hopes of one day recording a hip-hop hit and becoming a professional musician. Movement was Daphney's way of seeking a better life for herself and her son. Trapped, first under the debris, later in the street amid the devastation, she felt she was dying (*konsa lòk mwen santi m mouri*).

Macajou Street was now lined with dozens of tents. Sanitary conditions had quickly deteriorated, and a cholera outbreak worsened the situation, bringing the bacterial specter of death into all intimate spaces. The immensity of the tragedy—an "acute-on-chronic event," in Paul Farmer's apt rendering—evinced ways of dwelling and connections between persons and houses that had deep historical traces and would be reanimated in calamities yet to come, such as with Hurricane Matthew in 2016, the COVID-19 pandemic, and the social and political violence that exploded in the following years.[1] In each of these disastrous moments, the term *lòk* (literally, locked) took on a special density as a synthesis of both individual and collective experiences of calamity and immobility. Being forced to stay indoors to protect oneself from illness or violence. Being unable to move because of barricades or because of the shortage of fuel and the spike in fuel prices. Being unable to migrate due to walls (such as the one that began to be built on the border with the Dominican Republic) and increasingly severe legal restrictions on international mobility. Not only individual persons but the nation itself was denounced as "locked."[2] And, as Daphney herself expresses, lack of movement means no future, no life.[3]

In Plantationocene landscapes, mobility and immobility have always been forcefully entangled. Plantation and postplantation people have been inhabited by the tension between slavery and escape. In Haiti, this tension acquired even more intense modulations, permeated by a permanent sense of crisis and extreme poverty that impels movement.[4] This is true for those on the move as well as for those who remain at home in Haiti or who end up in the places that Haitians on the move inhabit in their diasporic routes. The very situation of immobility, reinforced by endless tragedy, drives movement—a permanent house-ing effort as a way to search for a life worth living.[5]

FIGURE 7.1. Refugee camp after the earthquake. Bel Air, Port-au-Prince, May 2010. Photo by the author.

A well-known Haitian proverb is "Kote ki gen grangou, kabrit pa mouri nan kòd" (Where there is hunger, no goats die tethered to their ropes). Being stuck, prevented from moving, is synonymous with an absence of life, such as in the extreme cases of people forced into slavery, those killed by magic, or those trapped in paralyzing tragedies. As I learned from my interlocutors in urban Haiti and in the Haitian diaspora, movement stabilizes relations between those at home and, even at a distance, supports bonds with kin and ancestors, between those residents in a place and those moving within and across national borders. Movement is relationally productive, and relationality is the condition of possibility for movement. Houses are inhabited by people in motion, and mobile people inhabit many houses. Contrary to the view of houses and the people who live in them as immobile, fixed in space and time, this chapter exploits the generative character of mobility in Haitian social landscapes, where houses and people are mutually constituted in movement in a permanent (de)house-ing through geographies and times, where people live together in movement and at a distance, in the ontogenetic space of lives and in-between generations.[6] Here, houses serve not only as places to stay but also as bases that enable continuous movement. Contrary to most common scholarly images and common sense about houses, this chapter shows how houses and people shape each other in movement. Instead of being a place to be in permanence, houses are here bases from which to continue life on the move.

Lakou Gina

Fritznel, Daphney's son, would never again live permanently with his mother. He stayed several months on the grounds of the NGO that had given him shelter, and when the flights and documents permitted, he was taken by a friend to Boston, where he lives to this day at his father's house, with his father's current wife and their son, Fritznel's half brother. Daphney was convinced that the boy's father could give their son a better life in the United States than she could in a country devastated by the earthquake and with an uncertain personal future. For several months before resuming her regular trips, she remained in Port-au-Prince, rebuilding her life and collaborating in the reconstruction of her family's place that had been destroyed by the earthquake: the *lakou* Gina, as it is known.

The space had been founded by Gina's husband, Leonard, Daphney's grandfather, first as a single house (*lakai*), then as a group of related houses in the same area, as predicated by the creole term *lakou*.[7] Gina and Leonard had migrated to Port-au-Prince from the town of Jérémie, in the southwest of the country, soon after they were married at the start of the 1970s. After his first odd job in the port region, Leonard found success in commerce, which allowed him to acquire the land on Macajou Street, but he fell ill and died soon after the birth of his second daughter. Some say he lost his mind, others that he was the victim of the sorcery of the lenders from whom he had borrowed money to obtain the property, and others still that it was the price he paid to the spirits who ensured his success. The *lakou* came to be known by the name of his widow, Gina. She likewise took the reins of her late husband's commercial activities with the help of one of her sisters, Daphney's aunt, who was still a prestigious voodoo priestess when I met her shortly after my first landing in Haiti, in 2007.

Like other *lakou* I got to know in the Bel Air region, in the center of Port-au-Prince, before the earthquake, *lakou* Gina had been made up of an aisle with houses on each side. The larger houses, situated toward the back, served as residences for the closest members of the Gina family. The houses nearest to the street were smaller, containing only one room. Some of these were inhabited by relatives, and others were rented out.

Bel Air has always been sensitive to the political geography of the capital, and it had seen other massive displacements of people prior to the January 2010 earthquake. During the 1990s, after the violent period that followed the first deposition of President Jean-Bertrand Aristide, Daphney herself left Bel Air along with other youngsters and children to live with relatives in Jérémie for a couple of years. The armed conflicts that spread after the second deposition of Aristide in 2004 caused the space of the *lakou* to be taken over by militias that charged rent for some of the rooms closest to the street. Many family members left once again for Jérémie; others migrated to the United States.[8] In 2007, the *lakou* Gina had only recently been reoccupied by the family.

Waves and Bases

The 2010 earthquake dramatically affected the relations between people and space. At least 250,000 individuals died and thousands more were mutilated

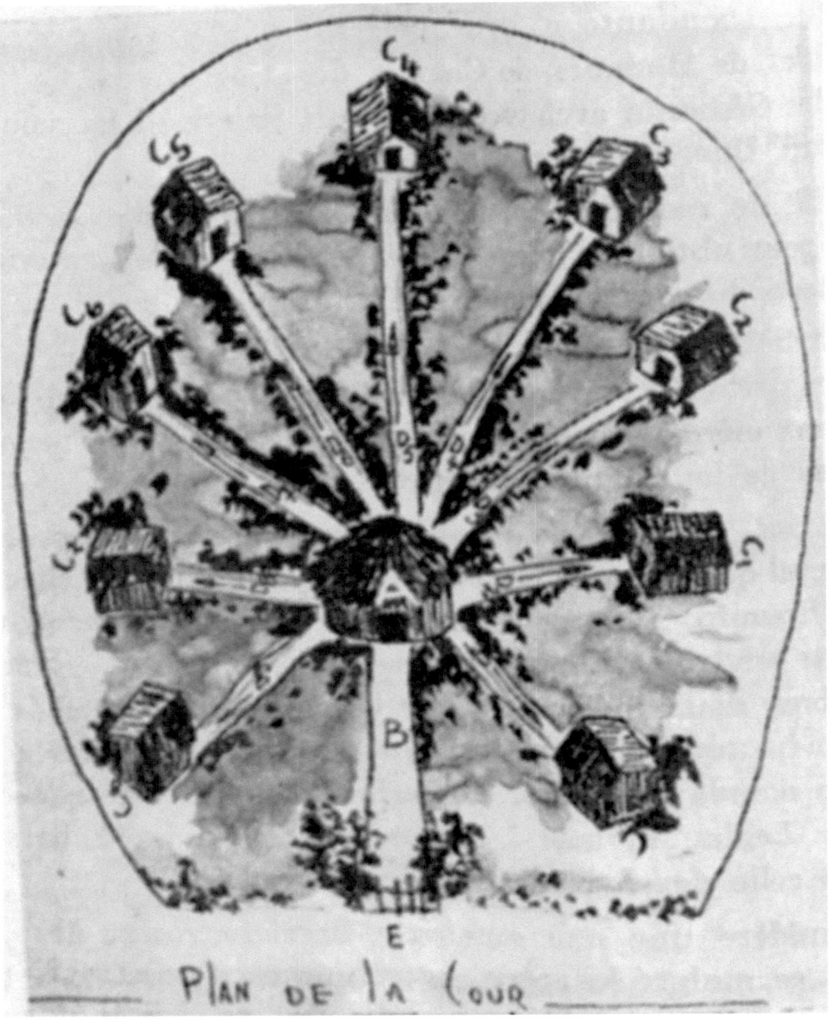

FIGURE 7.2. Idealized image of the traditional rural *lakou*. From Jean Baptiste Romain, *Quelques moeurs et coutumes des paysans Haïtiens* (Port-au-Prince: Imprimerie de l'État, 1959).

and injured, leaving an immeasurable trail of orphaned children, homeless families, and devastated infrastructure. It is estimated that more than 40 percent of the houses in some central districts of Port-au-Prince were destroyed or seriously damaged. Throughout the country, 1.5 million survivors left their homes. In the metropolitan zone of Port-au-Prince, with a population of some two million people, at least 300,000 fled, most heading for the countryside. Many left for the Dominican Republic and other destinations, composing a new wave in Haiti's diaspora.

The US occupation of the country (1915–34) was the first event to drive Haitian emigration, particularly to Cuba and the Dominican Republic. In the 1960s and 1970s, the consolidation of the dictatorship of François Duvalier produced the displacement of thousands of Haitians, mostly to the United States and Canada, but also to other parts of the Caribbean, such as the Bahamas, and to France and African Francophone countries that had recently gained independence, such as Senegal, Benin, and the Republic of the Congo. The well-known tragic phenomenon of the so-called boat people began around that time but intensified after the coup of 1991. The 2010 earthquake precipitated another wave of people that fed the diaspora, incorporating new geographies, including South America, which had not been a part of the previous routes of Haitian mobility.[9] It has since allowed me to receive and to live with Haitian friends—including some of Daphney's relatives—in Brazil, where I have my permanent residence.

When it is claimed that, at present, a little over eleven million people live in Haiti and at least two million more live abroad, we risk stabilizing a landscape that is marked by instability and movement.[10] The most recent statistics show that most of this total (approximately one million people) are in the United States; 400,000 are in the Dominican Republic; 200,000 are in Chile; 100,000 are in Brazil; and the rest are in Canada, France, and other Caribbean destinations.[11] These numbers reflect necessarily static images that evoke well the paradoxical incommensurability of mobility. Numbers are incapable of capturing people who cannot be counted—those who move illegally, invisibly, or routinely, coming and going. Numbers also have the effect of fixing at a geographical point people who are not stationary but passing through, who live in a place hoping to continue their journey at some point (days, weeks, months, years later) in search of better living conditions, of income in stronger currencies, especially US dollars (which make the value of remittances sent to their relatives in Haiti or elsewhere in the diaspora more significant), or of paths that will take them back to Haiti. The numbers likewise do not allow us to capture the coming and going of Haitians to and from the Dominican Republic. Traders and more or less temporary workers have made the recent project of the Dominican government to fix a physical limit between both countries impossible and porous, defying a wall built along more than three hundred kilometers of Haiti's only land border.

André Dumans Guedes has proposed the concept of "provisional forms of existence" to describe those dwellings of uncertain temporalities on the road that allow movement to continue: stops, barracks, hotels, more or less improvised lodgings, and the houses of hospitable people that can be transformed into one's own house where others, in turn, will find shelter.[12] Those houses in which one lives while passing through, even if one "passed through" for years in the imminence or the dream of continuing one's journey, are akin to what Ghassan Hage calls "diasporic lenticularity": a way of living, at the same time, several existences in different places.[13] This multiple inhabitance designs configurations of houses, the geographies of which accompany diasporic landscapes and routes. These landscapes and routes are, in turn, crossed by hierarchies: hierarchies between those who move and those who remain in Haiti or who stay on the road; hierarchies between men and women, between young and old, between adults and children; hierarchies between Haitians and other migrants with whom they interact along the way and with whom they may have strongly marked racial distances (as has been the case, for example, with Venezuelans in South America), which they may also have with locals, as sadly happened with white Brazilians who committed acts of violence against Haitian migrants; and hierarchies in relation to those who control the routes and borders, be it the infinite variety of so-called coyotes or the guards authorized by the states, armed with bureaucratic rules and weapons.

In Haitian Creole, the concept that indexes these places of rest and shelter, these more or less permanent or temporary houses, these "places for life" that enable one to live in motion, is the concept of *baz* (base).[14] It designates multiple spaces, from the materiality of the house itself to a street corner or spot where people feel emotionally and materially safe, at home, in the company of those close to them; a place where you are with your own people, where you feel safe, and where you can find a bed, some food, affection, and relevant information. The *baz* molds multi- or polycentric and rhizomatic configurations that include places in Haiti and along the diasporic landscapes.[15] The language of the family shapes the multiscale imaginary of Haitian bases: spaces of closeness and relatedness among neighbors and friends, among members of the same crew, village, city, or Haitian nationality, or even among a common humanity.[16] When we met after the earthquake, Daphney called the tent she occupied on Macajou Street her base. She also referred to her cousin's house where she used to stay in Miami, or the house of her relatives in Jérémie—where she spent different periods of her life—as her base. My own house in Rio de Janeiro was treated as a base by my friends, or by the friends of my friends, who visited or passed through in search of a better life after the earthquake. Bases are always liable to *housify* temporarily or permanently (see chapter 4 in this volume, by Eugênia Motta). Provisional rooms or shared spaces become houses. *House-ing* and *dehouse-ing* are two dimensions of the same landscape in movement.

Diasporic Routes and Persons

Handerson Joseph describes the differences between the so-called local houses (*kay local*) of those living in Haiti; the diaspora houses (*kay dyaspora*) built in Haiti by the diaspora people (*moun dyaspora*) who live abroad and maintain a home in the country; and the houses *in* the diaspora (*kay nan dyaspora*), these myriad places of life of uncertain duration, these more or less temporary or permanent bases that populate Haitian mobility.[17] Among them, not only people circulate or remain but also objects, money, debts and obligations, information, and care. The movement reinforces a sort of affective nationalism (rather than a political one, as in the 1990s, for example), which is nourished by tastes (Creole food that is reinvented on the road with available ingredients) and memories (objects, especially photos that are placed on the base's walls).[18] The relationships between these houses and bases are cultivated through the daily communication that digital networks allow.

Haitians on the move, like other diasporic subjects, used digital and remote media with intensity long before the great leap in long-distance communication produced by the COVID-19 pandemic. Those who maintain a more stable situation, in Haiti or elsewhere, monitor the routes of their relatives from a distance. Images and stories of journeys, successes, and difficulties circulate among them. They are informed about bureaucratic restrictions to crossing borders and about ways to legalize residential situations or work relationships. Contacts are passed on with intermediaries who can help in the journey, or with those who can provide shelter. Through digital networks, people can screen others' movements and know that they arrived safely at a certain point, that they received the expected help, that they found the contact who will give them housing. When someone stops communicating, the warning lights go on, and news is sought through others nearby. People talk about routes and travel plans, about news of loved ones, and about a plurality of geographies and homes.

And people talk about money, a constant presence in diasporic communication. Remittances are both a product and a condition of possibility of movement. The most intense circulation occurs through remittances from those in the diaspora to their Haitian homes in Haiti, fulfilling the main moral imperative of those who move: to help those who remain and those who cultivate the dream of one day also leaving. But there are other flows, too, such as the remittances that go to those on the move: the money sent by those who remain in Haiti or who live in the United States or in other regions of the diaspora to their loved ones who are in transit, who have not yet managed to establish themselves legally and to get a job along the way, or who are in unexpected situations of necessity. Data from 2019 show that 37 percent of the country's gross national product was composed of the remittances of Haitians who live in or were passing through other countries. It is not possible to measure the volume of remittances sent in the opposite direction, to those on the move. The fact is that mobility is a collective enterprise. It involves people who live in relative and uncertain temporariness and who, as Georg Simmel would say, tie their relationships together through multiple centers of gravity, "where purely ideal lines separate similar pieces of ground like a watershed below and beyond which each piece gravitates towards another center."[19]

Searching for Life

Edwidge, a cousin of Daphney's whom I met in Port-au-Prince on the Gina *lakou*, arrived in Brazil in 2014, accompanied by her eighteen-year-old son.

She entered the country by an Amazonian route on the border between Brazil, Colombia, and Peru. It didn't take long for her to find a base with other Haitian migrants who were then crowding the small city of Tabatinga: a school run by a parish priest with support from Caritas, the International Organization for Migration (IOM), and Brazilian government agencies. A year prior, Brazil had created a special type of "humanitarian refuge" visa to receive Haitian migrants and allow them to live and work legally in the country. New arrivals like Edwidge would stay for weeks or months at the Haitian house in Tabatinga until they obtained the visa and continued to other regions of the country where they would find friends, relatives, housing, and some way to earn money. After a couple of months, Edwidge traveled to São Paulo where, through an association of Haitian migrants, she got a job as a domestic worker. Her son decided to continue his journey to Santiago de Chile, which by then offered a better economic situation and a more advantageous currency exchange rate, making it a new destination for Haitians in South America.

Edwidge, by contrast, decided to stay in Brazil and travel to Rio de Janeiro, where her cousin and his wife had been settled for two years. The couple's two children were growing up and they needed help with them. Gradually she made her own way in the new city. Still living at her cousin's house, she began to take care of some elderly and sick people and other children. Eventually she moved to the Curicica neighborhood, which by then had become a Carioca "little Haiti." She shared her house with two Haitian men also from Jérémie. One of them had found a job as a night watchman, and the other worked in civil construction. The house consisted of two rooms: She occupied the bedroom, her roommates the living room, which also served as a kitchen. Among the few objects that adorned the house were a picture of the hero of Haitian independence—Jean Jacques Dessalines—and a Haitian flag. The kitchen space held some utensils for preparing Creole dishes (*banann pise, akra*) that were occasionally sold at Haitian gatherings or at immigrant events held in some squares of Rio de Janeiro, providing an always welcome additional source of cash.

At least once a month Edwidge and her two friends would go to the nearest Western Union agency to send money to their loved ones: US$25 one month, US$50 another, and when things were going well, US$100 or US$150.[20] One of her roommates was sending money to his wife, who was waiting in Port-au-Prince for the necessary papers to get her passport and her Brazilian visa, which, via "family reunion," would allow her to meet her husband in Rio de Janeiro. Edwidge was helping the man's daughter, who was finishing her nursing studies in Haiti and was, likewise, preparing to make her life in Rio de Janeiro with her mother.

Edwidge was then over forty years old and had three children: the eldest, who had been living with her own family on the outskirts of Paris for at least a decade, the boy who had gone on to Chile, and a girl who was studying in Port-au-Prince, hoping to come to Brazil. Her dream would not come true until 2020, after she received her diploma and, soon after, was able to come to Rio de Janeiro. She arrived in the middle of the pandemic, which made it very difficult for her to enter the job market. She helped her mother with the care of elderly people until she decided to sacrifice her nursing degree—temporarily, she thought at the time—to dedicate herself to street commerce, which, despite the restrictions imposed by COVID-19, was never abandoned in the city. They both moved to a new house, also in Curicica. They lived there for only a short time, as the young woman soon contracted the new coronavirus and died. The suffering Edwidge endured as a result of the death of her daughter was indescribable, and it was mixed with guilt for having "brought her to Brazil." Moreover, the pandemic did not allow for the weeks of mourning expected for coping with death in Haiti and always experienced with family and friends. As Edwidge told me more than once, on the few occasions we were able to put words to that tragic event: It all happened so fast; her daughter was buried far from home, unable to rest with her relatives in her own land, in Haiti.

The song "Lakou lakay," composed by the renowned Haitian musician Samba Kessy, was a carnival hit in 1991. Today it has many different versions that celebrate the ideals of coziness, protection, care, and stability that constitute the house as a physical space and as a moral concept amid the death, violence, and mobility that take place in Haiti. A chorus proclaims. "Lakay se lakou lakay" (The house is the *lakou* house), and it speaks of memories of mutuality that enable the continued quest for a better life at many bases, along different routes. The song seems to evoke the houses of memory and kinship that Janet Carsten writes about, the spaces of affect that are made as people live together, I would add, in movement and at a distance.[21] Among its many meanings, the house made in one's birthplace, or *lakou*, signals precisely this hope of return and a horizoning, a particular kind of intellectual labor that reconfigures possibilities for knowledge and action, reorganizing the moral and epistemological conditions of life—the goal of many of my Haitian interlocutors in Haiti and in the diaspora being to return to, or to remain in, a tranquil spot, with one's own, watching life go by.[22] The song also suggests that not all houses are alike, and that in configurations of houses in motion there are those that are more house than others: the house that recalls the memory of living and ancestral kinspeople. *Lakay se lakou lakay* can be an existing place or an idealized projection of a future that is often associated with the culmination of a life of fulfillment and fulfilled with movement, a point of arrival for the *chache lavi* (search for life): a place for serenity, the perspective of old age, and a good death, such as the land near which Edwidge would have liked to have buried her daughter.

Coda

I began this chapter by evoking the terrible earthquake of January 2010 and progressed to the tragedy of the COVID-19 pandemic, two situations that stress the relationship between stability and movement. I spent the first months of the pandemic in Princeton, New Jersey, beginning what should have been a sabbatical year and what ended up being a small fragment of a planetary-scale nightmare marked by confinement and uncertainty, particularly for those who, like me, were far from home.

In the months preceding the pandemic I met with some Haitian acquaintances who live in New Jersey, among them Willian, Daphney's brother and Edwidge's cousin, who also was in the *lakou* Gina on Macajou Street at the time of the earthquake and who moved to the United States a few years later. I was happy to hear that Daphney and her son Fritznel were safe and doing well. Willian and I met regularly to catch up until we had to go into quarantine. We continued to communicate through WhatsApp, a platform that, much like Skype or Facebook, had been constitutive of Haitians' mobile relatedness long before confinement. Mobility has also been a part of my own experience, having been distributed not only between the United States and Brazil but also Argentina, Belgium, and Mexico, where I have loved ones and, in some places, homes. Willian knew me well, which is why he used to refer to me as a "diaspora man," like himself.

While we followed each other at a distance during the acute uncertainty caused by the pandemic, I felt something of the great suffering that immobility triggered in Willian. The Uber service he was providing had to stop, affecting the livelihood of not only his home near Newark, where he lived with his Haitian wife, but also the other houses to which he regularly sent remittances: in Jérémie, where he had grown up in the care of an aunt and where his beloved nephew now lived, and in *lakou* Gina, on Macajou Street, which has been in constant reconstruction since the earthquake.

Like other Haitian friends with whom I kept in touch during the first months of the pandemic, Willian experienced the shadow of death associated with immobility, not only in the material aspects of money and remittances but also in the indefinite suspension of flights that kept him from his loved ones. Yet he persisted in "waiting for better times to search for a better life" (*retann yon bon moman pou chache lavi miyò*), to resume his goal of visiting his country and eventually of returning to live there. Digital communication partially mitigated his suffering, allowing him to be near while being afar, injecting life into confinement, reinserting him and his house in a multiscale and mobile vital landscape, and connecting him with close friends and family distributed in space (in several houses) and in time (with his ancestors, always present at the *lakou*). Macajou Street's *lakou* came back into view one Saturday, in April 2020, when a mobile phone positioned near the peristyle in Gina *lakou* allowed Willian in his Newark house, Daphney in her Miami house, me in my Princeton house, and "our people" in Port-au-Prince to be together, listening to drums, looking at dances, sharing time and affection, cultivating our virtual and desired human presence, and linking our homes and lives.

Despite the restrictions imposed by the pandemic, or even because of them, this scene intensely depicted how mobility involves geographic and temporal territories that constitute collective trajectories—experiences of personhood and belonging. These connections incorporate houses as physical, moral, and affective geographies. They constitute at once specific places and a conceptual field, a landscape of sorts where persons and houses are built in movement, bases to stay at and to keep in motion.

NOTES

1. On acute-on-chronic events, see Farmer, *Haiti After the Earthquake*, 21.
2. Danticat, "Demonstrators in Haiti"; Bulamah, "Lòk."

3. "We can think of Haiti after the 2010 earthquake as another kind of carceral space, in which most victims were unable to move away from the disaster zone but were instead trapped in IDP camps, as these places of physical and spiritual incarceration are." Sheller, *Island Futures*, 19.

4. Beckett, "Unlivable Life"; Neiburg and Joseph, "Searching for Life."

5. Montinard, "Pran wout la."

6. Anglade, *Espace et liberté*.

7. Since the beginning of the twentieth century, *lakou* refers to the traditional form of rural dwelling (Bastien, "Haitian Rural Family Organization"), later to an idealized way of living together with significant others, not in isolated units but in configurations of houses (Marcelin, "A linguagem da casa"), in rural spaces and also in contemporary urban forms of dwellings. Such living arrangements were often affected by the fragmented distribution of aid by the humanitarian system, as was the case in the postearthquake period (Joos, *Urban Dwellings, Haitian Citizenships*, 80ff.). Historical works have suggested that, emerging after independence (1804) and with the abolition of slavery, the *lakou* throughout the nineteenth century pointed at once to government policies for situating the population and to people's resistance to a return to the plantation (Casimir, *Haitians*; Dubois, *Haiti*).

8. According to the census of Bel Air carried out in 2007 by the Brazilian NGO Viva Rio, from 2004 to 2006, more than 30 percent of the population of Bel Air left and returned to the rural zone. Since then, many have stayed away, coming to dwell in the diasporic routes.

9. Joseph and Audebert, *El sistema migratório haitiano*.

10. Sheller, "New Mobilities Paradigm"; Olwig, *Caribbean Journeys*.

11. Joseph and Audebert, *El sistema migratório haitiano*, 23–24.

12. Guedes, "Dessubstancializando a casa."

13. Hage, *Diasporic Condition*.

14. On places of life, see Pietrafiesa de Godoi, "Mobilidades, encantamentos e pertença."

15. Braum, "Frustração"; Kivland, *Street Sovereigns*; Neiburg, "Serendipitous Involvement."

16. Marcelin, "Blood Symbolism."

17. Joseph, "Maisons diasporas."

18. Glick Schiller and Fouron, *George Woke Up Laughing*.

19. Simmel, "Sociologia do espaço."

20. According to some estimates, most of the money received in Haiti monthly is in quantities that vary from US$50 to US$200 (World Bank, "Response to the COVID-19 Pandemic"; Duroseau and Jean, "Haiti"). The importance of these funds becomes clear when we consider that in popular urban neighborhoods such as Bel Air, much more than 60 percent of the population subsists on less than US$60 a month (PNUD, "Programme des Nations Unies").

21. Carsten, *After Kinship*, 55.

22. Petryna, "Horizoning," 246–47.

THIAGO DA COSTA OLIVEIRA AND CARLOS FAUSTO

8

Dismantling and Reassembling Homes

"On a day like today, you would be right here running after a ball." While he talks to his son from the prow of the boat, Mr. Aranô dips an oar into the water in search of the bottom. Submerged below the boat is the field where the dwellers of Paratizão Island used to play soccer. It is May 4, 2019. The scene takes place at the lake of the Belo Monte Hydroelectric Plant, on the middle course of the Xingu River in the Brazilian state of Pará. Situated downriver of the city of Altamira, the dam was built on the Xingu's so-called Volta Grande (Big Turn) by the Consórcio Norte Energia (CNE), flooding 130 square kilometers of forest and altering the seasonal cycle of high and low river levels characteristic of the Amazonia basin. Construction work began in 2011 and the license of operation was issued in 2015, at which point parts of Altamira and its peri-urban settlements were flooded.

Paratizão Island, where Mr. Arанô was born, was one such settlement. In the lake formed by the damming of the river, the island, now submerged, stands out from the rest of the landscape due to the presence of the dry branches of the trees that once provided shade for its inhabitants. The Xingu River, once clear and shallow, is now brownish-dark and deep. The fish have vanished, having either swum away or been killed, intoxicated by the decomposition of the plants. As the boat scrapes its way past the trees' dry branches, Mr. Aranô lists their names—"mango, assai, moriche, guanandi, cashew trees"—while mentioning the former places of his neighbors' and relatives' houses.

To Mr. Aranô, this ruined landscape looks like the picture of a dead relative: "You can see the image, but you know he is no longer alive. You know that you will never be able to hug that person again." But even these phantom memories will eventually vanish away: "In another five years nobody is going to see anything. They will only be able to say, 'I think that the island where my brother lived was over there.' . . . It's very painful for us."

Like thousands of other river dwellers, Mr. Aranô was relocated to the periphery of Altamira. The *empresa* (company)—as CNE is called in the city—promised to cover his rental payments for a one-year period, after which he would have to survive by his own means. Turning to the MPF (Federal Public Prosecutor's Office) for help, Mr. Aranô managed to obtain a house located in a collective urban resettlement area (*reassentamento urbano coletivo*, or RUC).

The company presented these RUCs as a central element in Altamira's "urban requalification" (*requalificação urbana*). There, the residents would find a "house for the rest of their lives," with "three bedrooms, two bathrooms and an American kitchen," surrounded by "leisure areas, squares and paved streets" and equipped with "drinking water on tap" and "a sewage network."[1] The company contrasted this new type of settlement with the houses from which they had removed the residents, stigmatizing the latter as precarious homes built in unhealthy areas.

This visual essay describes the conflicts generated by this resettlement process, which came to oppose two modes of habitation: that of river dwellers and inhabitants of Altamira's peri- and semiurban areas, and the one imposed by Belo Monte's large-scale development project. We aim to explore the equivocations that characterized this process, arguing that the imposition of

FIGURES 8.1 AND 8.2. The last summer at Altamira's river beaches, 2015. All photos in this chapter by the authors.

FIGURES 8.3 AND 8.4. Interior of Ms. Rosa's house, 2015.

an external housing model allows us to devise, as a background figure, a form of dwelling we call Amazonian urban housing, which emerges as a distillation of a moment of dissolution and reassembling. As we shall see, dismissed as a sign of poverty and backwardness by the company's technocrats, Amazonian urban housing resurfaced through people's practices of dismounting and remounting their houses.

The Faces of "Development"

To understand how Altamira looked on the eve of its "urban requalification" and the characteristics of the housing process taking place there, we need to start with a brief overview of the city's history. In comparison with other contemporary medium-sized cities of Amazonia, Altamira was born late. The Xingu's Volta Grande, a long section of the river full of rocks and rapids, served as a major obstacle to colonial expansion. It was only toward the end of the nineteenth century that the situation began to change due to the construction of a road that allowed Volta Grande to be bypassed.

Altamira gained the status of *vila* (town) in 1911 and *cidade* (city) in 1917.[2] Nonetheless, until the mid-twentieth century, the city was still a small town in a vast region occupied by a modest population whose economic activity revolved around the tides of extractivism: rubber, animal skins, Brazil nuts, wood, and some gold. Depending on the cycle, this population of diverse origin—many of them descendants of Amerindians, others arriving from the Brazilian Northeast—shuttled between different activities and residences (situated in the forest, on islands, and in the city), which afforded them flexibility and a relatively autonomous existence vis-à-vis the regional economy.[3]

Altamira's turning point, however, came in the 1970s, with the construction of the Trans-Amazonian Highway, projected, at the height of the military dictatorship, to connect the North and Northeast Regions and to occupy what was perceived—by the Brazilian government—as a demographic vacuum. The construction led to a huge influx of migrants, provoking drastic changes to the urban plan and modes of habitation. This process was observed in practically all of Amazonia during the 1970s. In ten years, the population of the North Region increased by almost 59 percent, with the urban population growing by 80 percent and the rural by 40 percent. According to the 1970 census, there were approximately fifteen thousand inhabitants in Altamira, almost six thousand of them living in the city. A decade later, after the highway construction, this population had tripled to over forty-six thousand inhabitants, with almost twenty-seven thousand living in the urban area.[4]

The Trans-Amazonian Highway transformed Altamira at an astonishing speed. Many new districts sprang up, while stilt houses proliferated on the *baixões*, the seasonally inundated low-lying areas of Altamira. It did not take long, however, for the highway to shift from a symbol of progress to one of economic failure and environmental disaster. At the end of Brazil's military dictatorship, Altamira remained somewhat frozen in time, still awaiting the paving of the highway, hoping for a new project of regional development.

At that time, in the mid-1980s, the latter took the form of a complex of six dams, planned by Eletronorte, the state-owned company appointed to exploit the entire hydroelectric potential of the Xingu River, which was estimated at a firm capacity of 20,400 megawatts.[5] The plan was to form six large lakes by flooding eighteen thousand square kilometers of forest, from the north of Mato Grosso to the Volta Grande do Xingu.

At the end of the 1980s, although the studies were already advanced, with international funding already negotiated, a solid opposition to the project emerged, bringing together Indigenous peoples, environmentalists, and social movements. The paradigmatic moment of this movement was the historic meeting of Indigenous peoples in Altamira in February of 1989.[6] A new era seemed to be dawning, one in which Indigenous peoples took center stage in the environmental struggle.

Despite this partial victory, some ten years later Eletronorte returned with a new, less ambitious project, proposing only the construction of the first of the six dams previously planned: the Belo Monte plant. The project would take more than a decade to be implemented. After powerful lobbying, resistance to the construction of hydroelectric dams on the Xingu was overcome in the mid-2000s, just as Brazil elected its first left-wing government. This time the damming of the river could not be avoided.

100 Mark

Even before construction work began in 2011, the company demarcated the infamous Cota 100 (100 Mark)—a measure that defined the areas in the

FIGURES 8.5 AND 8.6. Ms. Rosa's kitchen and the interior of Ms. Francisca's house, 2015.

FIGURES 8.7 AND 8.8. Ms. Rosa's backyard garden, 2015.

FIGURES 8.9 AND 8.10. Semidismantled houses at Baixão das Olarias, 2015.

urban center that would be impacted by the damming of the river. This figure corresponded to the flood line on the urban waterfront of the Xingu River and Altamira's smaller watercourses. Around 25 percent of the city's area was below this level, meaning that about eight thousand families (or thirty-nine thousand people) would be affected by the forming of the lake necessary for the dam operation. Through this technical-political device, CNE's engineers loomed large in the imaginations of local inhabitants anticipating the presence of Belo Monte's lake and the spatial reorganization it would produce.

In 2015, when we arrived at Altamira to document the "urban requalification," the whole city resembled an enormous construction site, with its big machines and hurried workers. The urban landscape was a complex fabric marked by diverse temporalities. Within the area defined as being on or below the 100 Mark, there were still entire houses waiting for demolition but also partially or completely demolished houses, as well as vacant and leveled terrains, while on the new periphery of Altamira, the RUCs had just sprung up, and their first residents, like Mr. Aranô, had relocated to them.

When we started the photographic documentation, we had different experiences with the city. Fausto had carried out field research with the Apyterewa-Parakanã between 1988 and 1996. Altamira was then a transit point, his last port before navigating upriver for around three days to reach the Indigenous territory. In 2014, he returned to the region at the request of the Parakanã, who were then dealing with compensation projects for the construction of Belo Monte.

For Costa Oliveira, Amazonian urbanity had been a topic of interest since 2011, when he began visiting the region as an anthropologist and photographer. He first visited Altamira in 2014 with his then-partner, anthropologist Paula Lacerda, who was doing research in the city. After this first trip, he made four subsequent trips documenting the region (2015, 2016, 2017, and 2019) in partnership with Fausto, Lacerda, and the cinematographer Fabio Nascimento.

Altamira's rapid urban transformations became a topic of common interest for us when we realized the irreversibility of the processes the region was going through. In July 2015, we began documenting Altamira's "last summer," when the river beaches near the city—now permanently covered by the lake—were still exposed and full of beachgoers. It was urgent to carry out a kind of reverse archaeology: capturing images for the future, images that would no longer be repeated.

The novelty of the situation was also evident to the locals, who allowed us to photograph them without any embarrassment as we walked through the recent and fragile ruins of what had once been their lived world. People wanted to talk, not because they expected anything concrete from us, but because we showed an interest in their lives and places. We were witnessing, in the heat of the moment, the transformation of their lives caused by the impersonal forces of the company.

Our photographic relationship, open to words and memories, contrasted with the one implemented by the company as part of the process of registering the inhabitants and the houses to be removed. When inspecting these houses, the company's agents would produce a report. On the first page of the report would be a photo of the head of the house holding a white placard with the identification number and the date of the visit. The production of this type of image, which formally resembles that of suspects tagged by the police, constituted an initial violence in the resettlement process, as many of the people we visited confided to us. Ms. Rosa, for instance, an important social movement leader in the region, refused to undergo the humiliation of the technical portrait when her house was surveyed in 2011.

The report also had another effect. After the document was produced, the residents were legally required to remain "on hold" until further contact from the CNE technicians who defined the details of the eviction and the compensation applicable. Then a new phase began, technically called "freezing," that set a point in time after which any additional modifications to the area of residence would no longer be compensated.[7] Between the moment of freezing and the promised relocation, years could pass. The residents were left suspended in time, like their pictures displayed on the report's front page.

The freezing produced at least two effects: submission and expectation. On the one hand, as Lacerda observes, evoking Javier Auyero's *Pacientes del estado* (2013), the wait leads to a certain discipline and submission of bodies, producing orderly and at the same time inferior citizens; on the other hand, as the verb *esperar* evokes in Portuguese, waiting also implies a sense of expectation and hope, a certain openness to a future not entirely determined.[8]

FIGURES 8.11 AND 8.12. The last resident of Ferro Velho Street next to an abandoned house, 2015.

FIGURES 8.13 AND 8.14. Residents of Baixão das Olarias and Baixão do Tufi dismantling their houses, timber by timber, nail by nail, 2015.

BRASILIT
POLIETILENO 1000

FIGURES 8.15 AND 8.16. The surreal landscape of Baixão das Olarias during the dismantling process, 2015.

In our photographic gesture, we tried to enter into dialogue with both these dimensions of waiting, filtering them through images.

The Garden and the Roça

Ms. Rosa's house provides us with a useful example for presenting important features of urban domestic spaces in Amazonia: first, the presence of a garden linked to subsistence and sociability; second, the relationship between an urban and a rural unit; and finally, the collecting of industrialized objects in accordance with a logic of bricolage.

Ms. Rosa's house is, by local standards, a middle-class one. The front is separated from the street by a railing and by a garage space with a ceramic tile flooring. On entering, we pass through a living room whose profusion of scattered photos and colorful walls evokes the home interiors of Brazil's Northeast—the origin of most of Altamira's migrants. A second room serves as a pantry and kitchen, well provisioned with domestic appliances. Crossing the kitchen door, though, we enter another space with distinct characteristics. This is a second kitchen and service area separated from the extensive garden by a slatted wooden wall. On the right are twenty or so well-polished aluminum pans, a feature characteristic of various riverside kitchens we visited over the years.

The back garden is large. It was planted by Ms. Rosa's family over the last two decades and entailed landfilling sections of seasonally flooded forest on the shores of the *igarapé* Altamira. Cultivation slowly converted the flooded area into a backyard full of large trees and medicinal, edible, and ornamental plants. Ms. Rosa's back garden is typical of domestic gardens in Amazonia, in both riverside and urban areas. Plants are grown by women especially for consumption by the domestic unit, but they are also exchanged "among kin, neighbors, church members, and friends, [working as] a way of provisioning households without engaging the formal sector."[9] This is the case not only for food plants but also for medicinal and ornamental ones. The gardens enable residents to be inserted into a network of circulating plants.

Some Amazonian urban houses are also connected to rural units belonging to the same family. Ms. Rosa, for example, is married to Mr. Juarez, who most of the time resides on a small rural property on a branch of the Transasurini road. On this *roça*, or *sítio*, as the couple refers to the smallholding, Mr. Juarez raises a few livestock and grows food on a small scale for sale at the market as well as other crops intended for subsistence. From this property, Mr. Juarez takes produce to their urban house, where it cannot be cultivated in the back garden, and returns with produce from the garden as well as industrialized goods that complement his life on the smallholding.

These exchanges, invisible to macroeconomic indicators, constitute fundamental practices of existence in the Amazonian urban context.[10] Given the low degree of formalization of the economy in the region, double residence and domestic gardens point to an alternative form of urbanization. In this form, the work force is not "divorced from the soil" and, consequently, not entirely dominated by the economy of manufactured goods and services.[11] As Antoinette WinklerPrins and Perpétuo de Souza suggest, "The presence of gardens in the cities challenges what it means to be urban."[12]

However, from the point of view of the technical regulations adopted by CNE, a family had to choose between one or the other area of residence, especially when one residence was on the islands and the other in the urban area. The company simply did not recognize the dual habitation standard. For CNE, people could live in only one place, but as Mr. Antonio explained to a team conducting an inspection for the Federal Public Prosecutor's Office on his island: "If we chose to live here, we would lose our 'street house' (*casa da rua*). . . . And if we registered as living there, we would lose the right to live here."[13]

Dismantling Collection Houses

The third feature that seems to characterize Amazonian houses is a profusion of objects, something we had already observed in Ms. Rosa's house. The urban and peri-urban houses of Altamira that we visited were often full of useful (and temporarily unuseful) things: images lining the walls, dozens of photos stored on shelves, collections of glistening pans hanging in the kitchens, bottles filling bathrooms, toys and all kinds of objects waiting to be reused in the gardens.

In a context of economic vulnerability and restricted access to industrialized goods, these collections are both a reservoir that can be useful down the line and the material instantiation of living in a situation of structural insecurity. Even houses' materials can be subjected to this regime by being dismantled and reassembled elsewhere or in a different shape, a practice that was already part of residents' lifeways. In 2015, this practice was quite visible in the urban reconfiguration areas we visited. Before leaving their homes, residents carefully

FIGURES 8.17 AND 8.18. Ms. Francisca and Ms. Raimunda waiting to be relocated from their homes, declared unsafe because of their vicinity to the 100 Mark, 2015.

FIGURES 8.19 AND 8.20. A child playing amid the debris of demolished houses near the Igarapé Altamira, 2015.

dismantled them, leaving the landscape temporarily filled with piles of bricks and timber deposited in front of buildings in various stages of demolition.

In the Baixão das Olarias, we encountered the stilt houses almost entirely dismantled. The scene was that of a hallucinatory nightmare: a bridge leading to nowhere, a gate that closed on nothing, an unreachable bathroom. In this place, some residents were still disassembling their homes, plank by plank, nail by nail, under a scalding sun.

The dismantling operation showed the building process and the many lives of the construction materials in a context in which construction is permanent reconstruction.[14] Such a dynamic impacts the temporality of the houses and indeed of the whole neighborhood, which appears under the sign of impermanence and incompleteness, forever in a process of becoming. In the Altamira *baixões*, as much as in the favelas of Rio de Janeiro, houses evolve in dialogue with available materials, changes in the terrain, and the arrival of new residents.[15] Moreover, because of the challenging conditions of the terrain, these are also often themselves "constructed."

This point brings us to a final observation: Houses are also made of relations. They are part of an extended network that connects and separates. A home results from both cutting and making relations. Cutting produces an interiority we call "family," distinct from other homes to which, however, it is connected by means of neighborhood and friendship relations (see chapter 7 in this volume, by Federico Neiburg).

Such relations were integral to the dismantling process we documented. In the Baixão do Tufi, for instance, we encountered Silvestre and his friend Francisco helping one another dismantle the former's house: "They [the engineers] are in a hurry," Silvestre told us, "but as they can see I'm working, they haven't immediately flattened it." Like many other people, he feared what had happened to an evangelical pastor who, according to a story we heard multiple times, had left for a church service in the morning and, on returning home, found his house demolished and his furniture dumped in the road. But while the engineers could not wait, Ms. Maria Isabel, Silvestre's neighbor, had nothing to do but wait, since the company had not showed up again after the "freezing." She just sat in her backyard and waited.

Thus, these long-term neighbors were working together, perhaps for the last time, since they would soon be rehoused in different, and distant, parts of the city. Many people would soon lose their networks of solidarity constructed through gardens, plants, artifacts, work, and mutual care.

The Politics of Derecognition

It was CNE's plan to remove all the stilt houses and landfill these areas to transform them into public parks. The removals were presented not just as a result of the damming of the river but also as a measure for sanitizing the city, particularly in these *baixões*, described as "unsuitable," "high risk," and "irregular"—terminology that associated them mostly with illegality and precarity of life.[16]

We know little about the criteria CNE used to evaluate the properties (and lives) to be compensated, beyond what can be read between the lines of some official documents. Little or nothing was told to the residents. Moreover, since the rubber boom, writing and its secrets had served as a technical device of domination in the region. In the twenty-first century, the CNE's register and questionnaire contained language that was difficult for many residents to comprehend and that therefore hovered over their heads.

The questionnaires qualified the properties according to a dichotomous logic: One lives in either the *roça* or the city (dual residency was excluded); the property is situated either on the floodplain—raised on stilts—or on terra firma (mixed situations were simply nonexistent); the property is either residential or commercial (there cannot be cases in which the two overlap). In addition, networks of kinship and neighborhood, not to mention pets, plants and memories, were simply not considered—or were grossly underestimated. One thing became clear from the multiple complaints we heard: The compensation model did not match the objective and subjective experiences that it was supposed to indemnify. Moreover, in the context of Altamira, the company and the state had become one and the same thing. As an old local friend confided to us: "This is a dictatorship; a civil dictatorship, but nonetheless a dictatorship."

The construction of Belo Monte mobilized the old dichotomy between "backwardness" and "progress" so often reenacted in the Amazon, with its characteristic simplification of Indigenous and river dwellers' realities. This dichotomy—arranged temporally between a past to be overcome and a future to be achieved—is associated, in the case of Belo Monte, with an

FIGURES 8.21 AND 8.22. A demolished fish shop near the Igarapé Altamira and the Xingu River, 2015.

FIGURES 8.23 AND 8.24. Demolished houses in Altamira near the Igarapé Altamira, 2015.

FIGURES 8.25 AND 8.26. Recently built houses in the Laranjeiras and Jatobá RUCS, 2015–17.

anthropocentric and technocratic dream (or nightmare): that of reconfiguring the natural regime of a vast region, controlling the flow of the rivers, and thus promoting the "liquidation of the physical means of survival" of the population whose way of life aligns with this regime.[17]

This seems to be a recurring dynamic in large hydroelectric projects in Brazil, as Lygia Sigaud points out when discussing the case of the Sobradinho dam in Bahia, which flooded a vast stretch of the São Francisco River in the early 1980s.[18] Displaced, local farmers found themselves compelled to produce food within a market logic, having to take out bank loans to buy machinery and inputs that had been previously unnecessary in traditional agriculture. In Sobradinho, as in Altamira, the dream of progress sold by the megadevelopment projects failed to recognize the existence of other ways of life. The population was thus removed from the external margins of the system—where some autonomy remained—and thrust into its internal margins, where they had to occupy a peripheral and subordinate position.

A Nightmare Transformed

When Mr. Aranô arrived at the Jatobá resettlement area, a recently built RUC, on a hillside six kilometers from Altamira's center, he saw thousands of houses like the one he had just received lined up along the scalding asphalt recently baked by the company's machines. There was not a single tree in a radius of kilometers, nor even a stream with fresh water. It could not have been more different from Paratizão Island with its little soccer field, the shadows of bountiful trees, the constant presence of family members, and the quick access to the river and its fish. There was nothing more distant from the Amazonian ways of life than the grid of standardized houses geometrically disposed and painted in bright colors, or the wide sidewalks with no fences, all looking like the housing projects for deprived populations found at the margins of so many cities worldwide.

To make matters worse, Mr. Aranô, his wife, and his two married children received just one house for all of them to share, situated on an unfenced terrain. They soon realized there was no room for the *tralha da pesca*—the local term for the set of nets, polystyrene boxes, motors, oars, and other equipment used by fishermen—and it would need to be kept outside, next to the house. It was therefore urgent to fence off their plot. Cases of theft had grown exponentially alongside the demographic explosion caused by the construction of the dam. Moreover, the ties of solidarity and neighborliness, which had provided a feeling of safety, had been broken. There would be no one to watch your back.

Some features of the prefabricated houses clashed head-on with the Amazonian way of life. The best example is the sleeping hammock, which—despite its name—provides a place for people to rest during the daytime rather than at night. Although such hammocks are usually suspended where "the wind blows," the houses in the RUCs had been built with self-supporting prefabricated walls, making it impossible to tie up hammocks. Mr. Aranô tried hard before understanding that the walls would not accept any intervention. In fact, no modifications or repairs were allowed: Any alteration that a resident made to a house would nullify the compensation agreement's promise of five years of insurance coverage—which, in a way, prolonged the initial "freezing" imposed on the people affected by the dam.

However, after some time of bewilderment, the residents started to conspicuously transform the RUCs, violating the company's rules. They used the repertoire of skills they had possessed before being forced into this new housing model, making it clear why they had devoted so much time and energy to removing the material from their old houses: planks of wood, ironwork, tiles, bricks, and even nails. In a short time, they began to modify the RUC houses. At the backs of them, gardens began to sprout, chicken coops were erected, and new rooms were built with timber and bricks brought from the dismantled homes. Even the previous pattern of residence associated with commerce reemerged as small bars, grocery stores, hair salons, and tattoo studios popped out from the fronts of the houses, while evangelical pastors built small churches with the help of their followers.

The sterility of the engineering project was thus gradually contaminated by the practices of the garden and collection house. Using heteroclite materials, their only heirlooms from a dismantled world, the residents of the RUCs began, so to speak, to *re-Amazonize* their dwellings, modifying the urban landscape and recreating the elements of sociality that had informed their modes of habitation before Belo Monte. In the hustle and bustle of Altamira's "urban requalification," the engineers could not see life sprouting up again as

FIGURES 8.27 AND 8.28. Recently transformed backyards in the Jatobá RUC and front yards in the Laranjeiras RUC, 2015–17.

FIGURES 8.29 AND 8.30. Transformed backyard in the Jatobá RUC; Ms. Francisca fills her front yard with earth to level it with the street and avoid further flooding of her recently built house, 2015–17.

244
PeNA

Henrique e Yara
Eu Te Amo

FIGURES 8.31 AND 8.32. Ms. Raimunda and Mr. Luís in their transformed backyards, 2015–17.

the saplings grew, the hens laid eggs, and people wove new relationships to survive another cycle of regional development.

Surviving does not mean that nothing was lost. On the contrary, people were moved not only spatially but also socially and economically, losing the relative autonomy they had enjoyed in their previous lives. It would be a mistake, however, to close our eyes to the creative housing practices people can devise during these turbulent times.

NOTES

1. Consórcio Norte Energia, infographic, in *Projeto Básico Ambiental* (PBA), *Reassentamentos Urbanos Coletivos* (RUC), *Usina Hidrelétrica de Belo Monte*, no date.
2. Tourinho, "Estrutura urbana," 221.
3. Macedo, "Altamira," 89.
4. Miranda Neto and Herrera, "Altamira-PA."
5. Sevá [Filho], "Works on the Great Bend," 26.
6. Sevá Filho and Switkes, "Resumo executivo," 15.
7. Lacerda, "Reassentar e indenizar," 736.
8. Lacerda, "Reassentar e indenizar," 741; L'Éstoile, "'Money Is Good.'"
9. WinklerPrins and de Souza, "Surviving the City," 118.
10. Browder and Godfrey, *Rainforest Cities*; Lima and Saragoussi, "Floodplain Home Gardens"; Murrieta and WinklerPrins, "Flowers of Water."
11. Brunn et al., *Cities of the World*, 5.
12. WinklerPrins and de Souza, "Surviving the City," 121.
13. Ministério Público Federal (MPF), "Relatório de inspeção interinstitucional," 8.
14. Cavalcanti, "Do barraco à casa."
15. Jacques, *Estética da ginga*.
16. Lacerda, "Reassentar e indenizar," 736.
17. Sigaud, "O efeito das tecnologias."
18. Sigaud, "O efeito das tecnologias."

PART V

Domestic Experimentality

ANN H. KELLY AND JAVIER LEZAUN

9

The Immune Home

This chapter uses the example of mosquito repellents to reconsider the domestic orientation of global health immunologics. Spatial repellency, a volumetric mode of chemical action, seeks to reduce disease transmission by creating atmospheres inimical to mosquitoes and other insect vectors of disease. Unlike insecticides, which are expected to kill on contact, spatial repellency works by creating transitory chemical envelopes that keep potential biological threats at bay. Drawing inspiration from work by Tanzanian colleagues on new repellent products for malaria prevention, we explore the implications of untethering protection from the affordances of a physically enclosed domestic space. In Tanzania's Kilombero Valley, this untethering forces a reexamination of the self-contained, fully finished house as the conventional unit of global health action, drawing attention instead to modes of *house-ing* that encompass the spatial and temporal in-betweens of everyday life.

Introduction

It has been a long day. We have been driving around a network of rural villages across the river from the Ifakara Health Institute (IHI)—a Tanzanian center for global health research and a world leader in the study of mosquito-borne diseases. Our Land Rover carries a team of IHI scientists and a group of international collaborators looking to evaluate a new tool for malaria prevention: eave ribbons impregnated with the chemical transfluthrin. Designed by Arnold Mmbando, then a doctoral student at IHI, the ribbons are made of ten-centimeter bands of burlap that can be easily affixed to a house's exterior to cover the gaps between roof and walls that are common in many rural dwellings. Thanks to transfluthrin's spatial-repellent properties, the eave ribbons produce constant emanations that divert female mosquitoes when they approach houses in search of blood. Portable, cheaply made, and aesthetically pleasing, the combination of ribbon and chemical could, Arnold believes, transform the landscape of malaria prevention. It is a hope shared by those who have spent the last seven hours crammed in the car.

For the past two decades, the battle against malaria-carrying mosquitoes in sub-Saharan Africa has relied on two intradomiciliary interventions: the spraying of interior surfaces with residual chemicals (known as indoor residual spraying, or IRS) and the distribution of long-lasting insecticide-treated bed nets (LLINS). Integrated with antimalarial drugs and rapid diagnostic tests, these measures have significantly reduced the incidence of malaria across Africa. In recent years, however, case numbers have plateaued and, in some regions, started to rise again. Mosquitoes' increasing resistance to insecticides presents the most obvious challenge, but it has long been clear that the limitations of IRS and LLINS are inherent in their design. Key species of *Anopheles* mosquitoes are becoming behaviorally evasive, displaying a rising propensity to feed outdoors, or at times of day when residents are unlikely to be under the protection of a net. In rural Tanzania, a growing proportion of malaria transmission occurs through bites in peridomestic areas or during communal gatherings.

There is also the fundamental spatial question of *where* the house *is*, and whether a physically enclosed interior can effectively accommodate a household and all its domestic routines. In regions such as Ifakara's Kilombero Valley, the house does not always correspond to a singular, bounded material structure, and domestic activities rarely remain contained within the walls of a single dwelling. Residential space tends to spill out across thresholds, open spaces, and partial enclosures, encompassing multiple buildings in various stages of construction and (dis)repair.

This is where Arnold's impregnated ribbons come in. They are designed to create what he calls "bubbles of protection," invisible chemical envelopes shielding residents from malaria vectors. They work through passive dispersion, emitting into the ambient air vapors that irritate mosquitoes and disrupt their human-seeking abilities. Compared with other steps usually taken to repel mosquitoes—burning coils and herbs, applying topical formulations to skin and clothes—Arnold's emanators require minimal investment or compliance from the user, work effectively for months on end, and pose fewer health risks. The ribbons also travel light, and IHI researchers are testing their efficacy in a variety of locales; recently, they attached them to the temporary shelters, or shamba houses, where local farmers spend several weeks of the year while tending to their crops. Arnold is also exploring smaller repellent-dipped strips that could be distributed under verandas, partial walls, and outdoor kitchen pergolas (figure 9.1).[1]

Spatial repellents represent a peculiar form of *house-ing*, a practice of prophylaxis oriented toward the domestic routines that unfold across and beyond the house's walls. By strategically positioning transfluthrin-impregnated ribbons and strips, Arnold and his colleagues hope to extend the *oikos* by chemical means, encompassing those peridomestic locations and interdomiciliary events where the risk of infection is often highest. A seemingly modest intervention, this reformulation of chemical protection carries nevertheless huge significance. In the long and convoluted history of malaria prevention efforts in sub-Saharan Africa, spatial repellents bring into focus different forms of relationality and propinquity, directing our attention to the socio-material interstices of everyday life.[2]

Such a reimagining of global health does entail some trade-offs, however. The purpose of the day's road trip is to identify areas with very high rates of malaria transmission where a randomized controlled trial (RCT) could most easily demonstrate the ribbons' protective efficacy. For Arnold, this minor expedition to some of the poorest and most malaria-endemic villages in the Kilombero Valley has been dispiriting. That evening, around the dinner table at the institute's main house, he recounts to Lina Finda, a social scientist at IHI, a "heartbreaking" tour of houses with their backs open to the elements, mud

FIGURE 9.1. Arnold Mmbando affixing eave ribbons to an experimental hut, Ifakara Health Institute. Photo by the authors.

walls crumbling around sticks, children lying sick. Lina, who is researching the relationship between house construction and malaria risk, nods. "We are just going to go around putting ribbons on these homes?" she asks. "It is shameful." Even if they are effective in diverting mosquitoes, she implies, fixing chemically impregnated ribbons to houses in a state of dereliction will not bring any durable improvement to the residents' living conditions. In fact, by virtue of their very cheapness and ease of application, highly portable products such as the eave ribbons might help perpetuate chronic forms of destitution, "solving" the problem of exposure to mosquitoes at the expense of a proper consideration of the material infrastructures necessary to sustain a decent life.[3]

This chapter takes this ambivalence as its point of departure. What does the moral quandary of using chemo-atmospheric tools to tackle material inequities tell us about emerging paradigms of immunitary protection? How does it illuminate the relationship between global health interventions, commonly based on the distribution of finished products, and the living conditions of the populations those interventions seek to benefit? We begin by describing the history of the enclosed house as a site and instrument of early malariology, focusing on the architectural innovations and socio-material manipulations through which the movement of malaria parasites between humans and mosquitoes was first rendered visible. We then discuss the *domestication* of malaria control—how the house, understood as an interior contained by intersecting planes, made malaria control at scale a viable proposition. The repeated failure to eliminate malaria through indoor interventions provides the backdrop for the current appeal of spatial repellents and for the promise of grounding protection in a different topology of peridomestic spaces. We consider how the immune home is conjugated by this new paradigm of atmospheric action and the degree to which malaria can still be articulated as a problem of "improvement" or "development." Our interrogation closely tracks Lina and Arnold's own questioning of the affordances of spatial repellency and takes inspiration from their vision of *house-ing* to sketch out a more expansive imaginary of immunity in global health.

Domestic Surfacing

There is a close affinity between the organization of malaria control and the conceptualization of domestic space, and it goes back to the very moment the disease was first apprehended as mosquito borne. Ronald Ross's dissections of mosquitoes' *Plasmodium*-filled gut tissue proved the existence of a microbial pathogen associated with malarial fevers, but it was Patrick Manson's "model house" that ultimately settled the fundamental question of malaria epidemiology.

Manson conducted his famous experiment along the edge of a half-drained swamp in the Roman Campagna, an area in Italy both poor and intensely malarious. Constructed in London and then disassembled and shipped on to Ostia via Rome, Manson's model house consisted of four rooms adjoined by a single corridor. The windows were fitted with clear glass encasements and covered with cotton netting; the eaves, left open for ventilation, were secured with tight wire mesh. The netting-lined doors leading out of the house were further enclosed by a screened porch. A final set of netted curtains encircled each bed. They were affixed to the ceiling and anchored on the floor at a far enough distance to prevent mosquitoes from "biting through the meshes of the netting any limb which might be extended out of the bedclothes during sleep."[4] Four men took up residence in this experimental interior: two researchers from London, their domestic attendant, and an Italian artist commissioned to illustrate the experiment. They lived there for three months, moving freely around the swampy grounds during the day, returning home during the evening to be cocooned within its mosquito-proof walls. The study yielded incontrovertible evidence: For the duration of their stay, the four experimental subjects remained malaria free, while the surrounding population suffered repeated attacks of the disease (figure 9.2).

Manson's experiment was crucial in establishing malaria as a disease acquired predominantly indoors through the bite of a female mosquito that had entered the house in the evening in pursuit of a blood meal. This understanding of malaria as an intradomiciliary event would shape disease-control efforts for more than a century, allowing multiple answers to the question of how to improve the protective affordances of houses. In Italy, the strategy that would later be known as bonification conceived of malaria prevention as a consequence of "the improvement of the countryside in all its aspects."[5] According to this line of thinking, which was expressed with different nuances in other parts of the world, protection against malaria would emerge as the by-product of a generalized upgrading of the population's living conditions, specifically of the quality of the housing stock in rural areas.

FIGURE 9.2. Patrick Manson's experimental hut and its occupants from June to October 1900. Drawing by A. Terzi, ca. 1900. Wellcome Collection. Public Domain Mark. https://wellcomecollection.org/works/pz5qmgv2/images?id=dpztts8h.

British experimental hut at Ostia (Roman Campagna). June-October, 1900.

Programs of house improvement were adopted in other notoriously endemic areas, such as the mining towns of the Central African Copperbelt, or the new agricultural areas created under the jurisdiction of the Tennessee Valley Authority.[6]

Support for this sort of broad-based intervention into material living conditions was far from universal, however. Ross had promulgated a very different ideal of malaria control, one predicated on the targeting of mosquito breeding grounds. By systematically treating standing bodies of water with petroleum derivatives or poisons, he contended, it would be possible to suppress the relevant mosquito species and thus impede the transmission of the parasite. In contrast to the promotion of general economic improvement, targeting the aquatic habitats of mosquito larvae was presented as a properly scientific approach, a surgical intervention that would excise the vector of disease and, in so doing, disentangle malaria from a range of social issues that had only an ancillary bearing on its epidemiology. Critics of larval control methods, however, countered that seeking to uproot mosquitoes from malarious landscapes was often impractical and in many cases impossible. As the British malariologist Colonel Sidney P. James put it in his 1926 report to the League of Nations' Malaria Commission, "Malaria should be dealt with in the houses of people rather than in the environment."[7] For, regardless of the numbers of *Anopheles* mosquitoes present in any given area, the home was where malaria was typically contracted and should thus remain the central battleground of public health action.

The discovery of DDT in the 1940s radically changed the complexion of this debate. It reinforced the role of the house as the front line of antimalarial efforts, but at the expense of a broader understanding of "improvement" or "development." The extraordinary residual toxicity of DDT made it possible to interrupt malaria transmission by applying the chemical to interior domestic surfaces once or twice a year. The insecticide's low-cost efficiency disentangled malaria prevention from house upgrades or rural progress, while the possibility of concentrating efforts on walls and ceilings made control programs modular and scalable. This was the mode of chemical action that underpinned the World Health Organization's Global Malaria Eradication Programme (GMEP) carried out between 1955 and 1969. "Houses, unlike potential breeding places, are easy to locate," wrote Carlos Alvarado and Leonard Bruce-Chwatt, directors of the program. "Their area of wall surface can be closely estimated, and it is possible to forecast accurately requirements in materials, equipment, personnel and finance."[8]

The GMEP had its share of successes where homes conformed to the domestic topography of industrialized modernity. It struggled, however, in regions where residence was neither architecturally bounded nor geographically fixed. As WHO experts pointed out, a particularly intractable obstacle to GMEP's operations were those "habits of the population" that unsettled the assumption of the house as a stable material entity corresponding to an equally stable social unit. Recalcitrant behaviors, such as "outside sleeping during the hot season and frequent rebuilding, re-thatching and re-plastering of houses, related to special events (e.g., festivals) but carried out in an entirely irregular fashion," undermined the WHO's eradicationist ambitions.[9] The vernacular logics that drove these processes of "frequent rebuilding"—the need to rebuild houses made from materials incapable of surviving the rains, the aspiration to a larger family that explained the construction of adjoining rooms, the nature of the "special events" that triggered acts of structural upgrading, or the aesthetic choices that accounted for the "irregularity" of those improvements—went largely unacknowledged. Driven by a relentless preoccupation with the chemical treatment of interior surfaces, GMEP reduced the house to a set of intersecting planes within which a family spent the night—an *oikos* of invariable geometry averse to social or material recompositions.

Peridomestic Atmospheres

Transfluthrin-impregnated products partake in the long genealogy of chemical tools against malaria but index a different paradigm of protection. They reorient disease prevention away from the traditional insecticidal approach and toward the design, through repellency, of protective atmospheres. The site of operation is not the bounded, enclosed space of the physical house but the more fluid topography of the peridomestic, the spatiotemporal in-betweens that play such a critical role in the transmission of malaria in the Kilombero Valley. Key domestic practices that typically occur outside the walls of the house—washing, cooking, sleeping, and hosting or attending funerals and parties—move from the fringes of public health attention to become the very point of intervention. Kinship ties and social groupings external to the nuclear family begin to feature more prominently in public health action. With a strategic positioning of transfluthrin-impregnated ribbons, the ephemeral collective that gathers to watch a football game at an outdoor bar, or to pay its respects outside the house of the village leader, can do so under the invisible protection of chemical emanations. And the eave ribbon is just one among many customized repellent products currently under development in Ifakara—the team at IHI is trialing a range of transfluthrin-impregnated bags, sandals, football socks, prayer mats, and chairs, all capable of creating bubbles of protection around individuals as they go about their daily lives, moving in and out of interiors and joining in diverse social endeavors.[10]

As protection becomes more situational, however, the built environment begins to slip from view, and this creates, as we indicated, mixed feelings. The unease that Arnold and Lina felt at the remedial use of repellents in impoverished villages did not stem from any inherent limitations of the product but from their fear that the generalized use of these products would make living conditions irrelevant to malaria prevention.

It is telling that this moral concern crystallized in the context of preparations for an RCT, when IHI researchers and their foreign collaborators were embarking on the journey of producing robust scientific evidence of the ribbons' protective efficacy. Such data are necessary to sway the views of the international experts who determine whether a new product should become part of the global tool kit for malaria prevention. In this kind of study, the houses in the very worst shape often have the greatest evidentiary value—their crumbling mud walls and damaged thatch roofs leave their inhabitants so utterly defenseless that any protection afforded by the ribbon will become readily visible; against a backdrop of constant exposure, the null hypothesis of "no protection" can be refuted by the slightest of interventions. This requires that the houses remain in a state of suspended disrepair while the relevant data are collected (figure 9.3).

Dereliction as empirical baseline is not an uncommon feature of malariological research, or indeed of global health research more generally. Over a century ago, in another foundational study, the preeminent Italian parasitologist Angelo Celli was confronted with a similar predicament. Evolving in parallel to Manson's, Celli's research focused on the high rates of malaria infection among families of railway workers on the outskirts of Rome. To demonstrate the effectiveness of screening domestic dwellings, Celli affixed thick

FIGURE 9.3. Village dwelling, southern Kilombero Valley. Photo by the authors.

muslin strips along the windows, chimneys, doors, and porches of a select group of workers' houses. His results were as impressive as those obtained by Manson in Ostia. "It is as if in a book we had a white page and a black page, the first would represent our protected dwellings and families, the second would represent our unprotected dwellings and families."[11] The choice of which houses to screen and which ones to leave unprotected was not random, however. "Old dwellings," he wrote, "do not lend themselves to have protective modifications made, and as a consequence were left as controls."[12]

There is a ruthless scientific logic in these decisions, as trials are designed to produce evidence that can travel far and wide, contributing to the assessment not so much of interventions but of *commodities*, standardized objects that can be deployed in a variety of contexts and situations. Precisely for this reason, however, because they are oriented toward the epistemic needs of distant audiences rather than the material concerns of their participants, controlled trials tend to sharply delineate the moral issues at stake. When the matter under consideration is domestic living conditions, these concerns probe the boundaries of global health as a field of practice focused on the deployment of "scalable" solutions. The effort to prove the effectiveness of transfluthrin-impregnated ribbons as a generalizable solution thus confronted researchers at IHI with a version of humanitarianism wedded to what Peter Redfield describes as "minimal modernism," a preoccupation with the development of "replacement technologies meant to substitute for infrastructural norms."[13]

Windows in Waiting

In the end, and after much preparatory work, the planned RCT did not go ahead, as it failed to secure the necessary funding. The problem, it transpired, was the proposed scale of the trial. The funders were worried that the study would be too small to power a statistically significant effect.

Arnold has since pursued other avenues for his doctoral research, and this has involved him in the evaluation of a different approach to the immune home. The Star Homes are a series of prefabricated, single-family houses designed by a Danish architecture firm with the purpose of sharply reducing entry by disease-carrying insects. Originally inspired by the design of rural homes in Southeast Asia, the two-story structures use a prefabricated, lightweight-gauge steel framework. Erected on a raised concrete foundation and with mesh wire paneling for walls, the homes can be constructed relatively quickly and require far less concrete than houses with a typical cement block design. The mesh provides shade and facilitates airflow, keeping the house cool during the day and inhibiting mosquito entry by reducing indoor levels of carbon dioxide. Doors fitted with springs offer an additional layer of security against mosquitoes and other disease-carrying invaders. In contrast to most rural homes in the Kilombero Valley, the Star Homes have an elevated sleeping area, a dedicated cooking space fitted with a chimney, and roof gutters to collect rainwater and drain it into PVC water tanks. Each house also comes equipped with an outdoor latrine and a fly-proof septic tank.[14]

A randomized controlled trial to measure the public health benefits of this design was conducted over several years in Mtwara, a coastal region in southern Tanzania. A success, the trial demonstrated a significant reduction in both the number of mosquitoes in the home and the risk of malaria transmission, when the Star Homes were compared with traditional houses.[15] The design also appears to have reduced the abundance of domestic flies, suggesting a positive impact on the incidence of diarrheal and respiratory infections.

The project has not been without its challenges, however, and these are mostly due, once again, to those ever-unpredictable "habits of the population." Of the approximately 500 families in the trial area, 110 received identical Star Homes. The new houses were free, but the gift came with the expectation that participants would take up residence with their children for the duration of the study. Such generosity generated suspicions, and it took the research team considerable effort to convince residents that nothing untoward would befall them in their new homes. The houses also required significant changes to domestic routines: high tables for cooking, screens between bedrooms, and the expectation that animals would not be kept inside the house. For some, these accommodations were too costly. Unapproved alterations were made to screens and doors, cooking continued to take place outside the designated area, and children were secretly sent away at night to sleep with kin.

Hearing Arnold recount some of the project's challenges, Lina is not surprised. Over the past few years, she has worked with homeowners, masons,

FIGURE 9.4. House on the outskirts of Ifakara Town. Photo by the authors.

and builders to study local construction practices: what improvements residents prioritize and which ones they defer, and what the trade-offs are between cost and quality. As her research makes clear, building a house is a stepwise process drawn out over many years—if it can ever be said to be complete—directed and financed by the residents themselves, who source most of the materials locally and regularly postpone structural work until cash becomes available.

Lina, who has just completed her own house in Ifakara and is familiar with masonry costs per square meter, notes that many residents lay foundations that are far too large for what they can afford to build. Rather than a mark of imprudence, this appears to her as a show of commitment, care, and ingenuity: evidence of residents sketching out a future home that matches their aspirations, if not their current means. Many of these houses in the making boast steeply pitched roofs—the kind you might associate with a Swiss village—while their interiors wait empty until a propitious windfall brings the resources necessary to build up the walls. In the meantime, they sometimes serve as allotments for growing crops and vegetables (figure 9.4).

Here, as elsewhere, construction provides the primary idiom through which the home is articulated: a marker of adulthood and personal growth, social status, and economic advancement for which "affective materials" such as baked bricks, cement, or corrugated iron are as salient as the built form they take.[16] The shells of houses that dot the landscape across the Kilombero Valley stand as a testament to those dreams and reflect the tactical sacrifices residents make in the face of fluctuations in the costs of raw materials, crop failure following a drought, or changes in family composition. These "inside-out" houses, to borrow Caroline Melly's term, index ideals of the modern house—a large dwelling with large windows, brick walls, and screened doors—and the long and bumpy journey to get there.[17] They materialize what Claire Mercer, in her study of middle-class construction in Dar es Salaam, Tanzania, describes as "the familiar rhythms of cash flow, materials acquisition and the faster and slower phases of the development of the building."[18]

FIGURES 9.5 AND 9.6. Completely or partially blocked windows in the Kilombero Valley. Photos by the authors.

The incremental process of house building is perhaps most visible in the awkward squares that hover mid-wall in many otherwise seemingly finished houses (figures 9.5 and 9.6). These are windows in waiting, future apertures blocked for the time being while the house owner awaits an inflow of cash to install frames, grills, and screens. The temporary brickwork that fills in the space will often remain in place for years—in many cases, forever. In the meantime, light and ventilation are secured by creating brick lattices or leaving eaves open. These windows in waiting exemplify the ebbs and flows of aspirational *house-ing*. They also link vernaculars of house construction with the preoccupations that animate the search for better measures of chemical protection.

Homes in the Meantime

Arnold's experience with the Star Homes has reinforced his sense of the importance of spatial and temporal in-betweens in the fight against malaria. The fact that the new houses looked very different from traditional ones mattered, of course, as people struggled to adapt to novel features and predetermined designs. But more than any uncanniness residents felt about their form, it was the alienation from processes of incremental improvement that made these houses such a challenging proposition for many. Since they were erected in a short period of time from materials of unknown provenance, the nature of these houses as gifts, and their disassociation from everyday strategies of self-realization, made it difficult for people to grant them the status of proper homes.

These insights have renewed Arnold's optimism for his eave ribbons. Rather than operating as a "fix" for poor or derelict houses, they could be used, he believes, to mitigate the specific mosquito-borne dangers that are introduced by the drawn-out, stepwise nature of construction and improvement. Transfluthrin-impregnated ribbons and other portable repellent products could be deployed tactically during those periods in a house's extended life history when its inhabitants are particularly exposed to malaria. They would provide yet another temporary adjustment as residents strategize the next steps in the ongoing upgrading of their living conditions. In this way, the portability and lightness of the ribbons would be enfolded into a larger and longer-term project of material amelioration, rather than providing a justification for its abandonment. Affixed around a not-yet-finished window, for example, transfluthrin emanations would reduce the risks created by brick lattices or the eaves used for ventilation. Rather than an outline that registers an absence, the window in waiting could in this way acquire a double purpose—an opening not just to the outside but from the house onto the world and its contingencies; a platform for progressive *house-ing* to which the ribbons will meaningfully contribute.[19]

This volume reminds us that the house is a drawn-out vital project, a sustained endeavor—shaped by material constraints—to upgrade living conditions.[20] It also suggests that the *oikos* comes about through intensive boundary work, a product of social coordinations enacted through domestic space but independent of any permanent demarcation between the interior and the out-of-doors.[21] How we understand the home has a direct bearing on how we imagine the scope for solidarity within the immunitary configurations that constitute human existence. Peter Sloterdijk likens modern domestic architecture to "a spatial immune system" whereby individuals live adjacent to, yet insulated from, neighbors defined by a situation of co-isolation: "Residence is, immunologically speaking, a defensive measure designed to demarcate a sphere of well-being from invaders and other agents of unwellness."[22]

Yet while they might appear inoculated from the kind of intricate comings and goings that characterize the home, these "co-isolated associations" generate new connections, dependencies, and exposures by virtue of their sheer physical proximity and reliance on shared infrastructures. As we learn time and again when the private dwelling becomes our last line of defense against a common threat, the immunitary paradigm at the core of the high-modern security regime is inequitable, fragile, and ultimately dangerous.[23] When total seclusion is the price of safety, the most immediate danger may be refracted for a while, but new and unexpected threats emerge in the meantime. Lasting immunity cannot result from compartmentalization and exclusion but, as Roberto Esposito writes, from "something more complex that implicates and stimulates the common."[24]

The question we started this essay with is whether spatial repellents can conjugate a different vision of the home, one attuned to forms of mutual obligation that cut across physically bounded domestic enclosures and are congruent with the gradual, aspirational nature of house construction. In the morally charged endeavor to assess the value of transfluthrin-impregnated eave ribbons, we observe an effort to calibrate the diffuse power of this slight yet far-reaching innovation.[25] By virtue of their atmospheric effects, and of the ease with which they can be installed, the ribbons project protection into the spatial and temporal in-betweens of social life. Chemically active in the peridomestic areas that extend the private dwelling, and across the prolonged temporalities of houses in the making, repellent products intervene into the interstices of everyday life—those interim situations and circumstances that have historically been ignored by malaria prevention programs but are increasingly central to malaria epidemiology. Lina and Arnold's fear that this chemical power would be used to (yet again) discard more permanent forms of improvement or development speaks to the long legacies of material neglect that contextualize global health interventions. Their desire to integrate the ribbons into vernacular strategies of collective upgrade expresses the hope that these in-betweens can perhaps become spaces of *communitas*, moments of collective care and improvement, rather than simply gaps where danger lurks.

NOTES

1. Swai et al., "Protecting Migratory Farmers"; Mmbando et al., "Eave Ribbons."
2. See Zacka, "What's in a Balcony?"
3. Scott-Smith, *Fragments of Home*.
4. Sambon and Low, "Experiments on the Mosquito-Malaria Theory," 520.
5. Longobardi, *Land-Reclamation in Italy*, 8. See also Evans, "European Malaria Policy"; and Snowden, *Conquest of Malaria*.
6. Packard, *Making of a Tropical Disease*; Anne Wilson et al., "Importance of Vector Control."
7. James and Shute, "Report on the First Results."
8. Alvarado and Bruce-Chwatt, "Malaria," 90.
9. Pierre Bernard, "Remarks on the Eradication of Malaria in Inter-Tropical Africa," document no. WHO/Mal/403, World Health Organization, Geneva, 1963.
10. Masalu et al., "Potential Benefits."
11. Celli, quoted by Ferroni et al., "Angelo Celli," 37.
12. Celli, quoted by Ferroni et al., "Angelo Celli," 37.
13. Redfield, "Shacktopia," 18.
14. Mshamu et al., "Assessing the Impact"; Knudsen and von Seidlein, *Healthy Homes*.
15. Mmbando et al., "Effect of a Novel House Design."
16. Archambault, "'One Beer, One Block'"; Degani, "Air in Unexpected Places."

17. Melly, *Bottleneck*, 100. See also Brownell, *Gone to Ground*; Bofu et al., "Needs and Opportunities."

18. See Mercer, *Suburban Frontier*, 113.

19. Biehl, "Insurgent Archivings."

20. See Motta, "Dying Home"; Neiburg, "Multiscale Home."

21. Douglas, "Idea of a Home."

22. Sloterdijk, *Foams*, 535.

23. Sánchez-Criado, "Immunity Beyond the Home."

24. Esposito, *Immunitas*, 18.

25. See Kelly and Lezaun, *Mosquito Work*, ch. 4.

ALEXANDRA MIDDLETON

10

Home and the Human Machine

Amid an array of wires protruding from the neurostimulator to where his arm once was, electrical currents dancing like fluorescent light trails on the computer screen above, Olof was asked the simultaneously simplest and most complicated question: *What do you feel?* After fumbling for an answer that included the words "numb" and "electric," Olof would later explain to me, "Sitting in the laboratory, hooked up to the neurostimulator, you feel in a different way. You must take the prosthesis home, where there are more distractions, to see what changes."

Olof is one of five people in the world, all based in Sweden, living with a neuromusculoskeletal prosthetic arm—a cutting-edge technology at the frontier of the burgeoning neuroprosthetics field. It is intimately integrated with bone, with electrodes implanted on muscles and wrapped around nerves. These prostheses, developed in clinical trials run by an engineering laboratory and university hospital in Sweden, are intuitively steered through the person's thoughts and intentions, with the capacity to perceive sensory feedback (touch) via electrical stimulation delivered to the residual limb's nerves. While a range of sophisticated bionic limbs has flooded the prosthetics market in recent years, there remains a dearth of ways to functionally connect these with the human body to render them useful, particularly outside of controlled laboratory settings. The engineers and neuroscientists running these trials endeavor to engineer a system to interface body with machine and, in doing so, create a device that not only approximates a human limb but ultimately facilitates, in their words, "activities of daily living." Here, in the lab, Olof's prosthesis was being programmed with a "take-home system"—identifying settings and parameters of electrical waves to facilitate his use of the sensory feedback system independently in his daily life.

In this way, these clinical trials are not only a technoscientific frontier of human-machine integration. They also constitute the first cases in the world in which such intimately integrated prostheses are taken out of the lab and used freely by people at home, all while still being studied in an ongoing clinical trial. Patient-subjects such as Olof are at once both subjects of a trial and subjects of their own daily lives; the neuromusculoskeletal prosthesis moves with them as they navigate shifting terrains and subjectivities. How does the home, as Olof suggests, figure not as a peripheral site of use but as an integral site of this science in the making?

Over two years, from 2018 to 2020, I conducted ethnographic fieldwork, moving with patients and their prostheses recursively among laboratory, clinical, industrial, and home sites throughout Sweden. Early on, I began noticing the ways "the home" and "daily life" were continually invoked and construed by my interlocutors—both experimenters and patient-subjects. In the clinic, patients' homes were framed as zones of disappearance—"gray zones," as one physiotherapist called them. "They [patient and device] disappear for two months at home and then come back to the [lab/clinic], and we just don't know what happened in between," she told me. For my engineering interlocutors, the home was an enigmatic site of use, external to the experiment. Reflexive and aware of their own epistemic limits, they voiced genuine concerns I shared as an anthropologist. The principal investigator of the trials spoke of the tension between "making cool science" and "making something useful, functional, for people" and pondered the question "What matters most to these people, in their lives?" Yet seated at the lab bench that day, hooked up to the neurostimulator, with the claim that at home "you *feel* in a different way," Olof was pointing to something that exceeded the functional and technical concerns of the scientists, engineers, and physiotherapists. In their homes and with their bodies, patients complicated the promissory, at times normative, expectations embedded in this discourse—about both the body and the home.

In the lab's discourse of "at-home use," it was not only the technology that was getting domesticated, as narratives of biotechnology often go, but also the prosthesis itself that was rehoming life in the house by facilitating a return to "acts of daily living." Yet in visiting patients' homes from the southernmost to the northernmost reaches of Sweden, staying in their guest rooms and mobile homes, cooking and eating meals with their families and engaging in said activities of daily living alongside them, I came to perceive how homes were sites not only of use and function but also of relational and sensory intensities that placed demands on the experiment itself. At home, a prosthesis had to work in the way the lab experiments configured—first with the basics, such as opening and closing a hand, then with more sophisticated home tasks mimed in clinical tests, such as making a sandwich and pinning clothes to a clothesline and packing a suitcase. But it also needed to work in an entirely other sense: to fit into a constellation of relations and meaning making in home life in Sweden, not to mention the individual body and social life of its user. While actively folding the prosthesis into a vibrant web of ongoing activities and relations, homes and bodies were also sites of resistance and interference, surges and short circuits. It was not only the prosthetic hand that opened and closed, but the body and home too. In this chapter, I consider how the prosthesis becomes a core heuristic for the house and body as sites of opening and closing, making and breaking, negotiating and dissolving relations, as homes and bodies establish themselves as sites of ongoing experimentation.[1] The experiment of neuroprosthetic living involves coming home to the house with the prosthesis as well as coming home to the technologically mediated body in a way that is personal, specific, and agentive.

Sensory and Relational Intensities

Elsa and Moa never knew their father with two arms. Olof lost his right arm in a traumatic accident working on a Swedish sea barge off the coast of England more than a decade before Elsa, his first child, was born. For nearly twelve years, Olof abandoned his prosthesis, preferring to live without one. Olof's "stump," as the family collectively referred to his residual limb, was "cozy," as his youngest, Moa, put it, as we all sat around the family's kitchen table on a late Saturday morning sharing *fika*—coffee and pastries. "It was like a pillow," Elsa mused. "They would cuddle with it, even fall asleep on it," Olof's wife, Catrin, recounted.

Prior to his entry into the clinical trial and the implantation of the titanium rod into his humerus that would later harness his neuromusculoskeletal prosthesis, Olof told me, his daughters' touch on the surface of his stump would calm his raging phantom limb pain. I asked him if any touch would do, or if it was specifically his daughters' or wife's touch that provided relief. "Other than myself, they were the only ones who touched my stump," he explained.

Catrin turned to Elsa. "Elsa? Do you remember when Pappa had his operation and was home? Do you remember what that was like?"

"I remember . . . that it was really nice!" Elsa recalled with a smile. Olof and Catrin laughed, the creases of their eyes softening. "Cozy?" Catrin prodded. Elsa agreed. "Yes. We would just lie on the couch and watch films together."

"We talked a lot about the operation beforehand with the children," Catrin explained to me. "Because for them, it was totally natural that he had a stump. So after the surgery . . ."

"It was *weird*," Elsa finished her mother's sentence. "Because he didn't usually have a screw there, and then he had a screw. Also the stump was now shorter."

"A few centimeters," Olof clarified.

"There was a lot you didn't like about Pappa's screw," Catrin prodded Elsa.

"It was strange. Because I had never seen Dad with an arm. He was always without an arm," Elsa replied.

"When Elsa and Moa were small babies, normally when you lift babies this way," Olof said, demonstrating with his left arm and his prosthesis, grabbing Elsa below the armpits and mimicking a lift. "But I did it this way," he demonstrated with his stump. "The thing was, when I picked you up from school, you would run to me and want me to lift you up, and when you got to this position you would turn around," Olof recalled, while Elsa mimed: running toward her father in slow motion, slowly spinning around right as she reached him, approaching with her back turned. It was as if the two were rehearsing a play. "Now you're starting to get heavy!" he joked to Elsa. I saw, with her back turned, how Elsa's arms could drape over Olof's stump as it lay across her chest, creating an extra grip, allowing him to lift her more securely.

"Moa started in day care, and the teachers thought it was quite strange. Why are they turning their backs to their father?" Olof reminisced with a chuckle. The girls grinned. Here, Olof and his daughters were habituating their own bodies in relation to each another, an experimental creativity that defied social expectations of how bodies meet with their own practices of lived intimacy.

These descriptions of touch and intimacy between a father and his daughters made me recall an archetype I had often heard circulate in the neuroprosthetics sphere at industry conferences, touting the promises of prosthetic sensory feedback: the possibility of once again being able to touch (and feel) a child's hand in one's own. This affectively charged image seemed to speak directly to the heartstrings, conjuring up the most indelibly human sense of all—the ability to feel and share feeling with another. And yet, here Olof and his daughters were, creating these intimacies in alternative ways. How, then, did the sensory feedback system Olof was now test-driving at home square with this creative and deeply personal touch?

While the clinical trial's principal investigator would often claim that the very first patient-subject wore his prosthesis all day, "even while sleeping," as a testament to its integration in daily life, Olof developed a selective approach to when and where he used his prosthesis at home. For Olof, certain domains of social life did not need, or were even impeded by, prosthetic touch. Olof relayed to me that he preferred to shake hands using his biological hand, for the sake of the person he was greeting ("My prosthesis is cold; it's kind of strange") as well as his own ("I like the feeling of the handshake; with my prosthesis, it's impersonal"). An avid runner, he left his prosthesis at home during runs, citing an imbalance in weight that impeded a sense of moving unencumbered through the forest. Olof removed his prosthesis at night, he told me, because his wife lay to his right in the bed, the same side as his prosthesis. He didn't want the cold plastic to be a barrier between their warm bodies. His wife did not touch his prosthesis often, choosing instead to reach for his biological hand. What he lost in sensory feedback by removing the prosthesis, Olof explained, he gained in social intimacy.

I had anticipated that somehow, acquiring sensory feedback might change that relationship between cold plastic and one with feeling. Furthermore, I was expecting that sensory feedback would feature prominently in social relations at home. But when I asked Olof questions about the possibilities of social touch through a prosthetic hand, he diverted them—indicating these weren't the important questions to be asking. "For me the sensory feedback from the prosthesis is not connected to touching other people," he said decidedly. "It's more . . . when touching other objects. Object to object. Still, even with sensory feedback, it's very artificial." Here Olof underscored a stark difference between social touch, object touch, and what he called object-to-object touch. I took this to mean that, for Olof, the prosthesis in this touch encounter was itself an object touching another object, as opposed to an aspirational body part, and the sensory vibrancies of touch at home made this distinction all the more pronounced.

At that time, Olof had just received the take-home system from the lab. Despite the misgivings and continual state of becoming that characterized the sensory feedback system in its early years, Olof expressed ambivalence, carving out room for the possibility that these touch dynamics would change: "To find a sensation that feels natural, I think that's very difficult and won't happen during my lifetime. But to get a signal that is helpful, that can probably happen." Olof's hopes and expectations were measured, and they seemed to align with the lab's intention: not necessarily to recreate natural touch, however it was defined, but rather to facilitate a helpful transfer of sensory information, all with the goal of optimizing prosthetic function. But what function meant, and if it meant something entirely different in the home, was an open question.

A Malleable Interface

Most afternoons, when Olof returned home from work, he would remove the more anthropomorphic SensorHand, the one provided by the clinical trial, which he wore largely for social purposes to elicit less attention from colleagues. He would promptly exchange it for a claw-like prosthetic arm he had purchased online. Olof would connect this claw arm directly with his bone-integrated implanted interface, sans sensory feedback. The first time he showed the claw to me, at his kitchen table, I was struck by its resemblance to the head of a set of pliers, roughly the size of a human palm. Rolling down the skin-like rubber covering of his SensorHand, Olof removed the hand with its five articulated fingers and replaced it with the claw. I noticed how nonanthropomorphic it looked.

Olof showed me how he could intuitively open and close the claw in much the same way as the SensorHand. "These fingers"—he gestured to the fourth and fifth fingers of his SensorHand—"are pretty much useless. When you want to use these," he pointed to the second and middle fingers and the thumb, gesturing a grasp, "[the claw] is more robust." He described being able to help his wife trim plants in the garden with more precision than had been possible before. "And I have other hands, too, you know," he continued, referring to one his prosthetist had specifically designed for his participation in sports—namely skiing and paddling. Olof planned to build an entire deck in the backyard that summer and didn't intend to ask for help from his neighbor.

Substitutions such as Olof's claw were oriented toward his own sense of functionality and also served as a stopgap for the unevenness of scientific progress, when elements of the experiment didn't go as planned. While the sensory feedback take-home system was still in its early stages of development, Olof found that activating sensory feedback could inadvertently cause the prosthetic hand to open against his will, pitting function and feeling against one another. I heard other patients reference similar instances of electrical cross talk and signal interference. Just walking by a conduction stove or lifting the arm to the level of a microwave in a kitchen could trigger the hand to open on its own accord, a reminder that the home, too—just like the body—had its own electrical field.[2]

The environs of patients' homes introduced new interactions within the human-prosthesis relationship. Here, the two systems in communication (body and prosthesis) in the experiment were opening up to a third system—the home as a vibrant environment, a social-material domestic world—complicating the appearance of what the lab framed as a "bidirectional" interface.[3] I wondered if these were the "distractions" Olof was referring to when he said, "You must take the prosthesis home, where there are more distractions, to see what changes." Whereas the laboratory was set up particularly to limit confounding variables, the home was replete with them.

Olof described the prosthesis as *själv-villig* (self-willing) when it opened and closed on its own, without his intention. This influenced his and other patients' degree of trust in carrying fragile items in the home, such as a glass or a cell phone, or, even more fragile, an infant. More than one patient voiced concern that the prosthesis's mechanical strength, if acting aberrantly, might inadvertently harm another's hand during a handshake or a small child during a caress. Trust in prosthetic control was dependent on use, which was dependent on practice, but practice depended on trust. The three were entangled, and the home—where the bulk of neuroprosthetic living took place—was the testing ground of this entanglement.

Occasions of interference, however rare, were not inconsequential. They destabilized the sense of who was controlling whom: "Was that me? Or the prosthesis?" This cut—between subject and prosthesis—challenged what the lab called "prosthetic embodiment," defined as the extent to which a patient experienced a "sense of agency" and "ownership" over the arm as a part of the body.[4] A sense of embodiment in relation to a prosthesis, I would come to learn from my patient interlocutors, was experienced not as static, or even earned by time and practice, but rather as vacillating and intimately context dependent, unfolding in micromoments before disappearing once more; undone in instants where the prosthesis—or home or body—misbehaved.

When sensory feedback bristled against the reliability of prosthetic function, patients made their own interventions—such as turning off the feedback or substituting a more utilitarian claw for the SensorHand. Deciding when to use (opening the body to) and when not to use (closing the body to) the neuromusculoskeletal prosthesis in its intended way was not necessarily an outright rejection but a relational boundary working that wove an object of ongoing experimentation into the experiment of one's own life. Olof's chosen removals and substitutions seemed a small symbol of the ways in which a prosthesis, even among the most highly sophisticated and technologically advanced, does not always, nor need always, stand in for the missing arm.

Swedish Experimental and Domestic Aesthetics

Each of my visits to a patient's home would begin the same way: They would lead me on a tour of each room, proudly pointing out the details—renovated furniture, secondhand flea-market finds, a self-built kitchen. I

FIGURE 10.1. In the homes of prosthesis research subjects, tinkering projects–whether on cars, furniture, or gardens–were often underway. Photo by the author.

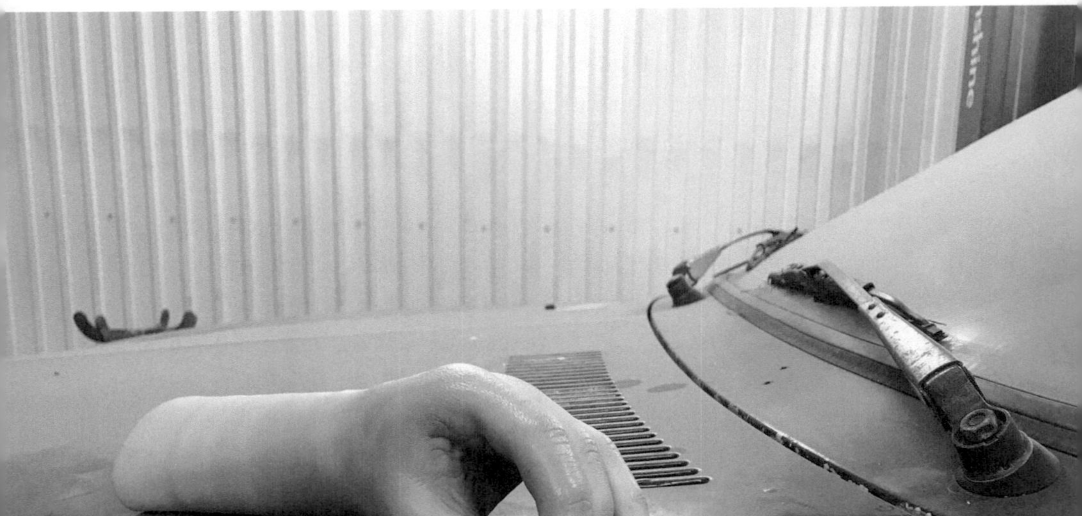

began to perceive how patients' own handiwork practices in their domestic landscape—Olof's garden and self-built deck among them—influenced how they interacted with their prosthetic limbs as ongoing sites of experimentation. Most of my patient-interlocutors were self-described manual laborers: electricians, truck drivers, mechanics, ship workers. In fact, the cases of limb loss in this trial were predominantly related to traumatic workplace accidents with machines, as opposed to causes such as chronic disease, congenital limb loss, or even war injury. Many lived in rural communities in which their local identities were tightly coupled with their manual labor. Their tinkering trickled into the home, where renovations and building projects were always underway.

There is a particularity here to the home in the context of manual labor in Sweden that cannot be overstated—rather, it must be emphasized to avoid essentializing the home as a homogenous and universalized site and instead tend to its situatedness as a locale of personal expression, a social ethic of discipline and improvement, and an aesthetics of self-building. While the laboratory running the trials was a high-level university lab made up of an international group of scientists and engineers coming and going, the first prototypes of the neuromusculoskeletal prosthesis landed squarely in the homes of these five Swedish citizens, four of whom were male. This, I argue, embeds specific ways of relating to and through the prosthesis-body-home as sites of production, renovation, discipline, aesthetics, making, and a particular form of masculinity and labor.

Sweden, itself home to a design aesthetic that emphasizes efficiency, functionality, and minimalism, has its own social history of space and subject making. In his ethnography of Swedish design, Keith Murphy traces historical political ideologies into domestic spaces to show how Swedish welfare politics and design aesthetics are entangled, and how everyday objects are imbued with social democratic ideologies.[5] The physical home in Sweden is a site of constant work, pride, updating, renovation, and improvement. Design, for Swedes, is not only a form of expertise; it is a diffuse and democratized practice in which everyone is a designer of their own domestic world (one need look no further than the now ubiquitous Swedish design house IKEA, whose motto roughly translates to "creating a better everyday life for the many people").

I witnessed this ethos bear out in the practices of my patient-interlocutors, each of whom seemed to be constantly building and renovating things in their domestic spheres (literal homes, but also beds, armoires, porches, cars, gardens). They demonstrated a notable degree of pride in and care for material possessions, a care that Murphy argues reflects the expectation that "the Swedish political system is organized to 'care' for its citizens."[6] These contexts—of work, homemaking, and belonging in Sweden—embed ideals of what a body (and hand) can and should do and, in turn, condition expectations for prosthetic function in the design of the neuromusculoskeletal prosthesis itself. They also implicitly establish certain taken-for-granted norms about body, labor, and identity—by virtue of a subject pool that is small, homogenous, overwhelmingly white, mostly male, and middle-aged—that bear consequence as these prostheses scale toward a future global market horizon, moving into other kinds of homes. Attending critically to this situatedness is essential to understanding how the home figures in this particular ethnographic context.

I mark this brief history here to situate the prosthesis within coexisting relations among homes, objects, repair, care, and the laboring body in Sweden. This circumstance, in which the home itself is a site of constant work and tinkering, influences the way people engage with their prostheses at home. In garages and workstations and gardens, as well as amid the intimacies of family life, the prosthesis figures not only as a limb but also as an object porous to intervention. For these patients, living in a postamputation body was also a process of restoring an identity tightly coupled with making and building (at) home.

Such was especially the case for Jesper, the last patient-subject enrolled in the clinical trial during my fieldwork. Jesper had lost his arm in a factory accident with a glass pellet grinder in a small town in southern Sweden. He was by many counts prolific, perhaps even more so after the accident: He had (literally) single-handedly renovated his sister's house down the road after his amputation and prior to receiving the neuromusculoskeletal prosthesis. Jesper and his wife often refurbished secondhand furniture together. After Jesper's implantation with the neuromusculoskeletal prosthesis, his wife would often send me videos of Jesper working in his garage using a pliers-like hand similar to Olof's, called a *Greifer*, to manipulate wires or pour liquid from a bottle into a glass. A hand-painted sign Jesper had made himself hung by the family's front door, imploring patience: "Nothing is impossible, some things just take a longer time"—Jesper's personal motto for overcoming adversity postamputation. This patience, however, was not inexhaustible. Once, frustrated by long waiting times at the clinic, Jesper took to using a soldering iron in his garage on his own skin, cauterizing a wound at the site where the titanium rod exited his residual limb. The prosthesis and the home were not Jesper's only sites of intervention; so, too, was his body itself.

On my final visit to a patient's home, right before the COVID-19 pandemic broke out, Jesper proudly, if not also somewhat shyly, led me to his garage to show me a contraption of his own making. Grabbing a stepladder to reach above a cabinet, he proffered a slick, black-and-silver prosthetic limb. The upper arm was made of black leather, with four thin silver buckles suturing the material together, up the outside of the arm. The lower forearm was a steel canister of sorts, featuring a pressure valve. The body of the hand was gear-like—a montage of hollowed-out, grease-stained screws with ringlike transparent centers—and the fingers were slightly rounded and claw-like, steel. "Steampunk," Jesper said proudly.

Jesper demonstrated how his steampunk limb was an assemblage of spare parts from his home projects. While it clearly did not function in the sophisticated manner of the neuromusculoskeletal prosthesis, it functioned in an altogether other way: providing an opening to incorporate Jesper's own artistry, with aesthetic nods to his own craft, materially sustained by the objects in his home. I was admittedly arrested by the subversive quality of the steampunk limb: the way it played with technoscientific posthuman imaginaries by anchoring itself in a certain nostalgia and antiquity, undeniably personal and specific to Jesper himself. It seemed, in a way, to speak back to the idealized limb, but also to the idealized home. It was greasy, excessive (in incorporating excess materials), and in some ways dystopic, upending narrower visions of both scientific and social progress as unequivocally forward moving. While his steampunk limb did not necessarily replace his neuromusculoskeletal one, it did gesture to a sliver of resistance to the reigning ideologies housed in the experiment—a playful entry, another opening.

FINILEC
DEKKTETT
TOUCH-UP PENCIL
FÄRGPENNA
STYLO-RETOUCHE
LACKSTIFT

FIGURE 10.2. In the garage of a research subject, a prosthetic glove literally points toward ongoing projects of making and building at home. Photo by the author.

The Labor of Laboratory and Locatory

Participating in the neuromusculoskeletal prosthesis clinical trial was not only an upfront commitment, even for the formal one-year parameter of study. It was, at its best, an entry into an ongoing, lifelong relationship with a device that would be, for the foreseeable future, under continual titration and improvement. A series of recommitments was continually remade, as in any relationship, and the home was the site where the consequences of this were dealt with and felt. As the first patient-subject to live with a neuromusculoskeletal prosthesis, Rasmus once told me, "In the lab, [the principal investigator] is the boss of my arm. But at *home*, in my world, *I* am the boss." Rasmus's cunning words have lingered with me, a reminder of how experimental subjectivity shifts in relation to a sense of place. I took being "the boss" to mean that, at home, Rasmus gained a sense of agency, control, and autonomy. The importance of the home as a key site of science in the making is not just an analytic device of interest to the anthropologist; it is of emic concern and curiosity to those living with the neuromusculoskeletal prosthesis. This confluence of highly experimental, yet simultaneously lived-with, science gives way to what I call a *domestic lived science*: the ways people improvise with, build relationships with (sometimes against), and affect technologies in everyday home life, and by doing so contribute to, even pioneer, material and conceptual makings of science.

Domestic lived science recasts the home from a lacuna or gray zone, into which the subjects and objects of science disappear between clinical visits, to a zone of generativity and emergence in its own right. The laboratory can no longer be taken for granted as the sole locus of the experiment, with everything else that happens beyond it as the margins. Traditional lab studies reinscribed the notion that homes exist peripherally to translational medicine's formal knowledge making, or at the end of a long teleological chain in which a device is prototyped in the lab and later used in the home.[7] Science and technology studies have productively troubled and dissolved the "inside/outside dichotomy," or the assumption that laboratories are contained by impermeable walls—black boxes producing indisputable scientific facts.[8] In seeking to account for domestic lived science, I was initially tempted to frame the

FIGURE 10.3. The “steampunk” limb. Photo by the author.

home as its own sort of laboratory, or an extension of it. Yet such a framing can verge toward a placelessness: that the laboratory is everywhere, and thus nowhere, all at once. And while digital surveillance, smart-home appliances, and self-tracking systems have accelerated a technical-industrial gaze into homes, user experience research tends to posit the user as consumer rather than maker, undercutting the value of their contributions to the interface itself.[9] In these myriad approaches, the plasticity and generativity, but also specificity, of domestic life are too often congealed. They also undercut the fact that homes are always already sites of experimentation, alongside the mundaneness of everyday life.

I interpret homes themselves as ongoing experimental spaces, rather than as laboratories. As experiments travel across sites (national, physical, digital), they bring affective, material, and social entanglements with them—and introduce new ones.[10] At the same time, a sedimentation occurs among a particular body-prosthesis-home that scales down the experiment, making local social and relational intensities matter. The home could be said to be a *locatory* as opposed to a laboratory. Michael Guggenheim describes locatories as "distinct spaces of doing science" in which "specific knowledge-claims can be made, which are not possible in other places."[11] Domestic lived science offers both a methodological and a theoretical lens to consider how everyday life contributes to knowledge making and materialization. Ethnographic attention to domestic lived science elucidates the relational labor of coming to live intimately with a device, as opposed to encountering the device (or body) as already made. Here, the home becomes not just a site of use but a site of invention and meaning making. Domestic lived science gathers from the margins less-than-accounted-for forms of knowledge—informal, embodied, social, material, local—that centrally participate in the making of biomedical technologies. In doing so, it expands our collective sense of where invention, knowledge, evidence, and the cutting edge come from to include the subjects, bodies, and homes of experimental science alongside its formal makers.

Olof's chosen removals and claw, Jesper's self-soldering and steampunk limb . . . these interventions with the prosthesis in the home far exceeded the lab's notion of "activities of daily living." Underlying these tweaks and substitutions were, of course, the patients' own sense of what facilitated involvement with daily life but also a sense of the prosthesis as part of their other ongoing home experiments. The neuromusculoskeletal prosthesis inhabits the home alongside (and within and through) the human body and subject.

Nerve, muscle, bone, titanium, electrodes, and flesh interface with one another but also, in different ways, with the experiment's many sites—laboratory, clinic, industry, and home. These multiple scales of interfacing and making point to the material, spatial, and relational entanglements of *embodiment* and *emplacement*. I approach embodiment as my patient-subjects describe living in a postamputation body with (and sometimes without) a prosthesis: vacillating, context dependent, subjective, profoundly fraught, worked on, both painful and pleasureful. By *emplacement*, I mean how the body is emplaced in the home and functions in particular ways in the domestic landscape that are meaningfully different from how it operates in the formal sites of experimental science.

To understand the relationship of embodiment with emplacement in neuroprosthetic living, I turn toward phenomenologist Martin Heidegger's framing of a relationship between *building* and *dwelling*. "We attain to dwelling, so it seems, only by means of building," writes Heidegger. "Building is not merely a means and a way toward dwelling—to build is itself already to dwell."[12] One could say that the experimental prosthesis makes possible a certain kind of dwelling through patients' own domestic practices of building. While the prosthesis prefigures a certain kind of dwelling through laboratory practices of making, its movement into the home opens a space for resistance to reigning technoscientific imaginaries about what a limb can and should be. I think through house-body-prosthesis as making life together in a scientific kinship that is produced and sustained through building and dwelling: making a limb to dwell with; dwelling with a limb porous to making.

There is something to the work of building that is recuperative for understanding how prosthesis and human come to meaningfully dwell together in a home, a body. In writing about the prosthesis as a heuristic for the home, I write away from several other framings that constrain theorizing and analysis of the relationships among bodies, technologies, and homes. I am acutely aware of the tendency to deploy the prosthesis as a trope or metaphor, making the device itself stand in for something else while erasing its user's agency and subjectivity, and of propensities to collapse the frictions between bodies and technologies with the gloss of a cyborgian hybridity.[13] What these rhetorical devices miss is the ongoing embodied labor that goes into producing and sustaining a relationship with a novel and unprecedented biotechnology, particularly one intimately entwined with the body. This labor is profoundly fraught and negotiated, and, importantly, the bulk of it takes place in the home. Domestic lived science makes tangible a different kind of labor performed by the patient-subject—and the home—beyond the clinical trial's own apparatus. In attuning to less-accounted-for forms of labor in clinical trials, I argue that experimental labor is done not only on the defined premises of the experiment, but more largely by patients' ongoing subjectivity and relation making with their prostheses at home.[14] In addition to the conceptual and material changes grounded in patients' home experiences and interventions, this labor also entails endurance and resilience when things, inevitably, fall apart.

In many ways, the home and the laboratory are united by their mundaneness. Living with a neuromusculoskeletal prosthesis entails maintenance, care, and upkeep. Long stretches of time in which the prosthesis was shipped out for repair, a spare part was in transit, an infection threatened the skeletal implant, or a patient's own neuromuscular signals failed to be read by the device demanded creativity and endurance. Through their own stories, patients show how this dwelling-with is continually renegotiated, the enactment of one relationship among the entanglements and demands of other relations. Things falling apart exposed just how much ongoing labor—social, emotional, and practical—took place in the home, outside the formal purview of the trial but necessarily a part of it. That the making of the neuromusculoskeletal prosthesis was, and still is, a process of false starts, troubleshooting, breakdown, and repair is perhaps no surprise to those intimately acquainted with the rhythms of biomedical engineering and technological development. But it is also the kind of narrative that gets easily glossed over in what Steven Jackson refers to as the "simplest *Wired* magazine form" of framing the "cutting-edge," in which "these stories posit a simple causal arrow: technology accelerates, and life adjusts."[15] This is the very underbelly of what gets missed when we ignore the home as a site of science in-the-making.

Interpreting the experimental prosthesis as an oikographic instrument is an effort to recuperate the prosthesis from its narrative extensions and technoscientific imaginaries, making it emic again—to the body, subject, and home in question. This approach attunes us to both the ongoing labor of making embodied human-machine relations—of its openings and closings—and the local emplacement in which this unfolds. It works against an essentialized prosthesis just as it works against an essentialized home, nuancing the question of how an individual comes to live with/among/against an embodied machine in the fabric of a life. This is precisely why we need to look closely at the home and, by doing so, expand the sense of what, who, and where counts as the experiment.

NOTES

This chapter draws on material in my book *The Connector: Living with Experimental Neuroprosthetics* (Durham, NC: Duke University Press, 2026).

1. Strathern, *Reproducing the Future*.

2. While this occurrence was more common with traditional prostheses with surface electrodes, the trials' implanted electrodes were not always impervious to such interactions.

3. Ortiz-Catalan et al., "Self-Contained Neuromusculoskeletal Arm Prostheses."

4. Zbinden et al., "Prosthetic Embodiment."

5. Murphy, *Swedish Design*. The centrality of the home to Swedish political ideology is apparent in the concept of *folkhemmet* (the people's home)—a particular sociopolitical configuration of belonging and citizenship that emerged with the Social Democratic Party's rise in the 1920s. The political reforms that emerged from this period extend to Sweden's present-day universal health care system and ethos of a science-state nexus (see Asdal and Gradmann, "Introduction") with generous public funding, making clinical trial participation possible for these patient-subjects in particular, localized ways.

6. Murphy, *Swedish Design*, 2.

7. Knorr Cetina, "Laboratory Studies."

8. Latour, "Give Me a Laboratory," 153.

9. Zuboff, *Age of Surveillance Capitalism*; Lupton, *Quantified Self*; Hassenzahl and Tractinsky, "User Experience."

10. Petryna, *When Experiments Travel*; Martin, "Anthropology and the Cultural Study"; Song, *Biomedical Odysseys*.

11. Guggenheim, "Laboratizing and De-Laboratizing," 111.

12. Heidegger, "Building Dwelling Thinking," 143.

13. Jain, "Prosthetic Imagination"; Sobchack, "Leg to Stand On"; Kurzman, "Presence and Prosthesis"; Haraway, "Cyborg Manifesto."

14. Petryna, *When Experiments Travel*; Cooper and Waldby, *Clinical Labor*.

15. Jackson, "Speed, Time, Infrastructure," 170.

PART VI

Toxic Environs

CATHERINE FENNELL

11

The House Underfoot

Before the pandemic sent all its proceedings online, the Housing Section of the Circuit Court of Cook County in Chicago was a place where you could witness one of that county's estimated fifty thousand vacant residential buildings come to one kind of end. In a series of windowless rooms off a main corridor, judges would hear cases concerning code violations: everything from collapsing walls and missing window boards to the refuse, weeds, rodents, and dogs that accumulated in and around vacant buildings. If compounding fines and repair orders remained unresolved, a building's file would eventually land around the corner in a room reserved for the most stubborn cases. Over the year and a half that I observed the "Demolition Call" operate in this room, presiding judges would offer a final grace period to those responsible for a building. If these parties could still not achieve compliance over the ensuing months, or if they stopped appearing, or if they had never appeared in the first place because the city could never locate them, then a five-minute trial would ensue. The judge would almost always approve the city's request for forfeiture and demolition. Many residential buildings that landed in the Demolition Call lie on the South and West Sides—that is, in places that racial violence, discrimination, and segregationist policies have fashioned into "Black neighborhoods."[1]

If you walked down the side corridor and turned another corner, you could land in a room whose origins also lie in attempts to manage uncertain presences on Chicago's streets: the antechamber adjacent to the women's toilets. Progressive Era reformers once pushed for the installation of such rooms in municipal, educational, and civic buildings throughout the region. They argued that such rooms provided respectable women with a place to relax and be shielded from the dangers of street life while out on the town to travel, shop, learn, or settle affairs. On occasion you'll still come across lavish "ladies' resting rooms" throughout the city, some still boasting the trappings of respectable domestic comfort: armchairs, settees, even writing desks. Few would mistake the Housing Section's tiny resting room as an invitation to stretch out or pen a letter. Yet when the Demolition Call would convene to hear cases from disinvested West Side neighborhoods, this seemingly superfluous room was a respite. Women would sometimes pause here to smooth a suit before the mirror, to organize and review documents at its ledge, or to rehearse pleas for a judge to grant more time to settle violations. One morning I hurried past a woman praying aloud for the judge to spare her family's onetime home from demolition.

The House Underfoot

To think and write about housing in a place like Chicago's West Side is to turn corners and land constantly amid narratives that conjure disintegrating, disappearing, lost, and longed-for homes. Sometimes these narratives are expected, emerging within court proceedings, community meetings, and political hearings devoted to housing matters. Yet they flow just as readily from those who still live and work in neighborhoods once dense with a mix of industrial, commercial, and residential buildings. They also emerge in washes of fascination, pity, outrage, fear, and disgust from those who observe such places at more of a remove: inspectors, advocates, wreckers, developers, gentrifiers, journalists, and scholars. In a city such as Chicago—that is, in a city that has long pursued the criminalization, prosecution, and destruction of homes occupied or owned by Black people as a means to manage anxieties about shifting demographics and economic downturns—narratives of disintegrating, disappearing, lost, and longed-for homes have saturated public life for six to seven decades. To think and write about housing in a place like this, then, is to turn corners and be prompted constantly to add yet another entry to such a sprawling catalog of loss.

My twenty years of coming and going to and from the West Side and places like it have schooled me in the importance of cataloging lost homes. Local public housing residents, for instance, moved in the 1990s to document how the federal neglect of their buildings resulted in a glut of vacant and increasingly uninhabitable apartments. Their efforts allowed some displaced through public housing demolition to secure a place within the limited subsidized housing rebuilt in the area. More recently, long-term renters and homeowners living in the area's private housing have organized around preventing further vacancy. Their efforts have yielded limited home-repair assistance and tax relief for seniors. Younger, more radical activists have moved to hold banks to account for lending practices that intensified vacancy, while advocating for financing models to support new affordable housing on vacant land. Here, the act of cataloging loss bolsters legal and ethical claims that allow some long-term residents to stay in their homes and others to advocate for housing models that might likewise keep them in place. At the moment some high-vacancy neighborhoods undergo revaluation, countering housing loss and displacement promises concrete gains—everything from the ability to retain an increasingly valuable asset to the ability to enjoy the amenities that accompany reinvestment.

The catalog of loss that grounds contemporary housing politics in the urban American Midwest warrants the attention and respect of anyone concerned with collective welfare and justice in late industrial America. Yet I worry that fixations on lost housing and homes serve to intensify the air of deficiency that already suffuses neighborhoods like the ones I focus on. It becomes difficult to appreciate what is *still present* in places predicated on so much loss, and what people do with such presences as they continue to inhabit these places. This chapter is a step toward such an appreciation through the examination of a kind of place that is diffuse, opaque, and ubiquitous in areas such as Chicago's West Side. This is a kind of place composed of things that once hung together as a home. Those components remain in the ground, just as they remain in the bodies of those who have moved within those homes and across the made ground they have become.

I didn't pay this place much notice for years, even though it grounded every moment I spent writing notes at a desk by a window that overlooked a vacant lot, walking desire lines locals had worn across lots as shortcuts, or socializing in the open spaces that abutted friends' homes. Sometimes those friends would, as they still do today, refer to the many gaps opening off the buildings they inhabit as "lots," "little fields," or "scattered" or "missing" teeth. This patchwork of open space did not emerge all at once. It opened little by little as spot demolitions and larger clearance projects began unfolding in the late 1940s. It has continued in fits and starts ever since. More concentrated periods clustered around urban renewal (known locally as "Negro removal") in the 1950s, a series of civil disturbances in the 1960s (known locally as "the Riots"), intensifying abandonment in the 1970s and 1980s, public housing demolition in the 1990s, and the years leading up to and following the subprime mortgage debacle. Each of these periods involved a mix of demolition practices. These practices have resulted in sites that for all the homogeneity implied by the term *vacancy* are characterized by considerable material heterogeneity.

Why did I lack curiosity about this place? The best I can say is that I had persuasive tools at hand that settled for me what these lots must be, so much so that I didn't watch or listen as carefully as I should have. I treated them as *stages* for personal and collective memories. Later I made them into *prompts* to elicit, distill, and—at my most mercenary—extract such memories. Or they were *indices* pointing to the political and economic forces that reached beyond these neighborhoods, the governmental strategies that wielded residential demolition to stimulate housing markets by attempting to contain racial and economic anxieties while safeguarding some people's investments. I would keep thinking and writing all this even as I would stand before students and insist that the issue with an anthropology of the house, and of built environments more broadly, was a stubborn tendency to keep reading power, order, meaning, habit, and practice *off* of material form. The durability and dynamism of domestic form itself, I would complain, keeps falling by the wayside. My complaints papered over a challenging problem and my inability to tackle it.

That all shifted in the fall of 2018 when I began trying a humbled hand at ethnographic research with a toddler in tow. Her presence shrank "the field" down for me, most days, to the three-block stretch that held our rental apartment, her day care, a playground, and a small farm from which we purchased vegetables. She would follow kittens that our neighbors let be in the hopes that they would join the feral clowder credited with keeping the local rat population in check. The kittens pulled us off the desire lines into what I was increasingly hearing our neighbors speak about as "weed trees"—an understory knitted with sumac shrubs and trees of heaven, tall grasses, blue chicory, and Queen Anne's lace, all of it clotted with plastic sacks, car parts, clothes, cans, nails, bits of glass, lumber, tile, and so many papers and cellophane wrappers. On laundry days I kept turning our pockets out to find what my daughter had plucked from the tumble: smoothed pieces of green or blue glass, toy figurines and marbles, but also bits of clinkers and slag—byproducts of yesteryear's domestic and industrial furnaces. She found ways to play with this clutch; I found ways to worry less about the grit it ushered into our home. As my attention slowed to match her studied movements through the fields, and over the brick, concrete, pipes, and wiring that poked up at our feet, I began to appreciate that we clambered on the roof of a place I had rushed across for years: the house underfoot.

Until the middle decades of the twentieth century, demolition had been a time-consuming process in the urban United States. It involved pulling a building apart piece by piece with tools and salvaging as many components as possible. Robust markets in reused building materials existed, which offset the considerable labor costs of demolition. By the 1950s, though, wrecking in urban America was well on its way to becoming quick and cheap. A small crew working in tandem with bulldozers or wrecking balls could have a single-family home or a smaller multiunit residential building down in a few days.[2] The process went even more quickly, and even more cheaply, if wreckers skipped salvage work or trips to the dump to deposit debris. They could pound a residential building down and fold its remains into what wreckers and inspectors I've observed refer to as "the hole," that is, into the foundations that, until quite recently, almost always remained on the site of a residential demolition. Wreckers could then apply a thin layer of soil or aggregate material, tamp the pile down, and move on. Mechanization rendered batch residential clearances thinkable and doable on a large scale, even as the

FIGURE 11.1. The house underfoot, Chicago's West Side, 2022. For decades, standard residential demolition practices in the region involved folding debris generated by mechanical wrecking into foundations that would remain on site. Over the years, this material subsides.

management of resulting refuse entered more shadowy realms. If inspectors or regulators turned their heads or had no strict policy on the matter, wreckers could forgo the work necessary to render fill "clean"—in this context, free not so much of toxins but of any organic materials that would decay quickly, namely wood. With the right connections or the boldness to bribe them into place, wreckers could dump anything that shouldn't go or didn't fit into "the hole" somewhere else. They could unload this stuff onto vacant neighborhoods whose residents did not command the clout to object. Some did just that; allegations and scandals concerning fly dumping have hounded demolition processes in the late industrial urban Midwest for decades.[3]

Many wreckers and salvagers I've spoken with in the region, as well as regulators, engineers, and also residents, recognize that historical and contemporary residential demolition practices present a range of problems that exceed scandal. Some focus on the immediate dispersal of hazardous debris and how it might compromise the health of those who live nearby. They also worry about those who take down a building, concerned that demolition laborers might take something dangerous "home" with them from work. The most thoughtful, technical, or simply litigation-minded have sought to suppress or contain debris dispersals. They recognize that health conditions related to exposure might take years to manifest, making it that much harder to tackle links between demolition and health. A handful take an even more capacious view when they speculate about what the practice of folding demolition's remains directly *into* the hole seeds over time. They point to depressions and concaves that have emerged across the surface of vacant lots as the voids in brick and stone-based fills subside, or the ponding that can occur on lots characterized by uneven compaction. They also suspect that when, or simply if, revaluation ever makes these lots an attractive prospect, developers with resources will just scoop demolition debris out and deposit it somewhere else, likely in or near another residential community lacking the resources or clout to refuse it. Gardeners and farmers attracted by the fields have taken comparable approaches. Those with time and resources will remove everything up to a foot and a half down and replace it with mulches, soil, and other amendments from sources they know or trust. Others will work with barriers, berms, raised beds, and grades to separate desired plants and animals from the suspect ground. When I visit with them, we climb *up* into their gardens and fields, several feet away from the house underfoot. Yet as the house underfoot settles and unfurls, it stands to usher all manner of dynamic, albeit uncertain, things into local domestic realms.

Long Footprints

One morning in the spring of 2005, I stood outside my neighbor's home in Chicago, a duplex built to house those displaced by the destruction of local housing projects. While waiting for Nayna, I absentmindedly traced shapes in the yellow film that had come over the past week to coat my kitchen windowsill, the cars parked along our street, and the railing leading up to her front door. She emerged, looked at my handiwork, and frowned. "We don't even know what was in those buildings," she muttered. "Now it's all over." What I had taken to be pollen from the vegetation that blanketed local lots, Nayna reframed as dust emanating from a large housing project undergoing demolition nearby. Nayna was active then in circles of displaced residents, the same groups who had pushed against unsafe building conditions within local projects. It was impossible to miss her drift: Neither relocated residents nor the new neighbors who tended to resent public housing residents' relocation to their blocks could outrun the risks, uncertainties, and insecurities of undermaintained public housing.

Nayna understated the case. Regulators, coordinators, and advocates I met years later while following efforts to develop guidelines for "safe" residential demolitions throughout the region have a name for the stuff that coated my finger that morning—"fugitive dusts": the particulate matter that escapes its emission source and becomes airborne through wind or human activities such as mining, agriculture, power production, or demolition. Over the two years they allowed me to observe them, their efforts focused on containment. They concerned themselves not so much with dusts emitted from a single, spectacular demolition like the one that preoccupied Nayna in 2005 but with high-vacancy residential neighborhoods being "hit," "dusted," or "dosed" again and again as wreckers intermittently took down smaller residential buildings. Almost everyone involved understood that total dust containment was a fantasy, even with elaborate and costly practices that included tents, sprays, chutes, tarps, and protective gear. Yet they disagreed profoundly about the long-term effects of such noncontainment and efforts to make demolition processes more accountable to public health.

Nayna underscored the stakes of such disagreements while attending a workshop with me in late 2021 regarding environmental hazards within public housing. During the discussion, she began wondering aloud how lead remediation could be considered a relatively settled issue in housing circles if new cases of lead poisoning kept plaguing local communities. She mentioned two small children recently diagnosed with learning and behavioral disorders attributed to lead poisoning. They had been living and playing in a redevelopment built to replace a housing project demolished over twenty years ago. A health scientist present observed that dispersed lead from past demolitions or car exhaust might still be present in the surrounds. It's the *exposure*, not the *presence*, that mattered most, he emphasized. Instances of childhood lead poisoning, he pointed out, had been steadily dropping in the United States. That drop coincided with regulations emerging in the 1970s that restricted the use of lead in residential paints and some gasolines. Housing advocates had also become more cognizant of effective remediation techniques. There are real achievements here, he insisted, real lessons.

The big picture that the scientist painted was right. Yet Nayna's comments danced around what this expert didn't say. Prevention strategies in his field tend to place responsibility for the everyday management of "legacy pollutants" on those who now live with them. Unless substantial negligence can be established on the part of, say, the manufacturer who created the substance and kept on distributing it despite growing knowledge of its harms, it is the current property owner who must manage its potential hazards. In places such as the West Side, a pollutant of particular concern is lead, a heavy metal that transformed paints and, with them, domestic interiors and tastes in the early decades of the twentieth century.[4] My collaborative surveys and samplings of local vacant residential lots suggest the ubiquitous presence of lead, and also additional substances of concern to health scientists, including cadmium, chromium, and barium. What's more, in places such as Chicago's West Side, an emphasis on property owners' responsibility goes hand in glove with established narratives about the presumed irresponsibility, ignorance, and incorrigibility of impoverished tenants—namely, women of color and their children.

In particular, lower-income Black women who rent within undermaintained housing stocks relayed to me a drumbeat of advice from health workers and advocates to monitor their children vigilantly lest they eat paint chips. Better informed health advocates and workers recognize "pica"—the compulsive eating of things like paint or dirt—to be a somewhat less common route into childhood lead poisoning. Small children engage in normal developmental behaviors that have them exploring their worlds as much with their mouths as with their hands. As those living in undermaintained homes crawl, climb, teeter, and steady themselves around floorboards, baseboards, and windowsills, as they suck on their hands and fingers and chew on anything available to diminish teething's discomforts, they can and do ingest dusts. These children do not eat lead; they ingest it.

Pragmatic health workers and advocates encourage caregivers to clean better lest the leaded dusts that settle across everyday surfaces resettle into children's bones and brains. Health workers consistently emphasize to impoverished caregivers that lead can impair their children's long-term capacities to learn and self-regulate. Some recognize that cleaning is no solution for interiors that simply give off lead. For many decades homeowners and landlords in the United States have been advised that lead paint poses little danger when encapsulated behind a "clean" barrier—in this context, not so much something free of toxins but rather something that blocks their movement: new tile, new wallpaper, a new layer of unleaded paint. And yet chronic undermaintenance compromises these containment strategies. Health workers and advocates who recognize that not every renter can simply leave or fix undermaintained rental housing advise caregivers to increase children's intake of calcium-rich milk or leafy greens. Stronger bones, they reason, will help exposed children better clear lead from their bodies. This is because lead can simulate calcium in the body of a calcium-deprived child. Her malnourished body stores lead in her bones. Bones later release lead during growth spurts as they would calcium. At the very moments a child's neural networks bloom and reorganize, a potent neurotoxin washes through her body. As serious and well-meaning as advice to *avoid* lead exposure is, it treats brain damage primarily as an effect of imperfect caregiving. The uneven social and material legacies of "legacy pollutants" fall by the wayside.

Caregivers internalize explanations about a lead-addled child's long-term prospects with the help of physicians and teachers. I could not help but notice the marked difference in how I heard differently positioned caregivers parse those prospects. "He's *disabled*," a Black mother living in public housing insisted to me in 2006. She was speaking of her teenage son as I helped the case managers who regularly worked with her assemble renewal paperwork for "his SSI." Here she referenced Supplemental Security Income, a federal program in the United States that provides modest monthly benefits to impoverished children and adults with disabilities. She knew that local gossip branded her son "slow," "hyper," and "bad"—that is, intellectually *and* behaviorally deficient. She took pains to remind everyone that his apparent deficiencies emerged from childhood exposure to aging lead paint; little could be done for him now. He had been on SSI for years, and she expected him to remain on it. Consider, by way of contrast, the remarks that a middle-class white father made to me in 2015. "She's OK now," he insisted of his then-teenaged daughter, with conviction that matched that of the mother I mention above. He recalled his family's early years in an intentional urban community, all of them renting a grand yet ramshackle home, all of them eating from a garden into which paint peeling from the siding regularly fell. They didn't think anything of it until a doctor flagged his daughter's blood test. His family leapt into immediate action. They left the community and relocated to a solidly upper-middle-class suburb known for its well-appointed homes and schools: "She's gotten so good at science." One group of caregivers I have spoken with holds fast to the idea of a child's permanent neurological damage, the other to its interruption and transcendence.

I also cannot help but notice the terms in which my own conversations with caregivers, health advocates, and educators mirror broader discourses about lead poisoning in the urban United States. Psychologists understand that impaired executive functioning in a growing child can manifest itself in a range of ways that include diminished focus, heightened distractibility, and impulsive behaviors. Yet teachers, health advocates, journalists, and criminologists focused on low-income, racialized urban communities tend to move quickly from these general qualities into discussions about lead's *criminogenic* horizons. Their fixations on impoverished lead-addled children who cannot clear this neurotoxin converge with presumptions that their impaired executive functioning portends adulthoods defined by erratic, even criminal, behaviors.

Like all dusts, particles that flake or rise off a building shift between states of suspension and settlement. Such materials will always shift, as anthropologists Jerry Zee and Timothy Choy observe, "up, out, and down [and] maybe up again." As they shift and resettle across terrains, dust particles have the potential to fall into other arrangements.[5] Yet if circulation is a defining quality of dust, so is durability. Carolyn Steedman emphasizes this point throughout *Dust*, her extended meditation on historiography: "Nothing *can be* destroyed. The fundamental lessons of physiology, of cell-theory, and of neurology were to do with this ceaseless making and unmaking, the movement and transmutation of one thing to another. Nothing goes away."[6] What exactly remains durable in conversations about childhood lead poisoning, even as something so mobile as dust drifts up, out, down, and maybe up again?

Nowadays, arguments that children can be *born* criminals have lost much of their sway in urban America. Yet where I work, something like a concept of race as permanent and heritable bodily difference rears its head again in converging public anxieties about ecological degradation and maternal vigilance. Here, durable investments in bodily deficiencies made and fixed if not by nature then by imperfect nurture suggest the outlines of a renewed eugenics focused on the daily rhythms of inhabiting place, of making relatedness, of feeding and caring, and of ingestion and incorporation. Nothing can be destroyed in racialized urban neighborhoods shaped by decades of residential demolition for the simple reason that nothing has really gone away—not the house itself, which has settled underfoot; not the economic processes that disperse and resettle its components; not the racism that authorized so much mundane neglect and physical violence visited routinely on residential buildings. What these residential demolitions and their material redistributions challenge me to think about, then, is not really the problem of suspension or potential but rather that of domestication. How do people come to make and inhabit residential spaces in concert with entities that might seem to have little to do with a house's solid physical form, be they animals or plants but also children and other dynamic, albeit uncertain, things, such as dust?

In the fall of 2018, I stepped back into the fieldwork I had abandoned two years earlier. I had lost research access after several of my interlocutors became anxious about additional scrutiny of their efforts to incorporate lead-safe measures into residential demolition programs. Yet my abandonment of previous fieldwork hadn't been only a matter of changing access. Shortly after I returned from a stretch of fieldwork in 2015, a physician posed some sobering questions to me. Was there "anything at home" that could be dangerous to my pregnancy? she asked. "*Anyone*?" she said as she directed my gaze to a side table stacked with pamphlets focused on maternal and infant health.

One featured a photograph of a pregnant woman sitting on an exam table, her brow furrowed, her hands wrung. Another drew a baby in loose strokes, laid out on a forearm, its jaw gripped in one hand, the heel of the other hovering above its back. I shook my head in the direction of these images and she was satisfied. I was apparently not the kind who gets beaten at home or skips an infant first aid class.

"What about work?" they physician continued. "What is it that you do?" Her lips pursed when I explained that my research had recently focused on efforts to mitigate lead dust during residential demolitions. "You know," she observed as she took notes, "there's no safe level [of lead exposure]." Something in her chiding reminded me of all those facts and statistics I had seen pinned to bulletin boards at social services and community centers during my field research, all those Z-folded photocopies stacked on tables at affordable housing fairs: the kind meant to educate caregivers about childhood lead poisoning or obesity *and* their responsibility to prevent both. Maybe, she added brightly, I could get back to "it" [research] after I weaned? Because, as I probably already knew, "breast is best." I was annoyed with all the rote advice laced with assumptions about what and who makes for good and responsible caregiving. Yet hadn't I already known before I stepped into that room that my questions about housing demolition and its aftermaths would have to change, along with my own paths into them?

When I returned to fieldwork in Chicago with my then-toddler in 2018, I did so with a "lead safe" research plan: to focus on the legal proceedings that had helped to dislodge residential buildings from their lots. My regular route to court took me past a corner composed of eight vacant lots. I knew these particular lots well. You had to pass them to get to the local transit stop. I had passed them many times in a decade of research. Yet their situation had changed.

In 2014, the city had started selling off its substantial vacant landholdings in the area. For a dollar and a commitment to meet future tax obligations while also keeping one's newly acquired property fenced, mowed, and clear of debris, as well as a promise to wait five years before selling off one's lot, local property owners could acquire additional vacant lots on the block where they already owned property. Titles to the lots would come "clean"—in this context, free not so much of debris but of debts and liens that tend also to accumulate: all the financial stuff that can make these lots challenging to acquire

FIGURE 11.2. The author's toddler searching for cats in the fields, Chicago, 2018. While this child has lived in urban housing that contains leaded paints, her likelihood of being poisoned by such housing is significantly less than that of low-income children of color living in undermaintained urban housing and attending undermaintained schools.

and develop. Local property owners, including recently arrived gentrifiers but also those who had never resided in the area and had no intention of ever doing so, moved to acquire additional lots. Best seen as providing land transfers that shore up a municipal tax base through speculation and revaluation, Chicago's "dollar lot" program converged with the city's effort to enforce regulations concerning vacant properties.

By the fall of 2018, the familiar "fields" had begun taking on a less incoherent feel. Many boasted newly installed chain-link fences marking reasserted property lines, less litter, and even clipped weeds that could sometimes, almost look lawn-like. Garden beds had appeared in once-vacant lots, along with farm-like spaces replete with fruit trees, sunflowers, and beehives. Reports of wayward chickens entertained a neighborhood email group. A neighbor across the street from where I stayed kept a herd of goats on a newly acquired vacant lot, while an adjacent vacant lot had become a rat burrow. Rumor had it that rampant demolition and redevelopment just to the east and a highway widening project just to the south had reconcentrated rats in our midst. The rats that traversed the party wall that our building shared with the vacant one next door kept us up at night as they rummaged through our cabinets. *Goat*, *the big mouse*, and, later, *rat* settled into my toddler's growing vocabulary.

For all the changes that greeted me in the fall of 2018, the cluster of eight vacant lots by the train was still not fenced. However, it did look markedly different than it had when I first started passing it in 2005. At that time, the lots caught special ire in community meetings for attracting dumping but also hawkers whom neighbors associated with everything from unhealthy food and drinks to drugs. The entire vacant cluster stood at the center of a shadowy ecology they connected to noise, illegal substances, loitering, and litter. Police responded by stepping up surveillance; the hawkers moved on. For years to come, this expanse seemed given over to weeds and trash. One afternoon in 2018, though, I saw something that stopped me in my tracks. Someone was keeping a vegetable garden at the edge of this expanse. More surprising than

the existence of the garden in such a space was its position. Someone had laid it out directly in the ground, directly *within* the foundations of the residential building that had once stood there; directly *within* the concave formed as the house below continued to subside.

The gardener, a Black man in his seventies, I got to know a little on my way to and from court. In our conversations, Y. B. made it clear that he understood why advice for raised beds had become so standard in local gardening circles. This was, after all, a residential neighborhood once known for light manufacturing. Yet as a lifelong resident, he insisted that he could recall what had once stood on every vacant lot. That knowledge allowed him to select the one lot within the entire cluster that had been "only houses." Insurance maps from the early twentieth century confirm Y. B.'s recollections. Street-level storefronts with residences or offices stacked above had stood cheek by jowl with manufacturing buildings across this entire cluster. Y. B. was correct in having chosen for his garden the one lot devoted exclusively to residential use. Yet the maps also show that this lot had stood near a workshop that contained what a careful hand had labeled as a "japanning" oven—an oven used to bake protective and decorative lacquers onto metal fixtures, tools, and machines. The insurance assessor who had drawn this map made note of the oven's vents by way of mapping fire risks. Yet these vents would have also moved up, out, and around whatever had once made lacquers durable (hydrocarbons and turpentine). Y. B.'s garden did not stand on "only houses."

I sometimes heard other local gardeners criticize Y. B.'s in-ground growing techniques. They didn't appreciate his efforts to share what he grew. It was one thing to grow and eat food you knew likely to be contaminated, entirely another to feed it to others. Y. B. would shrug when these criticisms came up. He continued to surround his garden with blocks, bricks, and slabs he pulled from below. It would be possible to see Y. B.'s shrugging as a result of ignorance about how hazardous substances settle, or as an effect of modest circumstances that forced him to make do with whatever settled into his garden. Such conclusions, though, would have to ignore that Y. B. is far from the only long-term or recently arrived resident who grows directly in the concaves formed by the house underfoot. These conclusions would have to ignore how some growers extol these concaves' capacity to concentrate water that would otherwise pond or flood a basement. They would have to ignore just how often current residents come across materials that suggest both bygone domestic lives and the physical structures that held those lives together—the clothes, carpets, toys, bottles, and furnishings, but also the wiring, pipes, plaster walls, and bricks. And those conclusions would also have to ignore how some growers talk about their choices to work with these materials as a straightforward response not so much to the expense or hassle of removing or avoiding suspect materials but simply to their ubiquity.

"You cannot pick up all the glass," a white woman in her thirties complained to me in 2019. "It's impossible." Her avid and adventurous gardening had attracted the notice of her neighbors. She worried about tickets and fines issued after neighbors complained about her "weeds" and "trash," so she started monitoring the vacant lot she had acquired farther down the block. She hovered at odd hours, hoping to catch a fly dumper in the act. She never did, and she began to understand that the glass that arrived regularly was not being dumped. It emerged from the ground with the weather, along with so much she couldn't see yet suspected could be present in and around her home: the heavy metals from bygone residential and manufacturing buildings; the volatile compounds from the embanked train tracks that abut the back of her lots; whatever of this mix washes through her garden; whatever her dogs carry in and lick off their paws; and whatever they spread across the sofa, the sheets, and her own body when they all curl up together. But none of that, she insisted, was anything one could entirely avoid. When it rained, she observed, and when it thawed, "the earth just births glass."

Domestications

Anthropologist Bettina Stoetzer recently observed that scholars have turned to registers of ruin to make sense of urban life unfolding amid intensifying economic, political, and material upheavals. She argues that this register does not account for the forms of embodiment that characterize relations among intimates and strangers, both human and nonhuman, in urban ecologies forged through industrial capitalism, migration, and wartime destruction. These ecologies remain opaque, wrapped in images of weeds, rubble, and feral animals.[7] I read her critique with a sinking sense of familiarity, and also a sinking sense that the situation is even more dispiriting. Have we deferred analysis of such ecologies, but also the practical demands of inhabiting them, in favor of negative concept metaphors that evoke both our horrors about destruction and our desires to overcome them? For me, the house underfoot is nothing more than a placeholder for a more nuanced description and analysis that late industrial urban ecologies warrant but that I am not yet in a position to offer. Such a description would have to come to terms with the practices through which people *domesticate* their surrounds, but not in the way we might expect.

Anthropologists revisiting conversations about domestication have departed from debates about whether a specific relation meets the concept's classic rendering as human mastery, species-level transformation, or physical and economic domination. They have been asking instead about how these weighty themes, and the metanarratives that conjure them, can make it hard to entertain exactly *how* people come into tight relations with animals and plants.[8] Domesticative practices, they caution, are not exhausted by human efforts to instrumentalize a given entity. They also include activities through which humans build and maintain symbiotic relations or interdependencies with a range of dynamic entities.[9] Plants and animals have tended to anchor anthropologists' questions about domesticative practices and "more than human" kinships. Yet the dynamic entities and components that constitute contemporary domestic spheres, a number of which are the remainders of earlier domestic spheres, are also fodder for my interlocutors' domestication dramas. Bits of glass, paint, bricks, clinkers, and industrial by-products that imparted distinct qualities to nineteenth- and twentieth-century domestic life now form the ambient envelopes that hold and permeate those who raise homes in the late industrial urban Midwest. My interlocutors know they cannot avoid these envelopes and their residues. Some lay out tarps and blankets when they want to sit in the grass, they plant vegetables and fruits said to sequester heavy metals in their roots, and they serve up dairy and greens to children.

It took dashed research, an upended household, and the patience enforced by both to remind me that my interlocutors in the late industrial urban Midwest have long and self-consciously inhabited dynamic surrounds that are replete with uncertain entities and components. Such practices can open familiar problems associated with an anthropology of the house—habit, memory, embodiment, and social reproduction—onto the broader processes that degrade, devalue, and demolish some homes in the service of shoring up the soundness of others. Yet that opening must attend to what anthropologists alive to the ambivalences of kinship and kin care have long known: The act of making and inhabiting a home has always involved efforts to make sense of that which envelops, permeates, and also extends our bodies—the people, the creatures, and the substances that sometimes corrode and confound us even as they please, comfort, bind, sustain, and stick to us.[10]

NOTES

1. Ethnographic and archival research for this essay unfolded in Chicago and several other Midwestern American cities, especially Detroit, from 2005 to 2021.
2. Byles, *Rubble*; Ammon, *Bulldozer*.
3. Pellow, *Garbage Wars*.
4. Markowitz and Rosner, *Deceit and Denial*.
5. Choy and Zee, "Condition—Suspension," 212–13.
6. Steedman, *Dust*, 164.
7. Stoetzer, *Ruderal City*.
8. Chazin, *Live Stock*.
9. Russell, "Wild Side"; Russell, "Domestication of Anthropology"; Hartigan, *Aesop's Anthropology*.
10. Carsten, *Heat of the Hearth*; Geschiere, *Witchcraft, Intimacy, and Trust*; Garcia, *Pastoral Clinic*; Agard-Jones, "Racial Capitalism, Chemical Kin"; Roberts, "Grappling with Exposure in Mexico City."

RYO MORIMOTO

12

Post-Fallout Home

Dying Well (*Ii Shinikata*)

The millennia-old former National Route 6 that connects central Japan to northeastern Japan also connected Naoko's temporary residence in Kashima and her evacuated home in Odaka, Minamisōma, fifteen kilometers apart from each other, about a twenty-minute drive. For Naoko, a woman in her late seventies who farmed her family land when I first met her in 2013, the route had become an essential path of her post-fallout lifeworld. It was the path she would take to visit the local clinic and her relatives and friends, to transport her household waste to a neighborhood garbage station, and to access her former residence in Odaka, which sat within the twenty-kilometer evacuation zone.

My first encounter with Naoko was pure happenstance, which she later described as *en*, when I briefly participated in a documentary film project featuring her twenty-year-old grandson. By attributing our chance encounter to *en*, she signaled to the existence of some invisible force that had arranged our meeting. "One good thing about the TEPCO accident is," she said earnestly, "it brought you to my life. What would be the chance of meeting someone from western Japan who lives in the US?"

Like Naoko, many elderly residents in Minamisōma often used *en* to acknowledge some supernatural force that bundles people, things, land, and the environment together in a knot of relations. Originally drawn from the Buddhist concept of *pratyaya*, *en* means an indirect cause or a hidden condition of possibility for webs of interconnections.[1] Colloquially, Japanese people use the term *en* to indicate some form of connectedness ranging from biological kinship (*ketsu-en* / 血縁) to a chance encounter (*kaikou* / 邂逅). Anthropologist Shunsuke Nozawa discusses *en* as a floating signifier for "related, somehow."[2] From this Japanese folk perspective, living and house-ing are about both submitting to and weaving invisible threads of *en* by not questioning the cause and meaning of each encounter and instead letting each encounter be the guide.[3] *En* itself is not meaningful, but one's belief in its potential as the invisible infrastructure for meaningfulness is.

The closer I became to Naoko and her family during my fieldwork in coastal Fukushima from 2013 to 2019, the more often I would assist her in the tasks and activities that took her along Route 6. In the car, Naoko would tell me about her *en*-filled places we passed and share stories associated with them: a factory where her relative works, a small store that her old schoolmate runs, a family-owned hair salon where she used to get her hair dyed before the evacuation. New places on the route had also become significant to her. When we passed a crematory near her temporary residence, she would often communicate, half-jokingly and half-earnestly. her plan for others to follow after her death. "I tell my son that if I die in the temporary house," she would remark, "just go to that crematory and drop my remains off at my family grave in Odaka before coming back to the temporary house." Some days she would report these instructions cheerfully. Other days, she sounded less hopeful.

The March 2011 failure of the Tokyo Electric Company–owned Fukushima Daiichi Nuclear Power Plant displaced Naoko from her home for more than eight years. Given that length of time, her remark signified both the symbolic and the real distance between her temporary residence and evacuated home as well as the experiential rupture that the fallout produced in the minds of evacuees. Over the course of years, I heard multiple versions of the same narrative, especially among elderly residents—men and women alike—expressing the desire to live and die at their evacuated homes, in their own words and always with a hint of humor. Many elderly residents wished to die well, and for their desire to be fulfilled, they felt it necessary to return to their evacuated home regardless of contamination. How can people die well in post-fallout coastal Fukushima? How is people's desire to die well related to their idea of home and the act of maintaining the decaying evacuated home and acquiescing to *en*, despite and because of the fallout?

Finding Home in a Post-Fallout World

The Japanese state has been gradually reopening areas it originally deemed unhabitable by remediating the irradiated environment. In August 2011, the state's decontamination policy sketched a hopeful trajectory for Minamisōma's displaced residents, including Naoko, who wished to reclaim their land and livelihoods. Despite the higher risk of radiological exposure in their old homes, for the evacuees, the idea of home—as both an enduring, contaminated physical structure and nostalgic *en*-filled place—had become inseparable from their idea of dying well.

Exploring home and housing as a landscape of shaping human settlement, Jeanne Haffner argues that since the turn of the twentieth century, home and housing have been the central loci for the modern state to enact social welfare, promote public health and sanitation, discipline individuals, and (re)construct human relationships to the environment.[4] I suggest that thinking with the Japanese concept of home, or *ie*, expands this conceptual horizon of the home beyond the state and its biopolitics.[5]

In Japanese conceptualization, *ie* is a historical collection of relationalities and affects that extends across the living, the dead, and the not yet born. Home is not just a physical structure in which one lives and is sheltered from the outside world and that can be (de)contaminated. It is also a semiotic and affective contour where concepts such as lineage, genealogy, kinship, memory, and belonging manifest and are performed, negotiated, and (re)produced through individual, social, economic, material, religious, cultural, and repair work.[6] As a living, processually unfolding archive of multiple *en*-filled relationalities, the home remains a vital resource through which coastal Fukushima evacuees make sense of the protracted afterlife of the triple disaster of March 2011—earthquake, tsunami, and nuclear fallout. More importantly, *ie* is the ground on which residents envision *en*'s continuity to the intergenerational—the biological, semiotic, affective, and environmental chain of being that outlives residents' individual lives. As I will show, for Naoko, dying well meant the negotiation of preserving her past while not burdening those who would remain after she departed this world.

By following Naoko's struggles to ground herself in a post-fallout world, I explore the home/*ie* as an archive of *en* and the nexus of the intergenerational. Situating our attention at the scale of the home in the planetary-level fallout demonstrates that (de)contamination is a more than biopolitical process negotiated through the act of making, unmaking, and remaking home.[7] *Ie* is the base from which residents reoriented themselves to the post-fallout environment and acted on their sense of duty for those who would follow after them, whom residents such as Naoko believed to be loosely but ineffably connected in their *en*-folded worldview.

Naoko's Dream

I often drove Naoko to a local medical clinic, situated in central Minamisōma, between her temporary house and her evacuated house, for a routine monthly checkup for her general health as an elderly person. The first time I took her to the clinic, I observed that there were many other elderly people in the waiting room. Naoko talked with a couple of them, chatting about who was in which temporary housing complex, whether they had plans to return to the "old" houses once the evacuation order was lifted, and so on. She told them that another friend had become sick and so could not make it for their checkup.

The clinic had become a place of gathering and socialization for healthy people who had been dispersed through forced evacuation. Each of Naoko's friends asked if she had come with her grandson, to which she responded that I was her friend and that I drove her places because she had no means of commuting. Her friends all thanked me for doing a great deed and lamented that young adults had become scarce in Minamisōma. Many young adults, willingly or not, had abandoned their now-contaminated hometowns and left the elders, who were more physically and psychologically bound to their birthplace. In a more immediate and tangible impact than any scientifically discernible biological effects on the individual body, the accident had disintegrated social organization, most palpably at the level of the household.[8]

One woman waiting at the clinic remarked that her children would never come back because they must have realized the convenience of living in a bigger city. "Radiation is a good excuse for them not to come back to this countryside," she told us. "I am saying this because we all know that the radiation levels in many places in Fukushima and Koriyama city in the west [to which many young people had evacuated] are, in reality, higher than here, though we cannot tell them that." When I asked why her children had moved to a more contaminated area, she guessed that it was because of the physical distance from the nuclear plant. "We are closer to the plant here," she offered, "so they think it has to be more dangerous."

Another chimed in: "If I had an option to cut my *en* [relation] with my mother-in-law when I was young, I would have." Everyone chuckled, signaling the still-standard extended family structure in this rural region. The threat of radiation exposure since March 2011 had apparently become an excuse for some locals to resolve many preexisting social and domestic issues and to circumvent moral judgments based on the region's traditions and norms. Disagreements over the perceived risk of radiation exposure had discouraged many locals from talking about radiation in private and in public. "We do not want to cause any trouble at home or outside by talking about it," Naoko lamented as she got up to wait in line to see a doctor.

Naoko herself had thoughts and experiences she refrained from sharing with her family. On our way to the clinic that day, Naoko had confessed to me unexpectedly that she had been having the same recurring dream for some time now. She asked me not to tell her family, because she did not want them to think she had gone crazy. "In the dream," she started, "I am in Odaka, but I am not inside my home [*ie*]. From where I stand, a big forest surrounds me, and it is very dark in there. From somewhere in the darkness,

I start hearing voices of people, the voices I recognize. I realize that they are dead people in my family, like my grandparents, mother-in-law, and close relatives. In the forest, I am feeling guilty that I am in the forest and cannot come out from it."

When she finished reporting her dream, Naoko looked somewhat relieved. I tried not to provide an interpretation. I instead offered a general validating comment that she must be tired from not sleeping well. Naoko nodded and said, "I will get some more sleeping pills from the doctor today, and that will help me to forget about it and sleep." It turned out that Naoko had been taking sleeping pills since not long after the accident in March 2011. As a farmer who farmed rice, grew vegetables and fruit in her garden, and had been continuously engaged in physical labor, she said that she never had any problem with her sleep before. By signaling her previous state of activeness and productivity at her Odaka home, Naoko implied that the limited space available at the temporary house in a more urban region of the city contributed to her current state of inactivity.

But what Naoko left unsaid, and what was also the common local sentiment, was this: The sudden awareness of the radiological danger and hypervisualized contamination in the post-fallout landscape across coastal Fukushima—the very reason she had to leave her home to begin with—made it undesirable for locals like her to stay active and engage in farming. The impacts of this significant lifestyle change manifested as extremely busy hospitals and clinics packed with elderly people with increased diagnoses of obesity, diabetes, high blood pressure, hypertension, hyperuricemia, rheumatic diseases, and mental health issues, ailments that are often glossed as stress-related misalignments.[9] The contamination posed a threat not just to people's lives but also to their livelihoods.

Noticing my concerned face as we drove back to her temporary residence, Naoko assured me that only half a pill would put her into a dreamless sleep. Listening to her, I wondered for a second which of Naoko's everyday life events—taking only half of a pill to produce a dreamless sleep or her realistic dream—was the new normal of a post-fallout existence. One thing was clear from Naoko's dream: The fallout and ensuing state-enforced evacuation and environmental remediation thwarted her desire to be at her *ie* and maintain her *en* with living and deceased family members. Before she was able to get out of the forest, however, her home had to be "cleaned up."

Decontaminating a Decaying House

Naoko was one of many evacuees from Odaka who clung to the state's promise to clean up the contaminated region by removing radioactive materials.[10] To be in a position to return promptly once decontamination was completed, after several relocations she and her family eventually settled into a temporary residence in the northern part of Minamisōma in April 2011. This final housing location was ideal—Kashima is roughly fifteen kilometers from Odaka, a short distance that Naoko hoped would enable her periodically to tend to the family's empty, evacuated home. "A house is alive," she often said. "It will decay quickly if no one breathes in it."

Although the effectiveness and purpose of decontamination have been much debated, scientific literature testifies to the gradual decrease of contaminants in formerly uninhabitable areas of coastal Fukushima and its surrounding regions.[11] Long-term environmental survey data suggest that the natural decay process of radioisotopes (i.e., half-life) and decontamination efforts have reduced the ambient radiation level by up to 70 percent in many regions of coastal Fukushima.[12] However, decontamination does not achieve the actual *removal* of contaminants. Decontamination efforts amount to moving contaminants away from a particular location to construct a physical and visible distance between people and these sources of radiation.[13]

The Act on Special Measures Concerning the Handling of Radioactive Pollution, issued in August 2011, defines decontamination as the removal of as many radioisotopes as possible from the environment: "In this Act, 'measures for decontamination of the soil, etc.' means measures taken for soil, vegetation, structure, etc., contaminated with radioactive materials discharged by the accident including the removal of the contaminated soil, fallen leaves and twigs, sludge accumulated in ditches, etc., preventive measures to keep the pollution from spreading, and other measures."[14]

For any space to be decontaminated, the invisible radioisotopes must first be "captured" using material objects in the vicinity. In the decontamination framework, dirt or any other tangible material in the environment is not a pollutant in its own right. These materials become toxic waste inasmuch as they are carriers—nonhuman hosts—of invisible contaminants. Radioactive contaminants are not only "matters out of place"; they are also matter deemed unnecessary to a given place.[15] In time, what is being removed from the zone becomes contaminated regardless of the degree of actual contamination, indicating that the main function of decontamination is to spatially carve out and articulate the geographical as well as the psychosocial boundary between safe and unsafe.

The processual nature of contamination is particularly evident in the case of coastal Fukushima, by the accumulative amount of earth stuff and personal property removed from one location to another. Regardless of the effectiveness of decontamination, which was often communicated with technical language the residents found almost impossible to decipher, the state-led decontamination and gradual opening of evacuation zones provided a semblance of order for the evacuees still interested in reclaiming their homes. At the same time, by framing contamination as a provisional and reversible condition that would constrain evacuees such as Naoko for only a set amount of time, the decontamination policy foregrounded radiation as the only issue while ignoring collateral social and individual issues in coastal Fukushima.

Decontamination engages with what I call *half-life politics*—a scientized politics that foregrounds the presence and absence of radiation in the environment and its potential harm to humans above all other things, such as the residents' quality of life, cultural and historical continuity, personal belongings, sustainability of livelihood, and biodiversity.[16] This type of radiation damage–centered politics ends up reproducing the kind of subjects and objects whose perceived value or lack thereof becomes dependent on actual, claimable damage.[17] In other words, half-life politics generates a prism through which the residents of coastal Fukushima and anything else in the environment become visible and meaningful if, and only if, their bodies indicate evidence for or against the adverse effects of radiological exposure.[18]

In contrast, I look beyond half-life politics and instead focus on the residents' desire to live as fully as possible by returning to their original homes despite the perceived contamination and the elevated risk of radiation exposure. To do so, in the remainder of the chapter I explore yet another kind of halving: the split between evacuees' original residences, which they were forced to abandon, and the residences they lived in during their evacuation, homes that the state and residents themselves identified as "temporary." In the case of Naoko, who was made sleepless and inactive and who was racked with guilt over abandoning her ancestral land, I examine how her *en* with things, land, the living, the dead, and the environment helped remake her contaminated home and reincarnate it as her *ie*, despite and because of the fallout.

FIGURE 12.1. Naoko in the front yard of her original residence in 2014. Photo by the author.

The Home Reincarnates

In the aftermath of the 2004 Indian Ocean tsunami, Frida Hastrup observed, tsunami victims used objects to articulate their sense of self and to delimit their territory from that of others as they processed the disaster.[19] Ruined or not, personal possessions such as clothing, furniture, and tools help to (re)articulate the boundary between self and other in social worlds.[20] From this perspective, making decontamination the necessary condition of evacuees' return posed a threat to their sense of self and territory by prioritizing the removal of contaminants in the "environment," a depersonalized framing of space and the very personal things inhabiting that space.

From 2013 to 2016, I accompanied Naoko into the evacuation zone to tend to her Odaka house and till her land. Upon each visit to her house, Naoko would enter her former bedroom, open the dresser drawers, and quietly contemplate the items within. She would remove a few things from a drawer and lay them on the floor, as if to indicate her willingness to transfer them somewhere. Then, she would clean up around the family Buddhist altar in the adjacent room. As she offered incense, the smoke would rise to the wall where memorial portraits of her deceased family members hung.

Since the fallout, she had thought about how her evacuated home had become not just an important place to live but also the only place where she desired to rest after her death. Naoko never doubted that she would eventually join the cremated remains of her deceased family in the family grave on their property, a few hundred meters from the house. The altar, memorial portraits, and nearby grave articulated Naoko's and her family's multiple *en*, temporalities, and territories archived in the place she called home. The accident threatened to sever her tie to those not easily quantifiable relationalities—what made the place her *ie*—as it had denied her the right to choose where to live and die.

Before leaving, she would return to her bedroom and return the items laid out on the floor to their respective drawers. Her temporary residence was too small to hold the bedroom dresser or the family altar, she would tell me. And it was only "temporary"; soon, she would be able to resume living in her old house, in her old room, surrounded by her clothes and her family, both the living and the dead.

FIGURE 12.2. Naoko praying in front of the family altar at her original home in 2013. Photo by the author.

Although the deceased in the altar had to remain in the contaminated residence, Naoko expressed how important it was that somebody take care of them. As material, semiotic, and affective proof of the groundedness of her personal lineage, the unmovable altar and grave were a primary reason she felt she must return to her home. With the family altar still in place, the dead continued to dwell at her evacuated home and haunt Naoko in her sleep at the temporary residence.

In late 2013, more than two years after the initial evacuation, the state began decontaminating the region around Naoko's home. Eventually, state officials proposed to demolish Naoko's home at no cost, and her family consented. The earthquake that had catalyzed the tsunami and the series of nuclear meltdowns had partially damaged the house. Thus, in 2014, as she turned eighty, I returned with Naoko to visit her home. This time, her task was to identify which items would be preserved from the demolition and which would be disposed of as contaminated "waste." The plan was to transfer the valuables to a warehouse next to the home, where farming tools and machinery were stored.

In this selection process, Naoko became more vocal about the items I had seen her unpack and repack many times before. Contemplating a kimono she had not worn in ages, she asked me, "What do I do with this? Even if I keep this kimono, no one is gonna wear it, including myself." She touched the faded gray fabric. "To tell you the truth," Naoko confessed, "I might have worn this only a few times. It was from sixty years ago, when I married in this house. It was the first and last good kimono I got from my parents."

Still holding the kimono that embodied her familial *en*, she said that in the old days, long before a nuclear power station was planned for coastal Fukushima in the 1950s, people wore kimonos every day. Naoko voiced her regret at leaving the crippled nuclear power plant and irradiated soil and environment to future generations. When I asked if she would throw away her kimono, Naoko replied, "The demolition date has not been set yet. I could keep it for the time being. I mean, isn't it a nice kimono?" She stroked the kimono before folding it with care and returning it to the dresser, closing the drawer with deliberate force. When she opened and closed the drawers, the chest gave off a musty, though familiar, fragrance of old clothes, of lost time.

FIGURE 12.3. Naoko moves her personal belongings from her home to storage in 2015. Photo by the author.

On the way back to her temporary residence, where her family waited, Naoko spoke about the difficulty of letting things go. She said, "My family said to throw away any unnecessary things in my life because I cannot take them with me when I die. But the more I thought about each item, the more I felt that my life was being taken away by the accident and reconstruction from it." Preserving personal belongings was Naoko's way of resisting the force of a particular kind of plot that the state had initiated with its reconstruction through decontamination.[21] Even though she desired to return to her home—and, by extension, longed for the place to be decontaminated—Naoko was not ready for her personal belongings to be "cleaned up" as carriers of contaminants and transformed into waste, along with the house she had lived in and the land she had cultivated. "It's not that I did not want my home to be less contaminated," Naoko explained. "It's just that whenever I go there, my *ie* looks less like how it used to be."

Although the state imagines decontamination to be the careful cleaning up of a house to protect its people, decontamination also takes on the face of large-scale destruction of residents' familiar environment and invisible *en*. Naoko's refusal to part with her personal effects, such as that unused kimono, exemplified the tension between her past and others' future. For her, these items stood for the anticipated loss of things past—her home that was marked by the sense of connectedness in her *en*-filled worldview. At the same time, Naoko wanted to die well by not leaving anything contaminated behind so that future generations could live well in the region. For Naoko, envisioning the intergenerational took a form of detachment from the things past.

The Proof of Living in the World

In June 2019, over eight years after the initial evacuation, Naoko was finally reunited with her inalienable belongings inside the warehouse. In place of her old one-story farmhouse now stood a modern two-story house with a shinier and more elaborate Buddhist altar. In the newly built house, Naoko secured a room right next to the altar. She told me that while the house was being rebuilt, she had to move the altar to the warehouse, where she kept her other

FIGURE 12.4. Naoko offers incense to the family altar moved to storage during the demolition of the original residence in 2017. Photo by the author.

personal belongings. As many people moving into a new house traditionally would, Naoko used her relocation as an opportunity to replace the altar to appease the spirits of the displacement, and the state compensated her for the cost of the replacement.

"It was challenging to move the spirits," she told me at her new residence at the end of June 2019, as she was cleaning the former altar in the warehouse while she waited for staff from the altar shop to remove it. She said that prior to this moving arrangement, "a Buddhist monk came and chanted in order to transfer the spirits from one altar to the other officially. It is funny how the deceased seemed to get better treatment than living ones like myself. No one prayed for me!" Naoko's sarcasm was a not-so-veiled critique of the state's half-life politics, which lacked any consideration for disaster-related damage beyond biomedically significant radiation exposure. For officials, her return to the supposedly decontaminated region signaled the success of their remediation efforts; Naoko was yet another statistic—one of over three thousand in Odaka—proving the efficacy of decontamination and the safety of the area.

When the altar movers arrived to dispose of the now-spiritless altar, Naoko proudly told them how carefully she had cleaned it as a gesture of bidding farewell to the object that archived her familial *en* and had marked her *ie* for over sixty years. One of the workers voiced his concern that the altar looked *too clean*; it did not look like a deserted altar in an evacuated home. After chatting among themselves, a younger staff member asked Naoko if it was all right to make the altar "look dirtier"; this was their routine way for documenting that an altar belonged to a displaced family. The procedure would allow Naoko's family to receive greater compensation for the altar's disposal, he said. "Is that so?" Naoko responded, pursing her lips together to protest in silence.

Without securing Naoko's consent, the worker grabbed the incense ash holder and spread ashes over the old altar. As he photographed the spoiled altar from multiple angles, he exclaimed, "It looks much better!" He then assured Naoko that the photos of the adequately "ruined" altar would garner her family the money, equivalent to US$10,000, that they deserved for the lost

time.[22] Watching the truck depart with the old altar, Naoko lamented, "The ruined altar is worth something, but what about my last eight years of waiting and more wrinkles on my face?" Yet a few seconds later, as she bowed to the disappearing truck, she told me that her loss would benefit her grandson.

Now there was one less item in the warehouse full of misplaced things from the past, including the chest that contained her kimono, for which Naoko was unable to find a place in her modernized residence. Without the old altar, those misplaced items looked stranger than before. When I asked Naoko about her plan for those stored items, she said, "I told my family that they could throw everything away when I die, but so long as I live, I need them as proof that I lived in Odaka."

The Earth and the Hearth

As Naoko implied, in an age when the increased frequency of disaster is leading to more displacement and misplacement of people and things, evacuees struggle to maintain a sense of continuity. The specific case of Naoko suggests that we must approach toxic environments by exploring how people engage with materialities to make homes, mark territories, and process changes despite and as a result of contamination. Being contaminated is far from the end of one's life story; instead, it is integral to the ongoing process of world making, which includes the desire to make life and land better for those who might follow. Home, in this sense, is not a mere field through which the state policy manages people and regiments its ideology; it is a dynamic entity—*ie*—that archives a plethora of relationalities, historicities, and materialities that are intertwined by *en*, however magically and invisibly.

In the grand Buddhist (and Hindu) scheme of the transmigration of the soul, *en* is as much about interweaving people, things, land, and nonhuman others in a knot of fate as it is about untangling the same knot so that when people depart to the other world, they can reincarnate as something new. Perhaps detachment is a general and pressing concern among elderly residents such as Naoko, for whom death feels more acute than the accumulative biological effects of radiation. For them, the moral reckoning of detachment depends more on their commitment to intergenerational succession: creating a good life for others.

Sometimes, it takes a useless kimono, an impractical piece of memorabilia, to keep one's sense of territoriality, to live and die well; at other times, it takes a form of intentional ruination of an intergenerational object like the altar to accept the irreversible flow of time. Meanwhile, radioisotopes continually decay, releasing radiation in the process, to achieve more atomic stability. Underneath the elderly residents' questions about their good death lies the question of good lives for new generations.

In the context of crisis and rupture, home becomes a particularly illuminating ethnographic object and scale of analysis. In the space of home, people use objects to negotiate not only their individual lives and livelihoods but also their deaths and what follows. Naoko's post-fallout life demonstrates that, as the archive of multiple material-semiotic-affective relationalities of people, things, and environments, home as an ethnographic site offers significant insight: into the process through which planetary contamination becomes experiential and into the processes through which people attempt to make home again in an already injured world. One insight Naoko provides is this: Whether contaminated or not, people still need proof to themselves and others that they live, that they had lived, and that their legacy will reincarnate and remain in the world.

NOTES

1. Jensen et al., "Attuning to the Webs"; Minakata and Nakazawa, *Minakata Mandala*; Rowe, *Bonds of the Dead.*

2. Nozawa, "Phatic Traces," 392.

3. Biehl and Neiburg, "Oikography."

4. Haffner, *Landscapes of Housing.*

5. Morioka, "Ancestor Worship"; Nakane, "'Ie' no kouzou bunseki"; Ochiai, "*Ie* (Family)"; Shimizu, "*Ie* and *Dōzoku.*"

6. Neiburg, "Multiscale Home"; Costa Oliveira and Fausto, "Amazonian House-ing."

7. Masco, "Age of Fallout."

8. Freudenburg, "Contamination"; T. Gill, "Spoiled Soil"; Minamisōma City, "Kouki Kihonkeikaku"; Morita, "Nihon no."

9. Hashimoto et al., "Influence of Post-Disaster Evacuation"; Tsubokura, "Secondary Health Issues."

10. About thirteen thousand residents evacuated Odaka in March 2011. As of June 2022, over eleven years after the disaster and six years after the reopening of

Odaka in July 2016, about 6,600 residents are registered and over 3,300 people are currently living in the area.

11. Kirby, "Slow Burn"; Morimoto, "Wild Boar Chase."

12. Saito et al., "Summary of Temporal Changes."

13. Morimoto, "From Nuclear Things."

14. For a tentative English translation of the act, see "Act on Special Measures Concerning the Handling of Environment Pollution by Radioactive Materials Discharged by the NPS Accident Associated with the Tohuku District—Off the Pacific Ocean Earthquake That Occurred on March 11, 2011," accessed March 2,2016, http://josen.env.go.jp/en/framework/pdf/special_act.pdf.

15. Douglas, *Purity and Danger*, 41.

16. Morimoto, "Wild Boar Chase"; Morimoto, "Nuclear Ghost."

17. Tuck, "Suspending Damage."

18. Compare Petryna, *Life Exposed*.

19. Hastrup, *Weathering the World*.

20. Goffman, "Territories of the Self."

21. In his discussion on the fear of radiation, Kai Erikson argues that the plotless nature of an atomic danger—there is no clear beginning and ending—is what makes radiation especially dreaded. See Erikson, "Radiation's Lingering Dread."

22. The fixed compensation for a family altar is around 400,000 yen, or around US$3,600.

Bibliography

Agard-Jones, Vanessa. “Racial Capitalism, Chemical Kin.” In *Histories of the Present*. Forthcoming.

Ally, Shireen Adam. *From Servants to Workers: South African Domestic Workers and the Democratic State*. Ithaca, NY: Cornell University Press, 2010.

Altenhofen, Cléo V. “O estudo de línguas de imigrantes no Brasil: O exemplo do ‘Hunsrückisch’ no Rio Grande do Sul.” *Cadernos do Instituto de Letras* 18 (1998): 17–26.

Alvarado, Carlos A., and L. J. Bruce-Chwatt. “Malaria.” *Scientific American* 206, no. 5 (1962): 86–101. https://www.scientificamerican.com/article/malaria-1962-05/.

Amado, Janaína. *Conflito social no Brasil*. São Paulo: Símbolo, 1978.

Ammon, Francesca. *Bulldozer: Demolition and Clearance of the Post-War Landscape*. New Haven, CT: Yale University Press, 2016.

Andrade, Felipe. “Comércio, mobilidade e dinheiro: A busca pela vida no Plateau Central Haitiano e na fronteira Dominicana.” PhD diss., PPGAS, Museu Nacional, UFRJ, 2019.

Anglade, Georges. *Espace et liberté en Haïti*. Montréal: ERCE, 1982.

Appadurai, Arjun. "Mediants, Materiality, Normativity." *Public Culture* 27, no. 2 (2015): 221–37.

Archambault, Julie Soleil. "'One Beer, One Block': Concrete Aspiration and the Stuff of Transformation in a Mozambican Suburb." *Journal of the Royal Anthropological Institute* 24, no. 4 (2018): 692–708.

Arendt, Hannah. *The Human Condition*. Chicago: University of Chicago Press, 1958.

Asdal, Kristin, and Christoph Gradmann. "Introduction: Science, Technology, Medicine—and the State: The Science-State Nexus in Scandinavia, 1850–1980." *Science in Context* 27, no. 2 (2014): 177–86.

Bachelard, Gaston. *The Poetics of Space*. Translated by Maria Jolas and John R. Stilgoe. Boston: Beacon Press, 1994.

Barragán Romano, Rossana. *Indios, mujeres y ciudadanos: Legislación y ejercicio de la ciudadanía en Bolivia (siglo XIX)*. La Paz: Fundación Diálogo, con el apoyo de la Embajada del Reino de Dinamarca en Bolivia, 1999.

Barthes, Roland. *The Eiffel Tower and Other Mythologies*. Berkeley: University of California Press, 1997.

Barthes, Roland. *How to Live Together: Novelistic Simulations of Some Everyday Spaces*. New York: Columbia University Press, 2012.

Bartram, William. *Travels Through North and South Carolina, Georgia, East and West Florida, the Cherokee Country, the Extensive Territories of the Muscogulges or Creek Confederacy, and the Country of the Chactaws*. Philadelphia: James and Johnson, 1791. https://www.loc.gov/item/rc01002676/.

Bastien, Remy. "Haitian Rural Family Organization." *Social and Economic Studies* 10, no. 4 (1961): 478–510.

Beckett, Greg. "Unlivable Life: Ordinary Disaster and the Atmosphere of Crisis in Haiti." *Small Axe: A Caribbean Journal of Criticism* 24, no. 2 (62) (2020): 78–95. https://doi.org/10.1215/07990537-8604502.

Beeckmans, Luce, Alessandra Gola, Ashika Singh, and Hilde Heynen, eds. *Making Home(s) in Displacement: Critical Reflections on a Spatial Practice*. Leuven: Leuven University Press, 2022.

Bellamy, Rhonda, ed. *Moving Forward Together: A Community Remembers 1898*. 1898 Memorial Foundation. Wilmington, NC: SlapDash Publishing, 2008.

Benedict, Ruth. *An Anthropologist at Work: Writings of Ruth Benedict*. Boston: Houghton Mifflin, 1959.

Benjamin, Walter. *The Arcades Project*. Translated by Howard Eiland and Kevin McLaughlin. Cambridge, MA: Harvard University Press, 2002.

Benjamin, Walter. "The Life of Students." In *Walter Benjamin: Selected Writings*, vol. 1, *1913–1926*, edited by Marcus Bullock and Michael W. Jennings, 37–47. Cambridge, MA: Harvard University Press, 2004.

Benjamin, Walter. "Theses on the Philosophy of History." In *Illuminations*, 253–64. New York: Schocken Books, 1968.

Bennett, Jane. *Vibrant Matter: A Political Ecology of Things*. Durham, NC: Duke University Press, 2010.

Berlant, Lauren. *Cruel Optimism*. Durham, NC: Duke University Press, 2011.

Biehl, João. "Insurgent Archivings: Sensing the Spirit of Nature and Reckoning with Traces of Our Dead." *Current Anthropology* 63, no. s25 (2022): s1–s47.

Biehl, João. *Jammerthal, o Vale da Lamentação: A minha Guerra Mucker*. São Leopoldo: Oikos, 2024.

Biehl, João. "The Mucker War: A History of Violence and Silence." In *Postcolonial Disorders*, edited by Mary-Jo DelVecchio Good, Sandra T. Hyde, Sarah Pinto, and Byron Good, 279–308. Berkeley: University of California Press, 2008.

Biehl, João, and Peter Locke, eds. "The Anthropology of Becoming." In *Unfinished: The Anthropology of Becoming*, 41–90. Durham, NC: Duke University Press, 2017.

Biehl, João, and Peter Locke, eds. *Unfinished: The Anthropology of Becoming*. Durham, NC: Duke University Press, 2017.

Biehl, João, Miqueias Mugge, and Ana Maria Goldani. "The Books of the Dead Revisited: Mortality and Morbidity in the German Colonies of Southern Brazil, 1850–1880." *História, Ciências, Saúde Manguinhos* 25, no. 4 (2018): 1197–217.

Biehl, João, and Federico Neiburg. "Oikography: Ethnographies of House-ing in Critical Times." *Cultural Anthropology* 36, no. 4 (2021): 539–47. https://doi.org/10.14506/ca36.4.01.

Boas, Franz. Foreword to *Mules and Men*. In *Folklore, Memoirs, and Other Writings*, by Zora Neale Hurston, 3. New York: Penguin Books, 1995.

Bofu, Ramadhani M., Ellen M. Santos, Betwel J. Msugupakulya, et al. "The Needs and Opportunities for Housing Improvement for Malaria Control in Southern Tanzania." *Malaria Journal* 22, no. 1 (2023): 69. https://doi.org/10.1186/s12936-023-04499-1.

Bourdieu, Pierre. "The Berber House or the World Reversed." *Social Science Information* 9, no. 2 (1970): 151–70.

Bourdieu, Pierre, and Abdelmalek Sayad. *Uprooting: The Crisis of Traditional Agriculture in Algeria*. Edited by P. A. Silverstein. Translated by S. Emanuel. New York: Polity Press, 2020.

Boym, Svetlana. *The Future of Nostalgia*. New York: Basic Books, 2001.

Braum, Pedro. "Frustração." In *Conversas etnográficas haitianas*, edited by Federico Neiburg, 131–57. Rio de Janeiro: Papeis Selvagens, 2019.

Braum, Pedro. "Rat pa kaka: Política, desenvolvimento e violência no coração de Porto Príncipe." PhD diss., PPGAS, Museu Nacional, UFRJ, 2014.

Braun, Felipe. *História de Linha Nova: 1847–1945*. São Leopoldo: Oikos, 2013.

Broom, Sarah M. *The Yellow House*. New York: Grove Press, 2019.

Browder, John O., and Brian J. Godfrey. *Rainforest Cities: Urbanization, Development, and Globalization of the Brazilian Amazon*. New York: Columbia University Press, 1997.

Brown, Margaret, dir. *Descendant*. 2022. Participant Media, 2022.

Brownell, Emily. *Gone to Ground: A History of Environment and Infrastructure in Dar es Salaam*. Pittsburgh, PA: University of Pittsburgh Press, 2020.

Brunn, Stanley D., Jack F. Williams, and Donald J. Ziegler. *Cities of the World: World Regional Urban Development*. Lanham, MD: Rowman and Littlefield, 2003.

Brunson, Deborah A., Linda L. Lampl, and Felicia F. Jordan-Jackson. *Interracial Communication: Contexts, Communities, and Choices*. Dubuque, IA: Kendall Hunt Publishing Company, 2010.

Buarque, Chico. "Pedaço de Mim." *Chico Buarque*. Rio de Janeiro: Polygram/Philips, 1978. Sound recording (approx. 3 min).

Bulamah, Rodrigo. "Lòk: Pandemics and (Im)mobility in Northern Haiti." *Global Perspectives* 2, no. 1 (2021): 29939. https://doi.org/10.1525/gp.2021.29939.

Byles, Jeff. *Rubble: Unearthing the History of Demolition*. New York: Harmony Books, 2005.

Cabezas Fernández, Marta. "'Diecinueve años de lucha por la ley, 11 en el parlamento': Las reivindicaciones de las trabajadoras asalariadas del hogar en Bolivia durante la etapa neoliberal." *Íconos-Revista de Ciencias Sociales* 44 (2012): 85–100.

Cabral de Melo Neto, João. "Psychology of Composition." In *Education by Stone: Selected Poems*, 27–32. New York: Archipelago Books, 2005.

Campbell, Emory S. *Gullah Cultural Legacies: A Synopsis of Gullah Traditions, Customary Beliefs, Art Forms and Speech on Hilton Head Island and Vicinial Sea Islands in South Carolina and Georgia*. 3rd ed. Hilton Head, SC: Gullah Heritage Consulting Services, 2008.

Carsten, Janet. *After Kinship*. Cambridge: Cambridge University Press, 2004.

Carsten, Janet. *The Heat of the Hearth: The Process of Kinship in a Malay Fishing Community*. New York: Oxford University Press, 1997.

Carsten, Janet, and Stephen Hugh-Jones, eds. *About the House: Lévi-Strauss and Beyond*. Cambridge: Cambridge University Press, 1995.

Carsten, Janet, and Stephen Hugh-Jones. "Introduction." In *About the House: Lévi-Strauss and Beyond*, edited by Janet Carsten and Stephen Hugh-Jones, 1–46. Cambridge: Cambridge University Press, 1995.

Casimir, Jean. *The Haitians: A Decolonial History*. Chapel Hill: University of North Carolina Press, 2020.

Castellanos, M. Bianet. *Indigenous Dispossession: Housing and Maya Indebtedness in Mexico*. Stanford, CA: Stanford University Press, 2020.

Cattelino, Jessica. *High Stakes: Florida Seminole Gaming and Sovereignty*. Durham, NC: Duke University Press, 2008.

Cavalcanti, Mariana. "Do barraco à casa: Tempo, espaço e valor(es) em uma favela consolidada." *Revista Brasileira de Ciências Sociais* 24, no. 69 (2009): 69–80.

Cavarero, Adriana. *Horrorism: Naming Contemporary Violence*. Translated by William McCuaig. New York: Columbia University Press, 2008.

Centro de Investigación y Educación Popular/Programa por la Paz. *Noche y niebla no. 58: Panorama de derechos humanos y violencia política en Colombia*. Bogotá: CINEP/PPP, 2019. http://archive.org/details/noche-y-niebla-n.0-58.

Centro Nacional de Memoria Histórica. *"Limpieza social": La principal arma de los paramilitares del Meta y el Vichada."* Informes sobre el orígen y la actuación de las agrupaciones paramilitares en las regiones, no. 3. Bogotá: Centro Nacional de Memoria Histórica, 2018.

Chavez, Leo R. *The Latino Threat: Constructing Immigrants, Citizens, and the Nation*. Stanford, CA: Stanford University Press, 2013.

Chazin, Hannah. *Live Stock and Dead Things: The Archaeology of Zoopolitics Between Domestication and Modernity*. Chicago: University of Chicago Press, 2024.

Choy, Timothy, and Jerry Zee. "Condition—Suspension." *Cultural Anthropology* 30, no. 2 (2015): 210–23.

Chuquimia, Jaime Durán, Verónica Karen Arias Díaz, and Gustavo Marcelo Rodríguez Cáceres. *Casa aunque en la punta del cerro: Vivienda y desarrollo de la ciudad de El Alto.* La Paz: Fundacion Pieb, 2007.

Civico, Aldo. *The Para-State: An Ethnography of Colombia's Death Squads.* Oakland: University of California Press, 2015.

Colloredo-Mansfeld, Rudolf. "Architectural Conspicuous Consumption and Economic Change in the Andes." *American Anthropologist* 96, no. 4 (1994): 845–65.

Colomina, Beatriz. "Domesticity at War." *Discourse* 14, no. 1 (1991–92): 3–22.

Comerford, John, and Federico Neiburg. "A casa e a invenção da família afro-americana vinte e cinco anos depois." *Mana* 27, no. 2 (2021): 1–5.

Connolly, William E. *A World of Becoming.* Durham, NC: Duke University Press, 2011.

Constable, Nicole. "At Home but Not at Home: Filipina Narratives of Ambivalent Returns." *Cultural Anthropology* 14, no. 2 (1999): 203–28.

Constable, Nicole. "Sexuality and Discipline Among Filipina Domestic Workers in Hong Kong." *American Ethnologist* 24, no. 3 (1997): 539–58.

Cooper, Melinda, and Catherine Waldby. *Clinical Labor: Tissue Donors and Research Subjects in the Global Bioeconomy.* Durham, NC: Duke University Press, 2014.

Cortado, Thomas. "La force du regard qu'a la petite fenêtre: La maison comme entrelacs de corps désirants dans un quartier d'habitat autoconstruit de Rio de Janeiro." *Gradhiva* 35 (2023): 28–47.

Costa Oliveira, Thiago da, and Carlos Fausto. "Amazonian House-ing: A Visual Anthropology Essay." *Cultural Anthropology* 46, no. 4 (2021): 580–88.

Dalmaso, Flavia. "Kijan moun yo ye? As pessoas, as casas e as dinâmicas da familiaridade em Jacmel/Haiti." PhD diss., PPGAS, Museu Nacional, UFRJ, 2014.

Danticat, Edwidge. "Demonstrators in Haiti Are Fighting for an Uncertain Future." *New Yorker*, October 10, 2019. https://www.newyorker.com/news/news-desk/demonstrators-in-haiti-are-fighting-for-an-uncertain-future.

Das, Veena, and Ranendra K. Das. "How the Body Speaks: Illness and the Lifeworld Among the Urban Poor." In *Subjectivity: Ethnographic Investigations*, edited by João Biehl, Byron Good, and Arthur Kleinman, 66–97. Los Angeles: University of California Press, 2007.

D'Avella, Nicholas. "Ecologies of Investment: Crisis Histories and Brick Futures in Argentina." *Cultural Anthropology* 29, no. 1 (2014): 173–99. https://doi.org/10.14506/ca29.1.10.

Davis, Angela Y. *Women, Race, and Class.* New York: Random House, 1981.

Dawson, Peter C. "Seeing Like an Inuit Family: The Relationship Between House Form and Culture in Northern Canada." *Études/Inuit/Studies* 3, no. 2 (2006): 113–35.

Dealdina, Selma dos Santos, ed. *Mulheres quilombolas: Territórios de existências negras femininas.* São Paulo: Editora Jandaíra, 2020.

Degani, Michael. "Air in Unexpected Places: Metabolism, Design, and the Making of an 'African' Aircrete." *Cambridge Journal of Anthropology* 38, no. 2 (2020): 125–45.

De León, Jason. *The Land of Open Graves: Living and Dying on the Migrant Trail.* Oakland: University of California Press, 2015.

Deleuze, Gilles. "Postscript on Control Societies." In *Negotiations*, 177–82. New York: Columbia University Press, 1995.

Deleuze, Gilles. "What Children Say." In *Essays: Critical and Clinical*, translated by Daniel W. Smith and Michael A. Greco, 61-67. Minneapolis: University of Minnesota Press, 1997.

Derrida, Jacques. *Archive Fever: A Freudian Impression.* Chicago: University of Chicago Press, 1996.

Desmond, Matthew. *Evicted: Poverty and Profit in the American City*. New York: Crown, 2016.

Dickey, Sara. "Permeable Homes: Domestic Service, Household Space, and the Vulnerability of Class Boundaries in Urban India." *American Ethnologist* 27, no. 2 (2000): 462–89.

Douglas, Mary. "The Idea of a Home: A Kind of Space." *Social Research* 58, no. 1 (1991): 287–307.

Douglas, Mary. *Purity and Danger: An Analysis of the Concepts of Pollution and Taboo.* London: Routledge, 2002.

Dubois, Laurent. *Haiti: The Aftershocks of History*. New York: Metropolitan Books, 2012.

Dufourmantelle, Anne. *Power of Gentleness: Meditations on the Risk of Living*. New York: Fordham University Press, 2018.

Dungy, Camille T. *Black Nature: Four Centuries of African American Nature Poetry*. Athens: University of Georgia Press, 2009.

Duroseau, Fritz, and Edwige Jean. "Haiti—The Productive Use of Remittances." Presentation to the Economic Commission for Latin America and the Caribbean (ECLAC), México, June 14, 2019.

Duvert, Tony. *District*. Cambridge, MA: Wakefield Press, 2017.

Ehrenreich, Barbara, Arlie Russell Hochschild, and Shara Kay, eds. *Global Woman: Nannies, Maids, and Sex Workers in the New Economy*. New York: Macmillan, 2003.

Elias, Norbert. *The Court Society*. New York: Pantheon Books, 1983.

Elias, Norbert. *Über die Einsamkeit der Sterbenden in unseren Tagen*. Berlin: Suhrkamp Verlag, 1982.

Eliot, T. S. *Four Quartets*. New York: Harcourt Brace, 1971.

Ellison, Susan Helen. *Domesticating Democracy: The Politics of Conflict Resolution in Bolivia*. Durham, NC: Duke University Press, 2018.

Ellison, Susan Helen. "Painted by Default: Public Shaming and Graffiti on the Homefront." *American Anthropologist* 121, no. 3 (2019): 694–707.

Erikson, Kai. "Radiation's Lingering Dread." *Bulletin of the Atomic Scientists* 2, no. 47 (1991): 34–39.

Esposito, Roberto. *Immunitas: The Protection and Negation of Life*. Translated by Zakiya Hanafi. New York: Polity, 2011.

Evans, Hughes. "European Malaria Policy in the 1920s and 1930s: The Epidemiology of Minutiae." *Isis* 80, no. 1 (1989): 40–59.

Fanon, Frantz. *The Wretched of the Earth*. New York: Grove Press, 2004.

Farmer, Paul. *Haiti After the Earthquake*. New York: Public Affairs, 2011.

Fassin, Didier, and Anne-Claire Defossez. *Exile: Chronicle of the Border*. Cambridge: Polity Press, 2025.

Ferdinand, Malcolm. *Decolonial Ecology: Thinking from the Caribbean World*. New York: Polity Press, 2022.

Ferroni, Eliana, Tom Jefferson, and Gabriel Gachelin. "Angelo Celli and Research on the Prevention of Malaria in Italy a Century Ago." *Journal of the Royal Society of Medicine* 105, no. 1 (2012): 35–40.

Finney, Carolyn. *Black Faces, White Spaces: Reimagining the Relationship of African Americans to the Great Outdoors*. Chapel Hill: University of North Carolina Press, 2014.

Fischer, Michael M. "The Peopling of Technologies." In *When People Come First: Critical Studies in Global Health*, edited by João Biehl and Adriana Petryna, 347–73. Princeton, NJ: Princeton University Press, 2013.

Foucault, Michel. *Discipline and Punish: The Birth of the Prison*. New York: Vintage Books, 1995.

Foucault, Michel. "Of Other Spaces: Utopias and Heterotopias." *Diacritics* 16 (1986): 22–27.

Freudenburg, William R. "Contamination, Corrosion and the Social Order: An Overview." *Current Sociology* 45, no. 3 (1997): 19–39.

Frost, Nicola, and Tom Selwyn, eds. *Travelling Towards Home: Mobilities and Homemaking*. New York: Berghahn Books, 2018.

Fuller, Sharon. "Don't Know Nothin' 'bout Subsistence. We Gullah! Construction of Self as Indigenous in the Americas." In *Relating Worlds of Racism: Dehumanization, Belonging, and the Normativity of Whiteness*, edited by Philomena Essed, Karen Farquharson, Kathryn Pillay, and Elisa Joy White, 89–111. Cham: Palgrave Macmillan, 2019.

Fuller, Sharon. "Indigenous Ontologies: Gullah Geechee Traditions and Cultural Practices of Abundance." *Human Ecology* 49, no. 2 (2021): 121–29.

Garcia, Angela. *The Pastoral Clinic: Addiction and Dispossession Along the Rio-Grande*. Berkeley: University of California Press, 2010.

Garcia, Angela. *The Way That Leads Among the Lost: Life, Death, and Hope in Mexico City's Anexos*. New York: Farrar, Straus and Giroux, 2024.

Geschiere, Peter. *Witchcraft, Intimacy, and Trust: Africa in Comparison*. Chicago: University of Chicago Press, 2013.

Gill, Lesley. "Painted Faces: Conflict and Ambiguity in Domestic Servant-Employer Relations in La Paz, 1930–1988." *Latin American Research Review* 25, no. 1 (1990): 119–36.

Gill, Lesley. *Precarious Dependencies: Gender, Class, and Domestic Service in Bolivia*. New York: Columbia University Press, 1994.

Gill, Tom. "The Spoiled Soil: Place, People and Community in an Irradiated Village in Fukushima Prefecture." In *Japan Copes with Calamity: Ethnographies of the Earthquake, Tsunami and Nuclear Disasters of March 2011*, edited by Tom Gill, Brigitte Steger, and David Slater, 201–34. Bern: Peter Lang, 2013.

Glick Schiller, Nina, and Georges Eugene Fouron. *George Woke Up Laughing: Long-Distance Nationalism and the Search for Home*. Durham, NC: Duke University Press, 2001.

Glissant, Édouard. "For Opacity." In *Poetics of Relation*, translated by Betsy Wing, 189–94. Ann Arbor: University of Michigan Press, 2010.

Glissant, Édouard. *Poetics of Relation*. Translated by Betsy Wing. Ann Arbor: University of Michigan Press, 2010.

Glissant, Édouard. "That Those Beings Be Not Being." In *Poetics of Relation*, translated by Betsy Wing, 185–88. Ann Arbor: University of Michigan Press, 2010.

Goffman, Erving. "The Territories of the Self." In *Relations in Public: Microstudies of the Public Order*, 28–61. New York: Basic Books, 1971.

Goldstein, Donna M. *Laughter Out of Place: Race, Class, Violence, and Sexuality in a Rio Shantytown*. Berkeley: University of California Press, 2013.

Goldstone, Brian. *There Is No Place for Us: A Story of Homelessness in America*. New York: Metropolitan Books, 2024.

Goodwine, Marquetta L. *The Legacy of Ibo Landing: Gullah Roots of African American Culture*. Atlanta: Clarity Press, 1998.

Grimmer, Anne. *The Secretary of the Interior's Standards for the Treatment of Historic Properties with Guidelines for Preserving, Rehabilitating, Restoring and Reconstructing Historic Buildings*. Washington, DC: United States Congress, National Park Service, Technical Preservation Services, 2017. https://www.nps.gov/orgs/1739/upload/treatment-guidelines-2017-part1-preservation-rehabilitation.pdf.

Guedes, André Dumans. "Dessubstancializando a casa via configurações e formas provisórias de existência." In *Casa, corpo, terra, violência: Abordagens etnográficas*, edited by John Comerford, Ana Carneiro, Dibe Ayoub, and Graziele Dainese, 71–95. Rio de Janeiro: Editora 7Letras, 2021.

Guedes, André Dumans. "Interstícios, distâncias e formas provisórias de existência." *Mana* 27, no. 2 (2021): 1–8.

Guedes, André Dumans. "Narrando, comparando e maldizendo andanças, pousos e alojamentos." *Ruris* 12, no. 2 (2020): 23–52.

Guggenheim, Michael. "Laboratizing and De-Laboratizing the World: Changing Sociological Concepts for Places of Knowledge Production." *History of the Human Sciences* 25, no. 1 (2012): 99–118.

Guyer, Jane. "Household and Community in African Studies." *African Studies Review* 24, no. 3 (1981): 87–137.

Haffner, Jeanne, ed. *Landscapes of Housing: Design and Planning in the History of Environmental Thought*. London: Routledge, 2022.

Hage, Ghassan. *The Diasporic Condition: Ethnographic Explorations of the Lebanese in the World*. Chicago: University of Chicago Press, 2021.

Haraway, Donna J. "A Cyborg Manifesto: Science, Technology, and Socialist-Feminism in the Late Twentieth Century." In *Simians, Cyborgs, and Women: The Reinvention of Nature*, 149–81. New York, Routledge, 1991.

Hartigan, John. *Aesop's Anthropology: A Multispecies Approach*. Minneapolis: University of Minnesota Press, 2014.

Hartman, Saidiya. *Lose Your Mother: A Journey Along the Atlantic Slave Route*. New York: Farrar, Straus and Giroux, 2007.

Hartman, Saidiya. *Scenes of Subjection: Terror, Slavery, and Self-Making in Nineteenth-Century America*. Oxford: Oxford University Press, 1997.

Hartman, Saidiya. "Venus in Two Acts." *Small Axe: A Caribbean Journal of Criticism* 12, no. 2 (2008): 1–14.

Hartman, Saidiya, and Frank B. Wilderson III. "The Position of the Unthought." *Qui Parle* 13, no. 2 (2003): 183–201.

Hashimoto, Shigeatsu, Masato Nagai, Tetsuya Ohira, et al. "Influence of Post-Disaster Evacuation on Incidence of Hyperuricemia in Residents of Fukushima Prefecture: The Fukushima Health Management Survey." *Clinical and Experimental Nephrology* 24, no. 11 (2020): 1025–32. https://doi.org/10.1007/s10157-020-01924-6.

Hassenzahl, Marc, and Noam Tractinsky. "User Experience—A Research Agenda." *Behaviour and Information Technology* 25, no. 2 (2006): 91–97.

Hastrup, Frida. *Weathering the World: Recovery in the Wake of the Tsunami in a Tamil Fishing Village*. New York: Berghahn Books, 2011.

Heidegger, Martin. "Building Dwelling Thinking." In *Poetry, Language, Thought*, translated by Albert Hofstadter, 141–61. New York: Harper Collins, 1971.

Holston, James. *Insurgent Citizenship: Disjunctions of Democracy and Modernity in Brazil*. Princeton, NJ: Princeton University Press, 2009.

Hondagneu-Sotelo, Pierrette. *Doméstica: Immigrant Workers Cleaning and Caring in the Shadows of Affluence*. Berkeley: University of California Press, 2007.

hooks, bell. "Black Vernacular: Architecture as Cultural Practice." In *Art on My Mind: Visual Politics*, 145–51. New York: New Press, 1995.

hooks, bell. "Homeplace: A Site of Resistance." In *Yearning: Race, Gender, and Cultural Politics*, 41–49. Boston: South End Press, 1990.

hooks, bell. *Yearning: Race, Gender, and Cultural Politics*. Boston: South End Press, 1990.

Hopkins, Dwight N. *Down, Up, and Over: Slave Religion and Black Theology*. Minneapolis: Fortress Press, 2000.

Human Rights Watch. *Paramilitaries' Heirs the New Face of Violence in Colombia*. New York: Americas Division of Human Rights Watch, 2010. https://www.hrw.org/sites/default/files/reports/colombia0210webwcover_1.pdf.

Humphrey, Caroline. "No Place Like Home: The Neglect of Architecture." *Anthropology Today* 4, no. 1 (1988): 16–28.

Hurston, Zora Neale. *Barracoon: The Story of the Last "Black Cargo."* New York: Amistad, 2018.

Hurston, Zora Neale. *Mules and Men*. In *Folklore, Memoirs, and Other Writings*. New York: Penguin Books, 1995.

Hurston, Zora Neale. "You Don't Know Us Negroes." In *You Don't Know Us Negroes and Other Essays*, edited by Henry Louis Gates Jr. and Genevieve West, 107–16. New York: HarperCollins, 2022.

Ingold, Tim. "Building, Dwelling, Living: How Animals and People Make Themselves at Home in the World." In *Shifting Contexts: Transformations in Anthropological Knowledge*, edited by M. Strathern, 57–80. London: Routledge, 1995.

Ingold, Tim. *The Perception of the Environment: Essays on Livelihood, Dwelling and Skill*. London: Routledge, 2011.

Jackson, Steven. "Speed, Time, Infrastructure: Temporalities of Breakdown, Maintenance, and Repair." In *The Sociology of Speed: Digital, Organizational, and Social Temporalities*, edited by Judy Wajcman and Nigel Dodd, 169–86. Oxford: Oxford University Press, 2016.

Jacques, P. B. *Estética da ginga: A arquitetura das favelas através da obra de Hélio Oiticica*. Rio de Janeiro: Casa da Palavra, 2001.

Jain, Sarah S. "The Prosthetic Imagination: Enabling and Disabling the Prosthesis Trope." *Science, Technology, and Human Values* 24, no. 1 (1999): 31–54.

James, S. P., and P. G. Shute. *Report on the First Results of Laboratory Work on Malaria in England*. Geneva: League of Nations, Health Organization, Malaria Commission, 1926.

Jensen, Casper Bruun, Miho Ishii, and Philip Swift. "Attuning to the Webs of *En*: Ontography, Japanese Spirit Worlds, and the 'Tact' of Minakata Kumagusu." HAU: *Journal of Ethnographic Theory* 6, no. 2 (2016): 149–72.

Joos, Vincent. *Urban Dwellings, Haitian Citizenships: Housing, Memory, and Daily Life in Haiti*. New Brunswick, NJ: Rutgers University Press, 2021.

Joseph, Handerson. "Maisons diasporas et maisons locales: Mobilités haïtiennes et réseaux transnationaux." *Etnográfica* 24, no. 3 (2020): 749–74.

Joseph, Handerson, and Cédric Audebert, eds. *El sistema migratorio haitiano en América del Sur: Proyectos, movilidades y políticas migratorias*. Buenos Aires: CLACSO, 2022.

Joyce, Rosemary A., and Susan D. Gillespie, eds. *Beyond Kinship: Social and Material Reproduction in House Societies*. Philadelphia: University of Pennsylvania Press, 2000.

Karim, Lamia. *Microfinance and Its Discontents: Women in Debt in Bangladesh*. Minneapolis: University of Minnesota Press, 2011.

Kelly, Ann H., and Javier Lezaun. *Mosquito Work: Vectors of Global Health*. Durham, NC: Duke University Press, 2026.

Khayyat, Munira. "Introduction: Another Season of War in South Lebanon." *Hot Spots, Fieldsights*, April 11, 2025. https://www.culanth.org/fieldsights/introduction-another-season-of-war-in-south-lebanon.

Khayyat, Munira. *A Landscape of War: Ecologies of Resistance and Survival in South Lebanon*. Oakland: University of California Press, 2022.

Kirby, Peter Wynn. "Slow Burn: Dirt, Radiation, and Power in Fukushima." *Asia-Pacific Journal, Japan Focus* 17, no. 19 (2019): e3. https://doi.org/10.1017/S1557466019015596.

Kivland, Chelsey L. *Street Sovereigns: Young Men and the Makeshift State in Urban Haiti*. Ithaca, NY: Cornell University Press, 2020.

Knorr Cetina, Karin. "Laboratory Studies: The Cultural Approach to the Study of Science." In *Handbook of Science and Technology Studies*, edited by Sheila Jasanoff, Gerald E. Markle, James C. Peterson, and Trevor Pinch, 140–67. Thousand Oaks, CA: Sage, 1995.

Knudsen, Jakob, and Lorenz von Seidlein. *Healthy Homes in Tropical Zones: Improving Rural Housing in Asia and Africa*. Berlin: Edition Axel Menges, 2014.

Kopper, Moisés. *Architectures of Hope: Infrastructural Citizenship and Class Mobility in Brazil's Public Housing*. Ann Arbor: University of Michigan Press, 2022.

Kurzman, Steven L. "Presence and Prosthesis: A Response to Nelson and Wright." *Cultural Anthropology* 16, no. 3 (2001): 374–87.

Lacan, Jacques. *The Four Fundamental Concepts of Psychoanalysis*. New York: W. W. Norton, 1981.

Lacerda, Paula. "Reassentar e indenizar: Formas de governo no contexto da implantação da usina hidroelétrica de Belo Monte, em Altamira, Brasil." *Etnográfica* 25, no. 3 (2021): 729–49. https://journals.openedition.org/etnografica/10328#quotation.

Landes, Joan B. "Further Thoughts on the Public/Private Distinction." *Journal of Women's History* 15, no. 2 (2003): 28–39.

Lanham, J. Drew. *The Home Place: Memoirs of a Colored Man's Love Affair with Nature.* Minneapolis: Milkweed Editions, 2016.

Lanham, J. Drew. "Joy Is the Justice (We Give Ourselves)." In *Joy Is the Justice We Give Ourselves*. Spartanburg, SC: Hub City Press, 2023.

Lanier, Michelle. "The Gullah Geechee Cultural Corridor." Talk delivered at the North Carolina Rice Festival 2023, Wilmington, NC, March 4, 2023.

Lanier, Michelle. "Rooted: Black Women, Southern Memory, and Womanist Cartographies." *Southern Cultures* 26, no. 2 (2020): 12–31. https://www.southerncultures.org/article/rooted.

Larson, Brooke. "Redeemed Indians, Barbarized Cholos." In *Political Cultures in the Andes, 1750–1950*, edited by Nils Jacobsen and Cristóbal Aljovín de Losada, 230–52. Durham, NC: Duke University Press, 2005.

La Silla Vacía. "Con la alerta por bacrim, Ciudad Bolívar se mira en el espejo de Soacha." May 4, 2018. https://www.lasillavacia.com/historias/silla-nacional/con-la-alerta-por-bacrim-ciudad-bolivar-se-mira-en-el-espejo-de-soacha/.

Latour, Bruno. "Give Me a Laboratory and I Will Raise the World." In *Science Observed: Perspectives on the Social Studies of Science*, edited by Karin Knorr-Cetina and Michael Joseph Mulkay, 141–70. London: Sage, 1983.

Latour, Bruno. *Reassembling the Social: An Introduction to Actor-Network-Theory*. Oxford: Oxford University Press, 2007.

Leinaweaver, Jessaca B. *The Circulation of Children*. Durham, NC: Duke University Press, 2008.

Leinaweaver, Jessaca B. "Raising the Roof in the Transnational Andes: Building Houses, Forging Kinship." *Journal of the Royal Anthropological Institute* 15, no. 4 (2009): 777–96.

L'Estoile, Benoît de. "Can Economic Anthropology Escape from Primitive Economics? Thinking Ethnographically from the Brazilian Oikos." In *One Hundred Years of Argonauts: Malinowski, Ethnography and Economic Anthropology*, edited by Chris Hann and Deborah James, 161–82. New York: Berghahn Books, 2024.

L'Estoile, Benoît de. "'Money Is Good, but a Friend Is Better': Uncertainty, Orientation to the Future, and 'the Economy.'" *Current Anthropology* 55, no. s9 (2014): s62–s73. https://doi.org/10.1086/676068.

L'Estoile, Benoît de, and Federico Neiburg. "Governing the House: An Ethnographic Approach." *Etnográfica* 24, no. 3 (2020): 655–64.

"'Let Justice Roll Down Like Waters': The Role of Spirituality in African American Environmental Activism in the US South." *Antipode Online*, May 21, 2019. https://antipodeonline.org/2019/05/21/let-justice-roll-down-like-waters-the-role-of-spirituality-in-african-american-environmental-activism-in-the-us-south/.

Lévi-Strauss, Claude. "Maison." In *Dictionnaire de l'ethnologie et de l'anthropologie*, edited by Michel Izard and Pierre Bonte, 434–36. Paris: Presses Universitaires de France, 1991.

Lévi-Strauss, Claude. *Paroles données*. Paris: Plon, 1984.

Lévi-Strauss, Claude. *The Savage Mind*. Chicago: University of Chicago Press, 1966.

Lévi-Strauss, Claude. "The Story of Asdiwal." In *Structural Anthropology*, 2:146–96. Chicago: University of Chicago Press, 1976.

Lewis, Jovan Scott. “Black Life Beyond Injury: Relational Repair and the Reparative Conjuncture.” *Political Geography* 108 (January 2024). https://doi.org/10.1016/j.polgeo.2023.102963.

Liboiron, Max, Manuel Tironi, and Nerea Calvillo. “Toxic Politics: Acting in a Permanently Polluted World.” *Social Studies of Science* 48, no. 3 (2018): 331–49.

Lima, R. M. B. de, and Saragoussi, M. “Floodplain Home Gardens on the Central Amazon Floodplain.” In *The Central Amazon Floodplain: Actual Use and Options for Sustainable Management*, edited by W. J. Junk, J. J. Ohly, M. T. F. Piedade, and M. G. M. Soares, 243–68. Leiden: Backhuys Publishers, 2000.

Lindsay-Poland, John. *Plan Colombia: U.S. Ally Atrocities and Community Activism*. Durham, NC: Duke University Press, 2018.

Longobardi, Cesare. *Land-Reclamation in Italy: Rural Revival in the Building of a Nation*. London: P. S. King, 1936.

Lorde, Audre. “School Note.” In *The Black Unicorn*, 217. New York: W. W. Norton, 1978.

Lowenthal, David. *The Heritage Crusade and the Spoils of History*. Cambridge: Cambridge University Press, 1996.

Lugones, María. “Heterosexualism and the Colonial/Modern Gender System.” *Hypatia* 22, no. 1 (2007): 186–219.

Lupton, Deborah. *The Quantified Self: A Sociology of Self-Tracking*. Cambridge: Polity Press, 2017.

Macedo, Eric. “Altamira: Ensaio histórico-maquínico sobre a colonização.” PhD diss., PPGAS, Museu Nacional, UFRJ, 2016.

Marcelin, Louis Herns. “A invenção da família afro-americana: Família, parentesco e domesticidade entre os negros do Recôncavo da Bahia, Brasil.” PhD diss., PPGAS, Museu Nacional, UFRJ, 1996.

Marcelin, Louis Herns. “A linguagem da casa entre os negros no Recôncavo Baiano.” *Mana: Estudos de Antropologia Social* 5, no. 2 (1999): 31–60.

Marcelin, Louis Herns. “Blood Symbolism and the Political Habitus of Violence in Haiti.” *American Anthropologist* 114, no. 2 (2012): 253–66.

Markowitz, Gerald, and David Rosner. *Deceit and Denial: The Deadly Politics of Industrial Pollution*. Berkeley: University of California Press, 2002.

Martin, Emily. “Anthropology and the Cultural Study of Science.” *Science, Technology, and Human Values* 23, no. 1 (1998): 24–44.

Masalu, John P., Fredros O. Okumu, Arnold S. Mmbando, Maggy T. Sikulu-Lord, and Sheila B. Ogoma. “Potential Benefits of Combining Transfluthrin-Treated Sisal Products and Long-Lasting Insecticidal Nets for Controlling Indoor-Biting Malaria Vectors.” *Parasites and Vectors* 11, no. 1 (2018): 231. https://doi.org/10.1186/s13071-018-2811-y.

Masco, Joseph. “The Age of Fallout.” *History of the Present: A Journal of Critical History* 5, no. 2 (2015): 137–68.

Mauss, Marcel. *Seasonal Variations of the Eskimo: A Study in Social Morphology*. London: Routledge, 2013.

Mbembe, Achille. “Necropolitics.” *Public Culture* 15, no. 1 (2003): 11–40.

McKittrick, Katherine. *Demonic Grounds: Black Women and the Cartographies of Struggle*. Minneapolis: University of Minnesota Press, 2006.

McKittrick, Katherine. "I Lost an Arm on My Last Trip Home: Black Geographies." In *Demonic Grounds: Black Women and the Cartographies of Struggle*, 1–35. Minneapolis: University of Minnesota Press, 2006.
McKittrick, Katherine. "Mathematics Black Life." *Black Scholar* 44, no. 2 (2014): 16–28. https://doi.org/10.1080/00064246.2014.11413684.
McKittrick, Katherine. "Plantation Futures." *Small Axe: A Caribbean Journal of Criticism* 17, no. 3 (2013): 1–15. https://doi.org/10.1215/07990537-2378892.
Mead, Margaret. *Coming of Age in Samoa: A Psychological Study of Primitive Youth for Western Civilization*. New York: William Morrow, 1928.
Medina Gallego, Carlos, and Mireya Téllez Ardila. *La violencia parainstitucional, paramilitar y parapolicial en Colombia*. Santafé de Bogotá: Rodríguez Quito Editores, 1994.
Mello e Souza, Laura de. "Formas provisórias de existência: A vida cotidiana nos caminhos, nas fronteiras e nas fortificações." In *História da vida privada no Brasil: Cotidiano e vida privada na América Portuguesa*, edited by Laura de Mello e Souza and Fernando A. Novais. São Paulo: Companhia das Letras, 1997.
Melly, Caroline. *Bottleneck: Moving, Building, and Belonging in an African City*. Chicago: University of Chicago Press, 2017.
Melnick, Robert Z., Andrea Roberts, and Julie McGilvray. "Integrity as Process and Feature: Cultural Landscapes of Underrepresented Communities." *Change over Time* 10, no. 2 (2021): 122–40. https://dx.doi.org/10.1353/cot.2021.0013.
Mercer, Claire. *The Suburban Frontier: Middle-Class Construction in Dar es Salaam*. Oakland: University of California Press, 2024.
Middleton, Alexandra. *The Connector: Living with Experimental Neuroprosthetics*. Durham, NC: Duke University Press, 2026.
Millar, Kathleen M. *Reclaiming the Discarded: Life and Labor on Rio's Garbage Dump*. Durham, NC: Duke University Press, 2018.
Miller, Daniel, ed. *Home Possessions: Material Culture Behind Closed Doors*. London: Routledge, 2002.
Minakata, Kumagusu, and Shinichi Nakazawa. *Minakata Mandala*. Tokyo: Kawade Shobo Shinsha, 2015.
Minamisōma City. "Kouki Kihonkeikaku no sakuteinimuketa Minamisoma-shi no genjyou to kadai." 2018. Internet Archive, accessed August 2022. https://web.archive.org/web/20190803013538/https://www.city.minamisoma.lg.jp/material/files/group/7/03_shiryou01-02.pdf.
Ministério Público Federal (MPF). *Relatório de inspeção interinstitucional: Áreas ribeirinhas atingidas pelo processo de remoção compulsória da UHE Belo Monte*. Altamira: MFP, 2015.
Miranda Neto, J. Queiroz de, and J. Antonio Herrera. "Altamira-PA: Novos papéis de centralidade e reestruturação urbana a partir da instalação da UHE Belo Monte." *Confins*, no. 28 (2016): 1–18.
Mitchell, Timothy. *Colonising Egypt*. Berkeley: University of California Press, 1991.
Mmbando, Arnold S., Amos J. Ngonzi, Salum Mshamu, John Bradley, Thomas Bøjstrup, and Halfan Ngowo. "Effect of a Novel House Design (Star Home) on Indoor Malaria Mosquito Abundance in Rural Tanzania: Secondary Outcomes of an Open-Label, Household, Randomised Controlled Trial." *Lancet Planetary Health*

9, no. 4 (2025): E253–E263. https://www.thelancet.com/journals/lanplh/article/PIIS2542-5196(25)00046-4/fulltext.
Mmbando, Arnold S., Halfan Ngowo, Alex Limwagu, Masoud Kilalangongono, Khamis Kifungo, and Fredros O. Okumu. "Eave Ribbons Treated with the Spatial Repellent, Transfluthrin, Can Effectively Protect Against Indoor-Biting and Outdoor-Biting Malaria Mosquitoes." *Malaria Journal* 17, no. 1 (2018): 368.
Mondragón, Héctor. "La economía rural y la guerra." In *Taller agrario y cultivos "ilícitos."* Bogotá, 2002. http://www.mamacoca.org/feb2002/art_mondragon_economia_rural_y_guerra.html.
Montinard, Mélanie. "Pran wout la: Expériences et dynamiques de la mobilité haïtienne." *Vibrant—Brazilian Virtual Anthropology* 17 (2020): 1–33.
Morduch, Jonathan, and Rachel Schneider. *The Financial Diaries: How American Families Cope in a World of Uncertainty*. Princeton, NJ: Princeton University Press, 2017.
Morimoto, Ryo. "From Nuclear Things to Things Nuclear: Minding the Gap at the Knowledge-Policy-Practice Nexus in Post-Fallout Fukushima." In *Disaster upon Disaster: Exploring the Gap Between Disaster Knowledge and What Enters Policy and Practice*, edited by Susanna Hoffman and Roberto Barrios, 218–40. New York: Berghahn, 2020.
Morimoto, Ryo. *Nuclear Ghost: Atomic Livelihoods in Fukushima's Gray Zone*. Oakland: University of California Press, 2023.
Morimoto, Ryo. "Wild Boar Chase: Ecology of Harm and Half-Life Politics in Coastal Fukushima." *Cultural Anthropology* 37, no. 1 (2022): 69–98.
Morioka, Kiyomi. "Ancestor Worship in Contemporary Japan: Continuity and Change." *Senri Ethnological Studies*, no. 11 (1984): 201–13.
Morita, Tomohiro. "Nihon no shouraiwosukuu Fukushimaken hamadori no koureikataisaku." April 20, 2015. Internet Archive, accessed August 5, 2022. https://web.archive.org/web/20150422204656/http://jbpress.ismedia.jp/articles/-/43570.
Morrison, Toni. "The Site of Memory." In *Inventing the Truth: The Art and Craft of Memoir*, 2nd ed., edited by William Zinsser, 83–102. Boston: Houghton Mifflin, 1995.
Motta, Eugênia. "The Dying Home: 'Bad Deaths' and Spatial Inscriptions of Mourning in a Favela." *Cultural Anthropology* 36, no. 4 (2021): 556–62. https://doi.org/10.14506/ca36.4.03.
Motta, Eugênia. "Houses and Economy in the Favela." *Vibrant—Virtual Brazilian Anthropology* 11, no. 1 (2014): 118–58.
Motta, Eugênia. "O que faz o dinheiro da casa." *Horizontes Antropológicos* 29, no. 66 (2023): 1–30.
Motta, Eugênia. "Resisting Numbers: The Favela as (Un)quantifiable Reality." In *The Real Economy: Essays in Ethnographic Theory*, edited by Federico Neiburg and Jane Guyer, 77–128. Chicago: Hau Books, 2019. https://doi.org/10.1186/s13063-022-06461-z.
Motta, Eugênia. "Uma casa boa, uma casa ruim e a morte no cotidiano." *Etnográfica* 24, no. 3 (2020): 775–95.
Mshamu, Salum, Arnold Mmbando, Judith Meta, et al. "Assessing the Impact of a Novel House Design on the Incidence of Malaria in Children in Rural Africa: Study Protocol for a Household-Cluster Randomized Controlled Superiority Trial." *Trials* 23, no. 1 (2022): 519. https://doi.org/10.1186/s13063-022-06461-z.

Muelle, Camila Esguerra. "Cómo hacer necropolíticas en casa: Ideología de género y acuerdos de paz en Colombia." *Sexualidad, salud y sociedad (Rio de Janeiro)*, no. 17 (2017): 172–98. https://doi.org/10.1590/1984-6487.sess.2017.27.10.a.

Munn, Nancy. "The 'Becoming-Past' of Places: Spacetime and Memory in Nineteenth-Century, Pre–Civil War New York." *HAU: Journal of Ethnographic Theory* 3, no. 2 (2013): 359–80.

Munn, Nancy. *The Fame of Gawa: A Symbolic Study of Value Transformation in a Massim Society*. Durham, NC: Duke University Press, 1992.

Murphy, Keith. *Swedish Design: An Ethnography*. Ithaca, NY: Cornell University Press, 2015.

Murrieta, Ruy S., and Antoinette WinklerPrins. "Flowers of Water: Home Gardens and Gender Roles in a Riverine Caboclo Community in the Lower Amazon, Brazil." *Culture and Agriculture* 25, no. 1 (2003): 35–47. https://doi.org/10.1525/cag.2003.25.1.35.

Nakane, Chie. "'Ie' no kouzou bunseki." In *Ishida Eiichiro kyoju kanreki kinen ronbunshu*, 101–13. Tokyo: Kadokawa, 1964.

Navaro-Yashin, Yael. *The Make-Believe Space: Affective Geography in a Postwar Polity*. Durham, NC: Duke University Press, 2012.

Neiburg, Federico. "Multiscale Home: Shifting Landscapes and Living-in-Movement in Haiti." *Cultural Anthropology* 36, no. 4 (2021): 548–55. https://doi.org/10.14506/ca36.4.02.

Neiburg, Federico. "Serendipitous Involvement: Making Peace in the Gueto." In *If Truth Be Told: The Politics of Public Ethnography*, edited by Didier Fassin, 170–98. Durham, NC: Duke University Press, 2017.

Neiburg, Federico, and Handerson Joseph. "Searching for Life in Time of Pandemics." In *Pandemic Exposures: Economy and Society in the Time of Coronavirus*, edited by Didier Fassin and Marion Fourcade, 321–41. Chicago: Hau Books, 2021.

Nietzsche, Friedrich. *The Use and Abuse of History*. New York: MacMillan, 1957.

Nixon, Rob. *Slow Violence and the Environmentalism of the Poor*. Cambridge, MA: Harvard University Press, 2013.

Noé, João Daniel. "História do ano de 1874." In *A nova face dos Muckers*, by Moacyr Domingues, 383–98. São Leopoldo: Rotermund, 1977.

Nozawa, Shunsuke. "Phatic Traces: Sociality in Contemporary Japan." *Anthropological Quarterly* 88, no. 2 (2015): 373–400. https://doi.10.1353/anq.2015.0014.

Ochiai, Emiko. "The *Ie* (Family) in Global Perspective." In *A Companion to the Anthropology of Japan*, edited by Jennifer Robertson, 355–79. Malden, MA: Blackwell, 2005.

Olwig, Karen Fog. *Caribbean Journeys: An Ethnography of Migration and Home in Three Family Networks*. Durham, NC: Duke University Press, 2007.

Ortiz-Catalan, Max, Enzo Mastinu, Paolo Sassu, Oskar Aszmann, and Rickard Brånemark. "Self-Contained Neuromusculoskeletal Arm Prostheses." *New England Journal of Medicine* 382 (April 2020): 1732–38.

Packard, Randall M. *The Making of a Tropical Disease: A Short History of Malaria*. Baltimore, MD: Johns Hopkins University Press, 2007.

Palacios, Marco. *Between Legitimacy and Violence: A History of Colombia, 1875–2002*. Latin America in Translation/En Traduccíon/Em Tradução. Durham, NC: Duke University Press, 2006.

Parreñas, Rhacel Salazar, and Eileen Boris, eds. *Intimate Labors: Cultures, Technologies, and the Politics of Care*. Redwood City, CA: Stanford University Press, 2010.

Pauli, Julia. "A House of One's Own: Gender, Migration, and Residence in Rural Mexico." *American Ethnologist* 35, no. 1 (2008): 171–87.

Pellow, David Naguib. *Garbage Wars: The Struggle for Environmental Justice in Chicago*. Cambridge, MA: MIT Press, 2002.

Peñaranda, Katrina, Ximena Flores, and Álvaro Arandia. *Se necesita empleada doméstica de preferencia cholita: Representaciones sociales de la trabajadora del hogar asalariada en Sucre*. La Paz: Fundacion Pieb, 2006.

Perea Restrepo, Carlos Mario. *Limpieza social: Una violencia mal nombrada*. Bogotá: Centro Nacional de Memoria Histórica, 2015. https://www.cervantesvirtual.com/obra/limpieza-social-una-violencia-mal-nombrada-879231/.

Peredo, Elizabeth, and Rogelio Mayta. *Perspectivas en la lucha de las trabajadoras del hogar en Bolivia*. La Paz: Fundación Solón, 2002.

Pérez, Amin. *Bourdieu and Sayad Against Empire: Forging Sociology in Anticolonial Struggle*. New York: Polity Press, 2024.

Periodismo Público. "La incertidumbre sobre la presencia de bacrim en Soacha." March 24, 2015. https://periodismopublico.com/la-incertidumbre-sobre-la-presencia-de-bacrim-en-soacha.

Perry, Imani. *South to America: A Journey Below the Mason-Dixon to Understand the Soul of a Nation*. New York: Ecco, 2022.

Pessoa, Fernando. *Quadras ao gosto popular*. Porto Alegre: L&PM, 2008.

Petryna, Adriana. "Horizoning," In *Unfinished: The Anthropology of Becoming*, edited by João Biehl and Peter Locke, 243–69. Durham, NC: Duke University Press, 2017.

Petryna, Adriana. *Horizon Work: At the Edges of Knowledge in an Age of Runaway Climate Change*. Princeton, NJ: Princeton University Press, 2022.

Petryna, Adriana. *Life Exposed: Biological Citizens After Chernobyl*. Princeton, NJ: Princeton University Press, 2013.

Petryna, Adriana. *When Experiments Travel: Clinical Trials and the Global Search for Human Subjects*. Princeton, NJ: Princeton University Press, 2009.

Philip, M. NourbeSe. "Testimony Stoops to Mother Tongue." In *She Tries Her Tongue, Her Silence Softly Breaks*, 52–56. Middletown, CT: Wesleyan University Press, 1988.

Philip, M. NourbeSe. "Universal Grammar." In *She Tries Her Tongue, Her Silence Softly Breaks*, 61–73. Middletown, CT: Wesleyan University Press, 1988.

Pietrafiesa de Godoi, Emília. "Mobilidades, encantamentos e pertença: O mundo ainda está rogando, porque ainda não acabou." *Revista de antropologia* 57, no. 2 (2014): 143–70.

Pina-Cabral, João de. "Partible Houses: Variants of Vicinage in Mozambique, Portugal and Brazil." *Articulo: Journal of Urban Research*, no. 20 (2019). https://doi.org/10.4000/articulo.4434.

Porteous, Douglas, and Sandra E. Smith. *Domicide: The Global Destruction of Home*. Montreal: McGill-Queen's University Press, 2001.

Povinelli, Elizabeth. *Economies of Abandonment*. Durham, NC: Duke University Press, 2011.

Prather, H. Leon, Sr. *We Have Taken a City: Wilmington Racial Massacre and Coup of 1898*. Rutherford, NJ: Fairleigh Dickinson University Press, 1984.

Price, Richard, ed. *Maroon Societies: Rebel Slave Communities in the Americas*. Baltimore, MD: Johns Hopkins University Press, 1996.
Programme des Nations Unies pour le Développement (PNUD). "Programme des Nations Unies pour le développement, République d'Haïti." In *Human Development Report 2014: Sustaining Human Progress; Reducing Vulnerabilities and Building Resilience*. New York: United Nations Development Programme, 2014.
Rajagopalm, Balakrishnan. "Domicide: The Mass Destruction of Homes Should Be a Crime Against Humanity." *New York Times*, January 29, 2024.
Ramírez, María Clemencia. "Maintaining Democracy in Colombia Through Political Exclusion, Sates of Exception, Counterinsurgency and Dirty War." In *Violent Democracies in Latin America*, edited by Enrique Desmond Arias and Daniel M. Goldstein. Durham, NC: Duke University Press, 2010.
Redfield, P. "Shacktopia: The Meantime Future of Humanitarian Design." *Social Anthropology* 30, no. 2 (2022): 16–33.

Ribeiro Corossacz, Valeria. "Sexual Harassment and Assault in Domestic Work: An Exploration of Domestic Workers and Union Organizers in Brazil." *Journal of Latin American and Caribbean Anthropology* 24, no. 2 (2019): 388–405.
Rivera Cusicanqui, Silvia. "Violence and Interculturality: Contemporary Indigenous in Bolivia." Translated by Isabel Dulfano. In *New World Colors: Ethnicity, Belonging, and Difference in the Americas*, edited by Josef Raab, 275–91. Tempe, AZ: Bilingual Press/Editorial Bilingüe, 2014.
Roberts, Elizabeth F. S. "Grappling with Exposure in Mexico City." *Current Anthropology* 66, no. 6 (2025): 891–915.
Romain, Jean Baptiste. *Quelques mœurs et coutumes des paysans Haïtiens: Travaux pratiques d'ethnographie sur la région de Milot à l'usage des étudiants*. Port-au-Prince: Imprimerie de l'État, 1959.
Rosenbaum, Susanna. *Domestic Economies: Women, Work, and the American Dream in Los Angeles*. Durham, NC: Duke University Press, 2017.
Rowe, Mark Michael. *Bonds of the Dead: Temples, Burial, and the Transformation of Contemporary Japanese Buddhism*. Chicago: University of Chicago Press, 2011.
Russell, Nerissa. "The Domestication of Anthropology." In *Where the Wild Things Are Now: Domestication Reconsidered*, edited by Rebecca Cassidy and Molly Mullin, 27–48. London: Routledge, 2007.
Russell, Nerissa. "The Wild Side of Animal Domestication." *Society and Animals* 10, no. 3 (2002): 285–302.
Sahlins, Marshall. "The Stranger-King or, Elementary Forms of the Politics of Life." *Indonesia and the Malay World* 36, no. 105 (2008): 177–99.
Said, Edward. *After the Last Sky: Palestinian Lives*. New York: Columbia University Press, 1998.
Saito, Kimiaki, Satoshi Mikami, Masaki Andoh, et al. "Summary of Temporal Changes in Air Dose Rates and Radionuclide Deposition Densities in the 80 km Zone over Five Years After the Fukushima Nuclear Power Plant Accident." *Journal of Environmental Radioactivity* 210 (2019): 105878_1–105878_12. https://doi.org/10.1016/j.jenvrad.2018.12.020.

Sambol-Tosco, Kimberly. "The Slave Experience: Religion." *Slavery and the Making of America*. PBS Thirteen, 2004. https://www.thirteen.org/wnet/slavery/experience/religion/history.html.

Sambon, Louis W., and George C. Low. "Report on Two Experiments on the Mosquito-Malaria Theory, Instituted by the Colonial Office and the London School of Tropical Medicine." *Medico-Chirurgical Transactions* 84 (1901): 497–552.

Sánchez-Criado, Tomás. "Immunity Beyond the Home: The Emergence of New Forms of Protection Through Telecare." Paper presented at the Care and the Art of Dwelling: Bodies, Technologies and Home symposium, conducted at the conference of EASST/4S: Acting with Science, Technology and Medicine, Rotterdam, 2008.

Santos, Antônio Bispo dos. *Colonização, quilombos: Modos e significações*. Brasília: Instituto Nacional de Ciéncia e Tecnologia, 2015.

Scott-Smith, Tom. *Fragments of Home: Refugee Housing and the Politics of Shelter*. Stanford, CA: Stanford University Press, 2024.

Sebald, W. G. "Le Promeneur Solitaire." In *The Tanners*, by Robert Walser, translated by Susan Bernofsky, 1–36. New York: New Directions, 2009.

Sevá [Filho], A. Oswaldo. "Works on the Great Bend of the Xingu—A Historic Trauma?" In *Hydroelectric Dams on Brazil's Xingu River and Indigenous Peoples*, edited by Leinad Ayer de O. Santos and Lúcia M. M. de Andrade, 19–41. Cambridge, MA: Cultural Survival, 1990. https://cpisp.org.br/wp-content/uploads/2019/02/HYDRO-ELECTRIC-DAMS.pdf.

Sevá Filho, A. Oswaldo, and Glenn Switkes. "Resumo executivo." In *Tenotã-mõ: Alertas sobre as conseqüências dos projetos hidrelétricos no rio Xingu, Pará, Brasil*, compiled by A. Oswaldo Sevá Filho, edited by Glenn Switkes, 13–28. São Paulo: International Rivers Network 2005. https://riverresourcehub.org/wp-content/uploads/files/attached-files/tenota_mo_portugues.pdf.

Shapiro, Nicholas. *Homesick*. Durham, NC: Duke University Press, 2025.

Sharpe, Christina Elizabeth. *In the Wake: On Blackness and Being*. Durham, NC: Duke University Press, 2016.

Sheller, Mimi. *Island Futures: Caribbean Survival in the Anthropocene*. Durham, NC: Duke University Press, 2020.

Sheller, Mimi. "The New Mobilities Paradigm for a Live Sociology." *Current Sociology Review* 62, no. 6 (2014): 789–811.

Shimizu, Akitoshi. "*Ie* and *Dōzoku*: Family and Descent in Japan." *Current Anthropology* 28, no. S4 (1987): S85–S90.

Sigaud, Lygia. "O efeito das tecnologias sobre as comunidades rurais: O caso das grandes barragens." *Revista Brasileira de Ciências Sociais* 7, no. 18 (1992): 18–28.

Simmel, Georg. "Sociologia do espaço." *Estudos avançados* 23, no. 79 (2013): 75–112.

Skrabut, Kristin. "Housing the Contingent Life Course: Domestic Aspiration and Extreme Poverty in Peruvian Shantytowns." *City and Society* 30, no. 2 (2018): 263–88.

Sloterdijk, Peter. *Foams*. Vol. 3 of *Spheres*. Translated by Wieland Hoban. Los Angeles: Semiotext(e), 2016.

Smith, Peggie R. "The Pitfalls of Home: Protecting the Health and Safety of Paid Domestic Workers." *Canadian Journal of Women and the Law* 23, no. 1 (2011): 309–39.

Snowden, Frank. *The Conquest of Malaria: Italy, 1900–1962*. New Haven, CT: Yale University Press, 2006.

Sobchack, Vivian. "A Leg to Stand On: Prosthetics, Metaphor, and Materiality." In *The Prosthetic Impulse: From a Posthuman Present to a Biocultural Future*, edited by Marquard Smith and Joanne Morra, 17–41. Cambridge, MA: MIT Press, 2006.

Soliz, Carmen. *Fields of Revolution: Agrarian Reform and Rural State Formation in Bolivia, 1935–1964*. Pittsburgh, PA: University of Pittsburgh Press, 2021.

Song, Priscilla. *Biomedical Odysseys: Fetal Cell Experiments from Cyberspace to China*. Princeton, NJ: Princeton University Press, 2017.

Spillers, Hortense J. "Mama's Baby, Papa's Maybe: An American Grammar Book." *Diacritics* 17, no. 2 (1987): 65–81.

Steedman, Carolyn. *Dust*. Manchester: Manchester University Press, 2001.

Steedman, Carolyn. *Landscape for a Good Woman*. London: Virago, 1986.

Stephenson, Marcia. *Gender and Modernity in Andean Bolivia*. Austin: University of Texas Press, 1999.

Stewart, Kathleen. "Precarity's Form." Paper presented at the annual meeting of the American Anthropological Association, November 25, 2011.

Stewart, Kathleen. "Window (Thinking the Unknown with João Biehl)." *Current Anthropology* 63, no. s25 (2022): s26–s27.

Stoetzer, Bettina. *The Ruderal City: Ecologies of Migration, Race, and Urban Nature in Berlin*. Durham, NC: Duke University Press, 2022.

Stoler, Ann Laura. *Carnal Knowledge and Imperial Power*. Berkeley: University of California Press, 2002.

Stolz, Rosalie, and Jonathan Alderman, eds. *Houses Transformed: Anthropological Perspectives on Changing Practices of Dwelling and Building*. New York: Berghahn Books, 2023.

Stout, Noelle. *Dispossessed: How Predatory Bureaucracy Foreclosed on the American Middle Class*. Berkeley: University of California Press, 2019.

Strathern, Marilyn. *Reproducing the Future: Anthropology, Kinship and the New Reproductive Technologies*. Manchester: Manchester University Press, 1992.

Swai, Johnson K., Arnold S. Mmbando, Halfan S. Ngowo, et al. "Protecting Migratory Farmers in Rural Tanzania Using Eave Ribbons Treated with the Spatial Mosquito Repellent, Transfluthrin." *Malaria Journal* 18, no. 1 (2019): 414.

Taussig, Michael. *Law in a Lawless Land: Diary of a Limpieza in Colombia*. Chicago: University of Chicago Press, 2005.

Thomas, Deborah A. *Exceptional Violence: Embodied Citizenship in Transnational Jamaica*. Durham, NC: Duke University Press, 2011.

Thomas, Deborah A. "Refusal (and Repair)." *Annual Review of Anthropology* 53, no. 1 (2024): 93–109. https://doi.org/10.1146/annurev-anthro-041422-020201.

Toomer, Jean. *Cane*. New York: Liveright Publishing, 2011.

Torrico Foronda, Escarley. *Emergencia urbana: Urbanización y libre mercado en Bolivia*. La Paz: CEDIB, Centro de Documentación e Información Bolivia, 2017.

Tourinho, Helena. "Estrutura urbana de cidades médias Amazônicas: Análise considerando a articulação das escalas interurbana e intraurbana." PhD diss., Universidade Federal de Pernambuco, 2011.

Tsubokura, Masaharu. "Secondary Health Issues Associated with the Fukushima Daiichi Nuclear Accident, Based on the Experiences of Soma and Minamisoma Cities." *Journal of the National Institute of Public Health* 67, no. 1 (2018): 71–83.

Tuck, Eve. "Suspending Damage: A Letter to Communities." *Harvard Educational Review* 79, no. 3 (2009): 409–28.

Umfleet, LeRae S. *A Day of Blood: The 1898 Wilmington Race Riot*. Raleigh: North Carolina Office of Archives and History, 2009.

Umfleet, LeRae S. *1898 Wilmington Race Riot Report*. Raleigh: North Carolina Office of Archives and History, Department of Natural and Cultural Resources, 1898 Race Riot Commission, May 31, 2006. https://digital.ncdcr.gov/Documents/Detail/1898-wilmington-race-riot-report/2257408.

Valderrama, Mario, and Héctor Mondragón. *Desarrollo y equidad con campesinos*. Bogotá: IICA, 1998.

Van Vleet, Krista E. *Performing Kinship: Narrative, Gender, and the Intimacies of Power in the Andes*. Austin: University of Texas Press, 2009.

Velásquez Rivera, Edgar de Jesús. "Historia del paramilitarismo en Colombia." *História (São Paulo, Brazil)* 26, no. 1 (2007): 134–53. https://doi.org/10.1590/S0101-90742007000100012.

von Koseritz, Carlos. "Der religiöse Wahnsinn." *Deutsche Zeitung* (Porto Alegre), May 17, 1873, p. 2.

Walley, Christine J. *Exit Zero: Family and Class in Post-Industrial Chicago*. Chicago: University of Chicago Press, 2013.

Warnock, Raphael G. *The Divided Mind of the Black Church: Theology, Piety, and Public Witness*. New York: New York University Press, 2013.

Weimer, Günter. *Arquitetura popular da imigração Alemã*. Porto Alegre: Editora da UFRGS, 2005.

Weiner, Annette. *Women of Value, Men of Renown: New Perspectives in Trobriand Exchange*. Austin: University of Texas Press, 1976.

Weiner, James F. "Anthropology Contra Heidegger Part I: Anthropology's Nihilism." *Critique of Anthropology* 12, no. 1 (1992): 75–90.

Weizman, Eyal. *Forensic Architecture: Violence at the Threshold of Detectability*. New York: Zone Books, 2017.

Weston, Kath. *Families We Choose: Lesbians, Gays, Kinship*. New York: Columbia University Press, 1991.

Wilson, Anne L., Orin Courtenay, Louise A. Kelly-Hope, et al. "The Importance of Vector Control for the Control and Elimination of Vector-Borne Diseases." *PLoS Neglected Tropical Diseases* 14, no. 1 (2020): e0007831. https://doi.org/10.1371/journal.pntd.0007831.

Wilson, Ara. "Intimacy." In *The Global and the Intimate*, edited by Geraldine Pratt and Victoria Rosner, 31–56. New York: Columbia University Press, 2012.

Winchell, Mareike. *After Servitude: Elusive Property and the Ethics of Kinship in Bolivia*. Berkeley: University of California Press, 2022.

WinklerPrins, Antoinette, and Perpétuo de Souza. "Surviving the City: Urban Home Gardens and the Economy of Affection in the Brazilian Amazon." *Journal of Latin American Geography* 4, no. 1 (2005): 107–26.

Womack, Autumn. "Contraband Flesh: On Zora Neale Hurston's *Barracoon*." *Paris Review*, May 7, 2018.

Woolf, Virginia. *A Room of One's Own*. London: Renard Press, 2020.

World Bank. "The World Bank Supports the Response to the COVID-19 Pandemic and Building Resilience to Health Shocks and Natural Disasters in Haiti." Press release, June 29, 2020. https://www.worldbank.org/en/news/press-release/2020/06/29/world-bank-supports-covid-19-response-and-increased-resilience-to-health-shocks-and-natural-hazards-in-haiti#:~:text=WASHINGTON%2C%20June%2029%2C%202020%20%E2%80%93,and%20Resilience%20Development%20Policy%20Operation.

Wynter, Sylvia. "Novel and History, Plot and Plantation." *Savacou* 5 (June 1971): 95–102.

Wynter, Sylvia. "Un-Settling the Coloniality of Being/Power/Truth/Freedom: Towards the Human, After Man, Its Overrepresentation." *New Centennial Review* 3, no. 3 (2003): 257–338.

Yanagisako, Sylvia. "Family and Household: The Analysis of Domestic Groups." *Annual Review of Anthropology* 8 (1970): 165–205.

Young, Grace Esther. "The Myth of Being 'Like a Daughter.'" *Latin American Perspectives* 14, no. 3 (1987): 365–80.

Zacka, Bernardo. "What's in a Balcony? The In-Between as Public Good." In *Political Theory and Architecture*, edited by Duncan Bell and Bernardo Zacka, 81–102. London: Bloomsbury Academic, 2020.

Zaloom, Caitlin, and Deborah James. "Financialization and the Household." *Annual Review of Anthropology* 52 (2023): 399–415.

Zamora, Romina. "Acerca de las discusiones sobre el salario de las criadas: Algunas reflexiones sobre el orden jurídico local en San Miguel de Tucumán a fines del siglo XVIII." *Revista de historia del derecho* 39 (2010): 1–25.

Zavaleta Mercado, René. *Lo nacional-popular en Bolivia*. Ciudad de México: Siglo XXI Editores, 1986.

Zbinden, Jan, Eva Lendaro, and Max Ortiz-Catalan. "Prosthetic Embodiment: Review and Perspective on Definitions, Measures, and Experimental Paradigms." *Journal of Neuroengineering and Rehabilitation* 19, no. 1 (March 2022): 37.

Zelizer, Viviana A. *The Social Meaning of Money*. Princeton, NJ: Princeton University Press, 2017.

Zuboff, Shoshanna. *The Age of Surveillance Capitalism: The Fight for a Human Future at the New Frontier of Power*. New York: Profile Books, 2019.

Zucchino, David. *Wilmington's Lie: The Murderous Coup of 1898 and the Rise of White Supremacy*. New York: Atlantic Monthly Press, 2020.

Contributors

JOÃO BIEHL is Susan Dod Brown Professor and director of the Brazil LAB at Princeton University. He is the author of the award-winning books *Vita: Life in a Zone of Social Abandonment* and *Will to Live: AIDS Therapies and the Politics of Survival.* Biehl has also coedited numerous collections, including *Arc of Interference: Medical Anthropology for Worlds on Edge* and *Unfinished: The Anthropology of Becoming.*

THIAGO DA COSTA OLIVEIRA is a documentarist and museum/media anthropologist. He has served as a Humboldt Fellow at the Ethnological Museum Berlin and is a co-founder of the Amazonian Future Lab. His collaborative research, curatorships, and documentaries focus on Indigenous material culture and on urban life in Amazonia. An experienced curator and collector, he has also worked with multiple museums and research institutions in Europe and the Americas.

SUSAN HELEN ELLISON is associate professor of anthropology at Wellesley College. She is the author of the award-winning book *Domesticating Democracy: The Politics of Conflict Resolution in Bolivia.*

CARLOS FAUSTO is professor of anthropology at the National Museum of the Federal University of Rio de Janeiro. He is the author of numerous books, including *Indios antes do Brasil, Warfare and Shamanism in Amazonia,* and *Art Effects: Image, Agency and Ritual in Amazonia.* He is also coeditor of the volume *Ownership and Nurture: Studies in Native Amazonian Property Relations* and codirector of the award-winning documentary film *The Hyperwomen.*

CATHERINE FENNELL is associate professor of anthropology with a joint appointment in the Center for the Study of Ethnicity and Race at Columbia University. She is the author of the award-winning book *Last Project Standing: Civics and Sympathy in Post-Welfare Chicago.*

ANGELA GARCIA is professor of anthropology at Stanford University. She is the author of the award-winning book *The Pastoral Clinic: Addiction and Dispossession Along the Rio Grande,* and she has recently published *The Way That Leads Among the Lost: Life, Death, and Hope in Mexico City's Anexos.*

ANN H. KELLY is a fellow in medical anthropology at Exeter College and a professor in Oxford's Department of Social Anthropology and Museum Ethnography. She has coauthored the book *The Anthropology of Epidemics,* and her work has recently appeared in *Cultural Anthropology, Social Studies of Science, Social Science and Medicine, Economy and Society, American Ethnologist,* and *Medical Anthropology.* Kelly is the coauthor, with Javier Lezaun, of *Mosquito Work: Global Health Vectors.*

JAVIER LEZAUN is associate professor in the School of Anthropology and Museum Ethnography and director of the Institute for Science, Innovation and Society at Oxford University. His recent work has appeared in *Nature Climate Change,* BMJ *Global Health, Cultural Anthropology, Social Studies of Science, Social Science and Medicine, Economy and Society,* and *Nature Communications.* Lezaun is the coauthor, with Ann H. Kelly, of *Mosquito Work: Global Health Vectors.*

ALEXANDRA MIDDLETON is assistant professor in the Centre for Medical Science and Technology Studies at the University of Copenhagen. She is coprincipal investigator of "Data Space," an ERC Advanced Grant–funded project, and a Marie Skłodowska-Curie Global Fellow. Middleton's work has appeared in *BioSocieties* and she has recently published the book *The Connector: Living with Experimental Neuroprosthetics.*

RYO MORIMOTO is assistant professor of anthropology at Harvard University. He is a member of the editorial collective of *Cultural Anthropology* and the author of the award-winning book *Nuclear Ghost: Atomic Livelihoods in Fukushima's Gray Zone.*

EUGÊNIA MOTTA is professor in the Department of Cultural Anthropology of the Federal University of Rio de Janeiro and at the Institute of Social and Political Studies of the State University of Rio de Janeiro. She directs two research groups: CASA—Social Studies on Housing and Cities and the Center for Research on Culture and Economy (NuCEC).

FEDERICO NEIBURG is professor of anthropology at the National Museum of the Federal University of Rio de Janeiro, where he is also the founder of the Center for Research on Culture and Economy (NuCEC). He has coauthored numerous books, including *The Real Economy: Essays in Ethnographic Theory*, *A Cultural History of Money in the Age of Empire*, *Conversas Etnográficas Haitianas*, and *Empires, Nations, and Natives: Anthropology and State-Making*.

SEBASTIÁN RAMÍREZ has been a lecturer in anthropology at Princeton University and is currently director of the Service Focus Initiative of Princeton's Pace Center for Civic Engagement. He recently published *Madres Terra* in collaboration with photographer Carlos Saavedra and the activist network MAFAPO.

AYLUONNE TXAI TERESZKIEWICZ is a PhD candidate in anthropology and the Interdisciplinary Doctoral Program in the Humanities at Princeton University. Her research is supported by the Charlotte Elizabeth Procter Honorific Fellowship and the Wenner-Gren Foundation. She is a contributing editor at the Society for Cultural Anthropology's *Visual and New Media Review*.

Index